DEVELOPMENTAL KINESICS
The
Emerging Paradigm

DEVELOPMENTAL KINESICS
The
Emerging Paradigm

Edited by

Bates L. Hoffer, Ph.D.
Trinity University

and

Robert N. St. Clair, Ph.D.
University of Louisville

University Park Press
Baltimore

UNIVERSITY PARK PRESS
International Publishers in Science, Medicine, and Education
300 North Charles Street
Baltimore, Maryland 21201

Typeset by The Oberlin Printing Company.
Manufactured in the United States of America by The Maple Press Company.

Library of Congress Cataloging in Publication Data
Main entry under title:

Developmental kinesics, the emerging paradigm.

Includes bibliographical references and indexes.
1. Nonverbal communication in children. I. Hoffer, Bates L. II. St.
Clair, Robert N. [DNLM: 1. Kinesics. 2. Psychology, Applied.
BF 637.C45 D489]
BF723.C57D48   155.4'13   80-28079
ISBN 0-8391-1651-9

Contents

Contributors

Marcie Dorfman, Ph.D.
Department of Psychology
University of California
Los Angeles, California 90024

Walburga von Raffler-Engel, Ph.D.
Program in Linguistics
Vanderbilt University
Nashville, Tennessee 37235

Gretchen Engquist-Seidenberg,
  Ph.D.
Center for Policy Research
National Governors Association
Hall of the States
444 North Capitol Street
Washington, D.C. 20001

Reuven Feuerstein, Ph.D.
Director, Hadassah-WIZO-Canada
  Research Institute
6 Karmon Street
Beit HaKerem, 96308 Jerusalem,
  Israel

Patrice French, Ph.D.
Department of Psychology
University of California
Los Angeles, California 90024

Ton van der Geest, Ph.D.
Psychologisches Institut
Ruhr-Universität Bochum
Postfach 102148
4630 BOCHUM 1, West Germany

Bates L. Hoffer, Ph.D.
Department of English
Trinity University, Box 165
San Antonio, Texas 78284

Robert H. Hutcheson, M.D., M.P.H.
Department of Public Health, State
  Office Building
Ben Allen Road
Nashville, Tennessee 37216

Luis R. Marcos, M.D., M.Sc.D.
Director, Department of Psychiatry
Gouverneur Hospital and
Professor of Psychiatry
New York University School of
  Medicine
550 First Avenue
New York, New York 10016

Howard M. Rosenfeld, Ph.D.
Department of Human Development
University of Kansas
Lawrence, Kansas 66045

Willard W. Remmers, M.A.
Department of Human Development
University of Kansas
Lawrence, Kansas 66045

Robert N. St. Clair, Ph.D.
Department of English
University of Louisville
Louisville, Kentucky 40292

I. M. Schlesinger, Ph.D.
Department of Psychology
The Faculty of Social Sciences
The Hebrew University of
  Jerusalem
Jerusalem, Israel

Richard G. Schwartz, Ph.D.
Department of Speech and Theatre
  Arts
University of Pittsburgh
Pittsburgh, Pennsylvania 15260

Karen F. Steckol, Ph.D.
Department of Surgery
Division of Communicative
  Disorders
University of Louisville
Louisville, Kentucky 40292

Cecelia K. Yoder
Program in Psycholinguistics
University of Michigan
Ann Arbor, Michigan 48104

Foreword

Research in linguistics has traditionally concerned only the verbal code itself. Structural linguistics and transformational grammar have both analyzed the human code of communication as a formal structure—that abstract system that sets humans apart from animals (see French, 1976, for a review). The nonverbal communication behaviors that animals and humans have in common were considered part of behavior, but not part of language. In the Platonic dualism of psyche and soma, the domain of the language researcher was clearly the mind and not the body. This end of the dualistic split was not peculiar to linguistics, however, but followed a trend that has continued for several centuries. In fact, a survey describes 2,000 years of Western European culture as based on the notion that "man is essentially a soul for mysterious and accidental reasons imprisoned in a body" (Brown, 1959).

The present interest in nonverbal communication as an integral component of language performance represents a basic and important shift in the language researcher's view of the phenomenon he or she studies. This trend toward the integration of psyche and soma, mind and body, formal code and actual performance is, finally, a more complete view of language. This is the view that has always been maintained by von Raffler-Engel, to whom this volume is dedicated. In this view, the focus is upon the complementary relationship between the verbal and nonverbal components of the linguistic code.

Like most shifts in science, this move to a more complete view of language is neither spontaneous nor anomalous. It is motivated by evidence that the goals of traditional language science are unattainable without consideration of the (nontraditional) nonverbal aspects of the phenomenon as well. This research suggests that nonverbal aspects of language are not just an "animal accompaniment" to the human verbal performance, but rather a necessary part of the signal for the human (animal) processor. For example, it has long been appreciated that variety of vocal phenomena such as acoustic markers of intonation, pause, and accent are necessary to the perception of syntactic structure (Trager and Smith, 1957; Chomsky and Halle, 1968). What is important here is the discovery that these markers are often perceived from the body movements of the speaker. Even trained linguists transcribing speech from videotapes wrote pauses and accents that were not in the verbal-acoustic channel at all. McQuown (1964) stressed the importance of body movement to the traditionally motivated linguist because "it will make them conscious, some of them for the first time, that they are picking up their stresses and their pitches not via the ears, although they fancy they are, but by the eyes (p. 124).

The first system for transcription of nonverbal information was devised by the American anthropologist, Ray Birdwhistell (1952). He coined the term *kinesics* for the study of body movements and derived much of its technical terminology from the field of linguistics. For example, analogous to the phone, phoneme, allophone, morph, and morpheme in linguistics are the *kine* (the basic unit of body motion), *kineme* (the smallest discriminable set of body movements), *allokine* (variant of the kine which, in combination with other allokines, constitutes the kineme), *kinemorph* (combinations of kinemes), and *kinemorpheme* (combinations of kinemorphs functioning as free or bound classes) or kinesics. The analysis of kinic movements also includes their co-occurrence with particular syntactic environments of speech. In American English, for example, distal extension of the head or hand is associated with pronominal forms such as *he, she,* and *it,* while proximal movements occur in association with the forms *I, me,* and *us.* Such motions are not instinctive, but learned systems of behavior, which differ from culture to culture (Birdwhistell, 1966).

Lomax (1968) developed a rather elaborate system of measurement known as Cantometrics. Cantometrics, originally a system for the description of song style, can also be applied to the analysis of styles of speaking. The parameters of the system include features of song performance such as embellishment, vocal noise, dynamics, and repetition. Following Trager's (1958) system of paralinguistic notation and Chapple and Arensberg's (1940) interaction theory, Lomax (1977) devised a rating system that correlates measurements of speech style with other culturally determined characteristics. For instance, Lomax related variation in the informational load of the verbal channel to measures of socioeconomic complexity, high verbal density, for example, being a factor typically associated with relatively complex social organizations and systems of production. Thus, it is suggested that particular features of speech style are not only learned, but correlated with specific sociocultural configurations.

A second type of nonverbal analysis falls under the rubric of *interactional synchrony,* or the description of rhythmically coordinated movements between speakers and hearers. This phenomenon was first observed by Condon and Ogston (1966) after viewing sound films of normal, aphasic, and schizophrenic interactants. An analysis of the films (taken at twice normal speed) revealed synchrony in the speech and movements of normal interactants, but not for autistic and schizophrenic patients. In addition, pathological interactants displayed a certain "tenseness" of posture and lack of variability in head movements and eye gaze, and the speech of depressed patients was characterized by a smaller degree of variation in pitch, stress, and length than typically observed in the vocalizations of normal interactants. Scheflen (1963), who has used sound film to study the behavior of interactants during psychotherapy, observed a complex of nonverbal regulatory devices that seem necessary for maintaining the stability of social interaction norms.

Further investigation of interactional synchrony was conducted by Kendon (1970), who focused upon the context of interaction. Following the segmentation method developed by Condon and Ogston, Kendon found that participants not directly addressed by the speaker displayed movements of different form and timing than actively engaged participants. Mirroring of the speaker's movements by the listener, for example, was only observed between speakers and actively involved listeners. One explanation for speaker/listener synchrony provided by Kendon is compatible with an analysis-by-synthesis model of speech perception. That is, by actively monitoring the speaker's movements, the listener is constructing a running hypothesis of the speaker's actions that can be checked against future actions and used as a means by which to decode future output.

From the viewpoint of information theory, or the mathematical theory of communication (Shannon and Weaver, 1949), the management of sequencing information in a separate channel increases the information load that can be carried by the verbal channel. Thus, the total channel capacity of the human communicator is greater than if such sequencing were handled in the verbal channel alone. The additional load carried by the verbal channel would make the information less discriminable if transmitted at the same rate. There is a neurological advantage to the nonverbal channel as well. Kimura's (1973) research suggests that kinesic movements are controlled by the hemisphere opposite that of language. Kinesic behaviors are in a different modality (visual) and so require the use of different "work space" in the brain. Thus, a person who is left-hemisphere dominant for speech has the kinesic aspects of the code controlled by the right hemisphere. (This opposite mapping is typical of neurological control or concomitant activities.) Thus, from the point of view of information theory, the usefulness of a separate channel for segmenting information finds empirical reality in the neurology of the speaker/hearer. The empirical reason that kinesic information allows for greater total information capacity is that nonverbal information is decoded by different equipment at the destination. Thus, neurological evidence also illuminates the integral nature of kinesic behavior to ongoing verbal behavior. Control of body movements unrelated to speech (such as adjusting one's dress or hair or rubbing the nose) reveals no reliable hemispheric assignment. Only kinesic behaviors were lateralized, mirroring in neurology what has long been observed in performance and decoding—that kinesics seems to be an integral part of both the code of language and its performance.

Similarly, the process of language acquisition reveals kinesics to be both a part of the code that is acquired and an important aspect of the acquisition process. In the early 1960s, when developmental psycholinguistics was emerging as one of the most exciting areas of language study, the focus of this field was transformational. Chomsky's Formal Theory of Syntax was exclusively a property of mind or psyche and dealt only with an abstract system. It is now clear that the complete study of language development must take into account all aspects of the interactional context, including maturational, biological, and cultural factors, as well as verbal and kinesic aspects of the linguistic code. Originally controversial, these points have since become common knowledge in language science. (See French, 1976, for a history of this evolution.)

Cross-cultural differences in kinesic code is one of the older areas of nonverbal communication, tracing back at least to Darwin (1872). He considered the evolution of nonverbal communication of wolves in the same manner as the evolution of other traits, and also collected data on cross-cultural expression of emotion (Darwin, 1872). Efron (1941), who provides one of the earlier modern comparisons of gesture, found that individuals learning a new language in a foreign community assimilate their gestural patterns to those of the target language group, and Hewes (1955), in a study of posture, found patterns of standing and sitting to differ from culture to culture. The general dependence of kinesics upon culture, both in the cultural diversity of kinemes and the sociocultural parameters regulating their use, suggests that kinesics is not as instinctive a system as once imagined. Clearly, although some aspects of facial expression may be genetic (Darwin, 1872; Izard, 1971), the cultural conditioning of kinesic behavior suggests that it is, in general, learned.

In kinesics, the Platonic dualism of soma and psyche, mind and body are becoming integrated. An empirical approach to language finds both psyche and soma—the code of language and the communicative behaviors of the living organism who uses it. Earlier paradigms viewed only one and, thus, were not really paradigms of language, only of a part of language. Transformational grammar was a theory of syntax. Chomsky (1965) stated clearly that his theory made no statement whatever about how a speaker/hearer would go about creating a sentence. At the other extreme, behaviorism considered only observable behavior—soma—and strictly discounted the existence of mind or psyche.

In other respects, kinesics is similar to any other new science. It has its founding fathers (e.g., Darwin), its popularizers (see the best seller list), its own innovators, eccentrics and outright nuts (make your own list), as well as a host of serious and productive theoreticians (e.g., Birdwhistell) and researchers (e.g., von Raffler-Engel). This cast of characters is typical of a new field. What is most promising and unusual about kinesics and nonverbal communication in general is its integration of psyche and soma, formal code, and empirical behavior. Although with only the beginning of a ruling paradigm, this integrative approach holds the promise unsuggested by either transformational theory or behaviorism—that of uniting both formal and empirical aspects of language in what has the potential to be a thorough-going theory of human communication—a complete picture of what the human animal is doing when he speaks his mind. It is this promise that makes the integrative approach to research a contribution beyond kinesics itself, and ultimately to the science of language as a whole.

Patrice French
Marcie Dorfman

Preface

Kinesics is that part of nonverbal behavior that is interrelated with language. It is, then, an integral part of human communication and as such has received critical attention over the past few decades. The broader, if overlapping, fields of nonverbal behavior and nonverbal communication have not only received wide scholarly attention but in the guise of body language have received much popular attention in books, magazines, Sunday supplements and the like. The more restricted field of kinesics is not yet so well circulated in the popular eye but is developing an imposing bibliography. Kinesic systems of various languages and clashes of kinesic systems across cultures are being described. The subarea of kinesics that has received perhaps the least attention to date is developmental kinesics, the study of the acquisition, development, and maturation of the kinesic system. This volume is a first step in the direction of this area of nonverbal studies.

The 70s saw a rapidly growing interest by ethologists, anthropologists, and comparative psychologists in the general field of nonverbal behavior, as in Hinde (1972). Weitz's (1974) collection on nonverbal communication highlighted, among other things, the especial interest of clinical psychologists and psychiatrists. Some linguists and other language specialists began turning their attention to the broader context of language as part of communication somewhat earlier, but recently their interest has intensified, as in von Raffler-Engel and Hoffer (1977) and the 1980 volumes by von Raffler-Engel and by Key. Currently many disciplines are studying the child's development of nonverbal behavior, and their possible convergence on a developmental pattern is an interesting prospect. As emphasized throughout this volume, it is the emergence of a paradigm from the independent work in different fields that has led us to prepare this volume on developmental kinesics.

Much of the study of kinesic development has paralleled the study of language development. The long history of language acquisition research and its current sophistication provide a natural model, especially because kinesics is intimately intertwined with language. Childhood acquisition patterns provide insights into the adult system and insight into the model we use to describe that system. Given the high level of language acquisition research, it is unfortunate that so many of the observations on kinesic development have been made as footnotes to language acquisition. The full system of kinesic patterning has needed a paradigm as the frame of reference within which the atomistic observations can be placed and interrelated. Attention to the bibliography will show the large amount of information—usually unconnected and from different fields using different premises and methodologies—we already have on the subject. It is the purpose of this volume to establish a frame of reference for developmental kinesics.

The organization of the volume begins with an overview and outline history of the field. The first section, "Toward an Integrated Model of Developmental Kinesics," contains three articles that chart a pattern for the acquisition and development of kinesics from neonate through adult system, especially as it parallels language development. The second section discusses the naturalness principle, one of the components of which is a search for the distinction between human universal features and cultural/conventional/learned features of human behavior and development. The core of the section is a search for universals in sign language systems, a search of interest herein because it deals with the development of a nonverbal system with many—some would say "all"—defining characteristics of human language. The third section, "Cognitive Kinesics," shows how the study of kinesics relates to the current interest in the cognitive sciences. The articles treat the development of behavioral perception and production as well as the study of modeling/imitation and teaching/learning in transmitting patterns of behavior and values from generation to generation. The fourth section, "Methodologies," gives examples of kinesics-related research from the different fields of early childhood development, linguistics, and epidemiology. Each section begins with its own introductory comments that provide an overview of the articles included.

Given the centrality of the notion of paradigm for this volume, it is appropriate to consider seriously the concept of a scientific paradigm and to draw on its implications for this volume. In his innovative approach to historiography, Thomas Kuhn (1970) discussed the concept of a scientific paradigm. He reviewed the positivistic tradition in which he was trained as a physicist and contended that, contrary to conventional wisdom, science does not progress by the mere accretion of new knowledge to already existing bodies of information and does not advance by the adding of new theories to old ones. What essentially takes place, he argued, is a spiral progress of growth with distinctive stages of development. The first stage in the cycle of progress he calls "normal science" and characterizes it in highly conservative terms as a protection of the *status quo*. As the findings of scientists in the field accrue, there is a gradual awareness among the scientific community that anomalies exist. This awareness gradually leads to his second stage of scientific progress known as "the period of crisis." During this interim, many competing models emerge and each of these provides an attempt at resolving those conflicts and anomalies that led to the failure of the traditional model. The focal point of Kuhn's model can be found in the emergence of the third stage of scientific growth. This occurs when one of the competing models is accepted by the community of scholars as the best model or paradigm. At this time in the spiral of growth, a scientific revolution takes place in which researchers find a new way of perceiving knowledge. This new theoretical framework is what Kuhn calls a "paradigm." It is indeed a new way of perceiving science, a recognition of data and theory.

Although this concept of a scientific paradigm is currently established in the literature, it is not adequate for conveying what we mean by paradigm in this volume. When Kuhn used the work, he meant it to apply to the growth of knowledge within an already established field of knowledge, such as physics or biology. In the case of developmental kinesics, however, there is no firmly established tradition from which new paradigms can emerge in the cycle of growth. Instead, the situation is more of a genesis of knowledge rather than a modification of current concepts by revisualizing them in a different framework. For this reason, the concept of a paradigm espoused in this volume is best understood within the framework of interdisciplinary research.

New disciplines have always developed within the natural and social sciences. Consider the case of social psychology. At one time there were sociolinguists who looked at the role of the individual in society and psychologists who attempted to study how society was incorporated within the goals and ideals of the individual. Each of these perspectives was on the fringe of the normal sciences of both psychology and sociology; from their interaction across both models of science there emerged the genesis of a separate autonomous discipline known as social psychology. It is apparent that the study of developmental kinesics is on the verge of a similar pattern of growth. Scholars from different disciplines have been concerned with how symbolic systems are acquired. They are not content merely to investigate psycholinguistic patterns of the emergence of language in children and have complemented their work with the study of nonverbal behavior. This shift in focus has been so promising for some that they have essentially been working fully within the paradigm of developmental kinesics discussed in this volume. Unfortunately, the work of a few isolated but enlightened individuals is not sufficient to comprise a full paradigm. This requires a concerted effort of numerous scholars, all converging on the same insights, theoretical claims, research findings, and methodological practices. The convergence of independent research using different premises and methods is the strongest of arguments for validity. It is with the expressed concern for the legitimization of a new and promising paradigm that this volume is presented. The contributors to this emerging model all share in this quest. We only hope that the reader will also become an active part of this effort.

Each section of the book is preceded by an overview and commentary. The references cited are given in a single Literature Cited section at the end of the volume. Neither the commentary nor the bibliography is designed to exhaust the literature in the field; they cite relevant research that the interested reader may explore at leisure.

Bates L. Hoffer
Robert N. St. Clair

*This book is dedicated to
Walburga von Raffler-Engel,
a pioneer in the field of developmental kinesics*

DEVELOPMENTAL KINESICS
The
Emerging Paradigm

Section I
TOWARD AN INTEGRATED MODEL OF DEVELOPMENTAL KINESICS

For too long, the artificial separation of verbal and nonverbal communication has led to intense and isolated investigations of common cognitive concerns. Linguists, for example, have developed explicit mathematical models of verbal expression in which lexical forms and grammatical patterns have virtually defined the parameters of their research interests. As a consequence, they have not been fully cognizant of how the same semantic intent can be formulated by means of different modalities of expression. When people feel close to one another, for instance, they reflect this verbally through the use of terms of endearment and the use of less formal syntactic expressions. However, this feeling of solidarity can also be expressed paralinguistically in the subtle use of intonation, or nonverbally by approaching another more closely while exchanging greater eye-gaze or contact, and through other forms of dyadic interaction. In contrast to the linguists, there are those within the scholarly tradition of nonverbal communications who conscientiously measure the minutest shifts of movement between people in a kinesic encounter, but who fail to see the larger framework of semantic intent on which their own quantitative research is based. They may overlook the parallel verbal expres-

1

sions that often accompany nonverbal behavior or the discourse structures that limit and constrain the agenda for both forms of interaction.

One of the few scholars to recognize the problems created by this superficial dichotomy of related disciplines is Walburga von Raffler-Engel of Vanderbilt University. She has effectively argued in several of her publications, for example, that this separation is spurious and counterproductive because it has frequently resulted in systematic distortion across related research paradigms. Her awareness of the need for more interdisciplinary research in kinesics has been reflected in her organizational efforts to arrange national and international conferences at which scholars from different disciplines have convened to work cooperatively toward an explanatory model of human development, verbal and nonverbal. Some of these concerns are outlined in her informative chapter at the beginning of this section.

The concern for integrating kinesic knowledge across disciplines is also shared by a number of other scholars and institutions. Of particular interest to the field of kinesic research is an open atmosphere of growth and progress expressed by such scholars as Albert Scheflen. He in particular has actively sought to work with linguistics, anthropologists, sociologists, and other psychiatrists to develop interdisciplinary insights into kinesic and proxemic behavior. His efforts stand out because he has not limited his search for knowledge to any one discipline, nor has his quest for insight been specifically bound to the academic community of psychiatrists. Hence, his research interests can exemplify how an integrated model of developmental kinesics can proceed.

In addition to the individuals who share the concern for integrating their efforts across disciplines, there are academic and service organizations that also merit recognition for their concerted efforts to communicate across different disciplines. One such group is the Institute of Nonverbal Communication Research in New York. It shares its knowledge and latest research findings through its publication, *The Kinesis Report*, edited by Martha Davis and Eden Graber; it also holds numerous workshops at various locations across the country. This organization has repeatedly sought to cooperate with other related disciplines in defining the parameters of developmental kinesics.

The cooperation of scholarship across related disciplines is crucial for the establishment of an integrated model of developmental kinesics. Each discipline has emerged from its own tradition of research based on different needs, methodologies, and concerns; for any one of these models of scientific knowledge to develop greater explanatory power, scholars must make a concerted effort to look beyond the traditional boundaries of their own disciplines. In this way, they can attempt to bridge the gap that separates their own views of science from those of others.

Perhaps this approach to an integrated model of developmental kinesics is best illustrated by means of the metaphor of a spotlight and its illuminating force when projected onto a darkened stage. When the beam of light is directed onto the stage it forms a circle of light, and everything within that circle becomes the data for which a discipline is responsible. What remains outside this circle of knowledge may also be important, but the information is not considered to be within the official purview of that discipline. Imagine a whole series of spotlights, each with its own illumination of knowledge, but also separated from the others. Each isolated model has its own areas of concern, separate methodologies, and disparate traditions.

What an integrated model of developmental kinesics would entail under these circumstances is best described as an enlargement of the various circles of knowledge until the insights and information from one tradition overlap with those of another. This would result, in effect, in a Venn diagram in which the enlarged areas of interest of each discipline intersect with those of others, forming a larger data base and providing a greater repertoire of research interests. As a case in point, consider the field of neurolinguistics, the study of motor and language development. Obviously, these are also the concerns of developmental kinesicists, but until these separate models of human growth actually share their own spotlights of knowledge with others and begin to create a common vocabulary of motives, the potential for a more integrated network of explanatory power will not be realized. Speech pathologists, it should be noted, have already demonstrated a cooperative concern in expanding their data base and enlarging their instruments of research methodology. They have shared in this venture of interdisciplinary scholarship and have worked closely with others or the paradigm of developmental linguistics. It is now time for linguists, experimental psychologists, communication scientists, and representatives of other related disciplines to broaden their perspectives of knowledge and join in this pursuit of enlightenment. They must actively make the effort to transcend the limits of their own disciplines.

In this section of the volume, Walburga von Raffler-Engel provides an interesting attempt to create an integrated model of developmental kinesics. She has ascertained the research problems of several related disciplines as they deal with aspects of nonverbal behavior, and she demonstrates the delicate interplay of maturational features across several cognitive sciences. Her model takes into account the nature of the mother and the child, their cultural environ-

ments, and their perceptual and productive capacities in the acquisition of kinesic behavior. Her model also considers the problems of the
bilingual child in acquiring more than one kinesic system, as well as
the needs of handicapped children (blind, deaf, mentally retarded,
emotionally disturbed, and so on) and focuses on their various stages
of adjustment along the maturational curve toward a full adult pattern
of nonverbal interaction strategies and experiences.

In formulating this integrated model, Walburga von Raffler-Engel
has drawn her insights from numerous research paradigms. She has
investigated the findings of social psychologists, neurolinguists, cultural anthropologists, speech therapists, psycholinguists, and developmental psychologists, and has incorporated them into her own theoretical and experimental framework. It is for this reason that her work
is best seen as a step in the development of an integrated model of
developmental kinesics.

Karen F. Steckol and Richard G. Schwartz draw on the work of von
Raffler-Engel, but, as specialists in learning disabilities, they are aware
of other research paradigms and share the complexity of their experiences in the relationship between movement and action in the acquisition of nonverbal behavior. Their own model reflects the research on speech acts in language and establishes them along a
maturational scale based on strong empirical research. They deal specifically with the relationships between actions and lexical concepts
and raise numerous issues that merit further investigation in the literature. In essence, the research of Steckol and Schwartz adds significantly to the integrated model of developmental kinesics that is emerging.

Bates Hoffer has also investigated the parameters of kinesic research and provides yet another perspective on how the model can be
substantially enhanced. He notes that recent research shows us that
some aspects of basic kinesic development are learned in the years
from 7 to 12. Much of the research in developmental kinesics has concentrated on the early years, even as did language acquisition studies
for so many decades. There is a rich and fruitful area of research in the
development of elementary school children, both within and across
cultures.

Chapter 1
DEVELOPMENTAL KINESICS
The Acquisition and Maturation of Conversational Nonverbal Behavior

Walburga von Raffler-Engel

Much research into the language development of the child, and particularly that which was accomplished during the recent past, has been conducted as if language acquisition were an isolated phenomenon. In reality, the capacity to understand spoken language and to express oneself verbally is acquired as an integral part of the total development of the child's sense of self and of his socialization.

Language serves to clarify one's own thoughts and to communicate them to others. This, however, does not imply a dichotomy. Our self-image and our inner emotions are in no way separable from our social life. Normalcy is just that: man as a social animal with rapport with others, beginning with the baby's rapport with his mother. Autism and schizophrenia are disturbances of self in relation to others; there is no normal self-awareness disjointed from human interaction. There are, of course, innate drives, such as the needs for food and shelter, and universal types of expression, such as the cry of pain. How these needs are satisfied, when these innate ways of expressing oneself are used and when they are suppressed, and what exact shape they take within the possible parameters of their natural framework are culturally determined. Because enculturation begins at birth, it is never possible to fully distinguish between biological and social factors.

An earlier and shorter version of this chapter appeared in von Raffler-Engel (1980).

There also was a tendency in the past to disassociate the physical and the cognitive elements of biological development. Correlates more so than parallels can be seen between, for example, beginning to walk and the onset of adult-type language. The child who walks can distance himself from his mother, feels more independent and needs more specificity in language. His physical contact is no longer so close that flow of communication is basically by touch and synchronized rhythm. Physiology and psychology are mutually reinforcing: one is not the cause and the other is not the effect; they develop jointly.

The process of learning how to communicate is one of interaction and thus cannot be described by focusing exclusively on the child. As Bullowa (1979) puts it, "It is possible to use language all by itself, although not to learn it. It is not possible to communicate, in the basic meaning of the word, alone." The interaction between mother and child is nonverbal and paralinguistic before it becomes verbal, and it would be absurd to study language acquisition by ignoring this earlier, simpler mode of infantile communication. Strange as it may seem now, this was the manner in which the development of language was studied, especially in the United States. The interactional model proposed by Bullowa (1975, 1979) and by von Raffler-Engel (1964, 1976d, e) was not well received at first, but gradually it has taken hold. Later books start speaking of "action" and "gesture" (Lock, 1978) and the model now seems to be so firmly established that it is taken for granted.

Science is certainly cumulative, but it is not necessarily always progressive. The psychologists of the turn of the century had more insight into language development than many linguists of the mid-1900's. Today, most researchers of the language development of the child have come to realize that language acquistion is achieved by communicative interaction and that verbal language is only part of the total communication. It is a component and not the whole, the other overt component being nonverbal behavior. This chapter explores the development of this particular facet of the child's acquisition of communicative competence.

RESEARCH CONSIDERATIONS

The case for the systematic study of the gradual acquisition of nonverbal behavior by the child was first made in a short documentary film presented at the Golden Anniversary meeting of the Linguistic Society of America in New York City in 1974 (von Raffler-Engel, 1974a). Four months later, in Chicago, this new area of research was called *developmental kinesics* in a paper delivered at the 25th Anniversary meeting of the International Communication Association (von Raffler-Engel, 1976a).

Once this new branch of the science of human behavior was opened up, the need for such research seemed so obvious that it is strange that this work had not been begun earlier. Although there was a plethora of hyphenated disciplines, such as psycho-linguistics, true interdisciplinary cooperation was very rare, and this may explain why the area of developmental kinesics had not emerged before 1974.

The science of kinesics is still in flux, and the terminology has not yet been fully established. In terms of basic definitions *body language* should be reserved for the bodily movements that express the mood of the individual, including such examples as nervously walking back and forth or crossing the legs for a more comfortable sitting position (von Raffler-Engel, 1977). The term *kinesics* should be restricted to message-related movements of the eye and other parts of the body as they function in an interactional exchange of a message, either in regulating that exchange or in supplying information about its message. In this respect, kinesics is similar to language whereas body language is not. The term *nonverbal behavior* is frequently used interchangeably with kinesics and could be a good term because it stresses the parallel with "verbal behavior," which is an established term, and is less ambiguous than the term *language*, which is sometimes used as a synonym of verbal behavior and sometimes as a synonym of communication. "Communication" encompasses verbal behavior, nonverbal behavior, and vocal nonverbal behavior, whch is synonymous with paralanguage. Unfortunately, "nonverbal behavior" is used, particularly by developmental psychologists, for any activity of the child, including behavior at play.

Linguists tended to analyze verbal language as if words were the only means of conveying and perceiving a message. For a time, their theories ignored the fact that human communication is a combination of words and gestures, and their theories of language acquisition were inadequate because eventually they attributed too much power to the verbal expression, including in it that which pertains to nonverbal expression. The psycholinguists did not ignore the movements of the child's face and body but categorized them only within the expression of emotional states. Whenever the affective and the regulatory function overlapped, the latter was subordinated to the former. Their charts showed parallel developments of words and body movements without showing kinesic interconnections (Lenneberg, 1967). Psychologists have concentrated mainly on the face and the emotional aspects of mother-child interaction. Much of their research is excellent but not within the domain covered here. They do, however, have a clear concept of child development within the interactive framework (Oster and Ekman, 1978). Anthropologists were frequently aware of the kinesics function of nonverbal behavior, but they had no particular interest in its ontogeny. Specialists in speech and communication who studied gestures in regard to their appropriateness in rhetoric were not concerned with spontaneous conversation. Lately, however, they have been in the forefront in analyzing natural gesticulation and bringing it to the attention of their students; but their concern is with adults, not with children.

Educators probably have observed children more closely than members of any other profession have. They have produced videotapes of classroom interactions in various school grades, and their material and personal knowledge could be of great value to the kinesicist. Their way of analyzing the data is of little help, however. For example, they did not distinguish between the general "body language" of their fidgety or sleepy charges and the systematized kinesic movements by which schoolchildren signal their desire for a speaking turn by raising a hand, or increase gesticulation to signal that they intend to keep that turn.

Among educators, however, those working in bilingual education became aware of the semiotic function of these body movements, which are conversation related, and observed that differences in kinesic systems can cause cross-cultural clashes (Hoffer and Santos, 1977, 1980). Although they rarely went beyond the listing of such misunderstandings, as a group of professionals they were probably the ones who brought the need for a systematic study of kinesics to the attention of the general public. For examples of cross-cultural differences, consider two reciprocal cases: Americans signal a positive response by nodding the head, whereas Greeks shake the head to express assent; in forming a negative reply, the movements are reversed. It cannot even be said that the use of head movements in some form or other for signaling the equivalents of *yes* and *no* is universal. The Japanese giggle politely when they are forced to reply in the negative. These culture-specific nonverbal expressions are as much learned as the language forms. The same holds true for the deictic motion. Americans point with the extended forefinger, whereas in another culture, speakers stick out the lower lip in the direction of the object (Nida, 1949:176). Americans count with the fingers exclusive of the thumb, and Germans start counting with the thumb. One and the same hand gesture thus signifies *two* to an American and *three* to a German.

Bilingual speakers must also be bikinesic if they want to function properly. As children grow up, they adjust to the kinesic behavior of the community. Eventually, they establish a pattern of expectance for gestural behavior similar to the expectancy that makes one's mother tongue understandable and other languages foreign. When in the Vanderbilt Linguistics Program this expectancy was tested by showing a videotape of a conversational interaction involving a certain amount of gesticulation, persons from low kinesic cultures hardly noticed any details of the ongoing gesticulations, whereas persons from high kinesic cultures—such as those of

South America—recalled most of the movements (von Raffler-Engel, 1977).

In 1969 my then student Patrice French (French and von Raffler-Engel, in press) tested gesture recognition across age groups ranging from first graders to adults. Her experiment showed that gestural communication is most effective within a speech community, and particularly between peers. Such communication is less effective outside one's speech community and between individuals differing in age by some 20 years. Culture and society mold kinesic behavior.

Cultures differ greatly in their determinations of what is socially acceptable to be expressed verbally and what is to be reserved for nonverbal expression. In Western society, derogatory remarks are frequently "left unsaid" and are conveyed through movements of the face and shoulders. Cultures differ also in the degree to which bodily expressions are socially acceptable. The emotional release of profound grief is expected to be contained in Great Britain, whereas Middle Eastern societies have codified wide body movements for the public display of sorrows.

From the examples above it is certain that conversational nonverbal behavior is culture specific. Therefore, given that it is not innate, it must be researched within a learning paradigm. There are also cultural differences in the way parents recognize the conversational function of nonverbal behavior. Most Western societies do not explicitly mention illustrators and emblems to their young, but in one African tribe such instruction is part of the child's training (Alexandre, 1972). General postural behavior is part of the education of the young in most societies. Among the well-known examples are the strict table manners requested of upper class children in Europe. In China, according to Nierenberg and Calero (1971:94) "girls are admonished not to put their hands behind their back because of the provocation of protruded breasts." Maoris in Indonesia believe that by limiting the use of the left hand; they suppress the evil powers of mind that are associated with the left side; their children are taught to restrain the use of the left hand "even to the point of binding it to the side of the body" (Ten-Houten, 1980). Our children are taught to wave goodbye with their right hand and some are scolded if they use the left hand, because this is considered impolite. If one is holding a cumbersome package in the right arm, the left hand can be used to greet people only with apologies and in any case, only with very close friends. Greeting formulas and the contingent nonverbal behavior are, of course, part of kinesics. It would be interesting to study how much of nonverbal interactional behavior is explicitly taught to children in our own society.

Teaching by example and explicit instruction does, of course, determine different learning strategies. This is, however, not the only reason for the failure of any single learning theory to properly account for the acquisition of kinesics. The phenomenon may be best explained by the combination of different types of learning discussed by Carson (1969). It is well known that even very small children scrutinize the behavior of their parents. In 1882, Preyer (1900:306) observed that small children watch the lips of the speaker.

CATEGORIES OF CONVERSATIONAL NONVERBAL BEHAVIOR

Conversational nonverbal behavior is divisible into three distinct—albeit not always clearly separable—categories. The *referential category* represents the object of the conversation, that which is said or implied, its most frequent gestures being illustrators and emblems. The *regulatory category* refers to the interactional aspects of the conversation, including turn-taking procedures and degree of formality. The choice of language or dialect and the use of code-switching may be related to either the referential or the regulatory function, or both simultaneously.

A third type of nonverbal behavior is the manifestation of the *affective, or emotional, category*. The relevance of this category to conversational behavior is incidental. Even an experienced poker player finds it hard to hide his ego state. The differences in societal rules governing the situational appropriateness of showing one's emotions have been noted. Within a culture, people also differ in their perception of emotional manifestations on the part of conversational interactants (von Raffler-Engel, 1980). Evidently, the speaker as well as the hearer is influenced by his own emotions, including the attempt to suppress them, and by the partner's emotions and the hearer's reaction to them, which will color his response. The fact remains that the spontaneous expression of one's emotion is not a purposeful part of conversational interaction.

The show of emotion—genuine or fake—becomes a conversational practice when it is produced on purpose. In that case, the affective function is utilized for regulatory purposes and should be classified within that category. It has been documented that tears caused by emotion and tears caused by a physical interference, such as peeling onions, differ chemically (Frey, 1980). Whether there is a chemical difference between tears resulting from genuine and from faked emotion has not been explored. Within the conversational context one has to keep in mind that the free expression of genuine emotion serves the regulatory function in the same manner as a faked show of emotion. Children are masters at using emotion in the regulatory function. When they start doing this and how they learn it remains to be researched.

The child perceives the visual and the verbal message at the same time. Even if they are not stored in the same area of the brain, they certainly are retrieved synchronously and connected meaningfully through the brain's electrical circuits. Pribram (personal communication) believes that communicative expressions, be they verbal or visual, are stored according to function. Storage for him is a matter of cognitive organization, not of physical sense modality. Following this theory, referential expressions are stored by themselves, whereas regulatory expressions are stored jointly in another part of the brain. With reference to the acquisition of communicative competence, the problem arises of how these expressions are transferred to different places of storage when the child gradually separates the three functions from an original global and possibly erroneous interpretation of these functions. Indeed, considerable research is still needed to clarify perception, storage, retrieval, and production of kinesics throughout the life of the individual.

In the child's acquisition of natural behavior, the bulk of learning probably takes place through osmosis, what Berlyne (1965) has called "incidental learning." This is particularly true for the regulatory category. As Dukoff (1979) put it: "The types of behavior which regulate and maintain the flow of conversation are far too rapid and involved to be imitated piecemeal. The child rarely, if ever, rehearses what he has seen performed by an adult or other model." As in language development, reinforcement is necessary for the maintenance of a gestural configuration. In a family group whose interactions were videotaped (von Raffler-Engel, 1974a, 1978a), the smallest member of the group, a 3½-year-old girl, is engaged in conversation with her father. At a certain moment she stretches her right arm out and extends the index finger in a pointing gesture. Soon thereafter her father points back toward the child in the same manner, confirming the social acceptability of his daughter's gesture.

The imitation of body motions differs from the imitation of vocalizations because of the influence of the physical surroundings on the freedom of movement. The lack of space between the interactants limits the range of the movements, and the orientation of the conversation partner channels the direction of the movement. The presence of artifacts close by causes additional constraints. Children are also smaller than adults, and even a perfect imitation will by necessity be in a smaller scale. Basically, if one wants to speak of a kinesic model and its imitation, one must define imitation not in terms of identity but in terms of sameness of proportions of the direction, duration, and intensity of the movement. The child's process of kinesic acquisition is basically similar to the adult's process of metakinesics, the description of a gesture in conversation by means of making that gesture. It begins with a model and ends with a reproduction of that model, mediated by a series of psychological and physical constraints (von Raffler-Engel and Weinstein, 1977:10).

Purposeful movements of the body also require physical coordination and therefore cannot be produced by children before they have acquired the coordination necessary for each movement. In this respect, the development of kinesics is similar to the development of sound articulation, which requires muscle control and a full set of teeth. The development of kinesics requires readiness in motor coordination, psychological intent, and knowledge of the proper form of nonverbal behavior. Among Arabs, showing the sole of one's foot or shoe to one's conversation partner is tantamount to an insult. To perform such an insulting gesture, however, one must be able to sit in adult fashion. It is evident that a baby lying on a table with his feet exposed will not be perceived as contemptuous. In an informal setting in America, putting one's feet on an ottoman does not carry communicative meaning.

Given that nonverbal behavior requires motor coordination and intent in performing movements that have meaning in a given culture, the acquisition of kinesics must be described in relation to a biological maturation curve, a curve of cognitive development, and the exposure to a given culture. Not all body movements are kinesic. Beyond a very early age, there is, however, no motion of the body that is not influenced by culture. Even small children model their body movements on those of their significant others, either in conformity with what they observe or in reaction to it. Girls are conscious of crossing their legs in cultures where such a seating posture is deemed inappropriate for females.

What is a non-speech-related body movement in one culture may be kinesic in another culture. All gestural configurations are culture specific. They can, nevertheless, be divided into two groups. Bolinger (1975:19–21) distinguishes between instinctive gestures and semiotic gestures. Although instinctive gestures, such as holding up one's hand—be it palm up or down or sidewise—may show great similarities across unrelated cultures, semiotic gestures are basically diverse; therefore it is not possible to interpret them correctly unless one has previously acquired knowledge of their meaning in a manner similar to learning a language. The dialects of southern Italy are especially rich in semiotic gestures, for example. The so-called instinctive gestures differ in both form and use (Birdwhistell, 1970:3–23). If indeed these gestures have underlying universals, it remains to be explored whether this factor causes them to be acquired by the child at the same stage or age cross-culturally.

Depending on the purpose of one's research, gestures can be classified together by the body part or parts involved (e.g., hand movements) or by the meaning they represent (e.g., manifestation of contempt).

CULTURAL VERSUS UNIVERSAL FEATURES

Children do not use identical strategies in learning the rules of their native language (or languages, if they grow up in a bilingual environment). The same holds true for the acquisition of kinesics. In addition, once the linguistic and the kinesic systems have been acquired, people do not necessarily use them in the same fashion. Differences between the sexes are partly biological and partly due to cultural influences.

Psychologists and educators have constantly tried to isolate what is attributable to universal innate human faculties from what makes languages different. Behavior is neither totally innate nor totally learned. All cultures have rhythmically cadenced nursery tales, lullabies, finger games, and dances for their children. It is the type of rhythm that varies extensively between cultures (von Raffler-Engel, 1978a).

Whether there is a critical age or an optimal age for language acquisition is a much debated question (Lenneberg, 1967; von Raffler-Engel, 1974b). In regard to that same question concerning the acquisition of kinesics, the current state of our knowledge is virtually nil. Given the inseparable relationship between words and gestures and the synchronous acquisition of the forms and the use of the means of communication, it is likely that the answer to the problem of critical age for language and for gestures might be the same (see chapter 3).

Kinesics, being an integral part of the whole of communicative behavior, cannot be adequately studied separately from verbal language and from paralanguage, and the study of each modality in isolation is only an artifact of analysis. Research in a day care center for lower class black and white children in Nashville, Tennessee, conducted in 1966 with a student, Lucy Long, showed that the most talkative children were also the most active kinesically, whereas the verbally quiet children were also kinesically quiet.

The intricate relationship of the verbal and the nonverbal component appears clearly from the case of a 3-year-old Italian boy who distinguished two homophones entirely by facial mimicry. Albertino had one word *kappa* for both Italian *scarpa* 'shoe,' and *schiaffo* 'slap.' *Kappa* in the meaning of 'shoe' was unmarked, whereas in the meaning of 'slap' it was consistently accompanied by a stern expression identical to the one Albertino's father displayed when telling the child that he was preparing to administer this kind of punishment. When the boy was observed in 1964, it was impossible to determine whether mimicry or lexicon was the primary agent of communication (von Raffler-Engel, 1964:68–69).

Many gestures have a verbal equivalent with exactly the same meaning. What causes the perception and/or production by the child of one modality before the other remains to be explored. It is possible that the child chooses to produce one modality of an intersemiotic synonym before the other simply because he finds that modality easier to produce. It is also possible that at certain stages of his cognitive maturation, the child is more advanced kinesically than verbally, or vice versa. Ultimately, it may be that the understanding of certain particular meanings is more readily grasped when perceived through the eye than when perceived through the ears, and vice versa. The answer lies probably in a combination of all these. One

Italian-speaking child who was followed longitudinally during his first year of life produced the leave-taking hand gesture at 7 months, first waving with one finger and then with the whole hand. At 7½ months he added the word *ča* (for *ciao*, bye-bye). This lasted for 1 month, after which the child discontinued saying *ča* without interrupting the use of the hand-waving motion. Eventually, when the child was almost a year old, he regained the use of the leave-taking word (von Raffler-Engel, 1964:66, 101–102).

Just as a small child's words are not pronounced perfectly, so his gestures are sometimes only imperfect replicas of the corresponding adult gestures. It may not always be easy to determine whether the child's hand movement does indeed represent an established gesture, or is only a simple movement that happens to resemble a gesture. It is also difficult at times to tell exactly which of two or more possible gestures the child intended to produce in his limited fashion.

One type of infantile gesture that is truly kinesic but difficult to classify is a meaningful and consistent gesture that, nevertheless, does not have its counterpart in the adult system. Such a gesture, observed by van der Geest (1978b) in his two children, consisted of grasping with one hand in the direction of a certain object. This motion originally was a natural gesture but eventually developed into an arbitrary sign that was later used to indicate that an object was beyond the child's reach. Such a gestural creation parallels word creations of the type where form precedes meaning. One such verbal creation was the sound *gigl* by a 6-month-old child. Originally, this was one of the child's babbling sounds. The father took a liking to that particular sound, and whenever he heard it he went and played with the infant and while playing, repeated the babbling sound. Eventually the child came to associate that sound with his father, and whenever he spied his father he uttered the sound *gigl* to gain his parent's attention (von Raffler-Engel, 1970b). Some child-created sound combinations persist within the family intimacy, and it would be interesting to find out whether some child-created gestures can be preserved in the same manner.

Perhaps we should not try to establish correlations between children's speech and regular adult speech, but rather between the speech of children of a certain age group and the forms of language adults use in conversing with them. When children reach maturity and speak adult language, they do not use the forms that were common to adult language when they were little but the current forms by which they are addressed now. This circumstance is only partially attributable to the influence of peer groups. It is also due to the changing patterns of parental speech. Children are expected to change as part of the normal process of growing up. They are expected to change in conformity with their age. A 1½-year-old is greeted with *hi* by the maid, and if he greets his father's boss by *hi*, he is applauded. His 12-year-old brother would not be praised for using this same greeting formula in a similar circumstance.

Greeting formulas are a good case in point. Fifty years ago, men bowed more formally than is customary now when greeting ladies. Men who were boys 50 years ago do not behave like their elders of that time, however. They had a parental model when they were 5 years old and a slightly different parental model when they were teenagers. Some men still conform to the parental model that existed when they reached adulthood; most men adjusted their greeting behavior to fit subsequent societal norms; none behave like the parental model of their earliest childhood. Lexicon, discourse styles, and modes of kinesic expressions change diachronically, and even the most conservative adults change their speech habits to adapt to society. The communicative model of a 5-year-old is geared to his age and represents the speech patterns that are prevalent at that time. Ten years later, the same child will be addressed not only in a manner suitable for a teenager, but also in the forms that are in use at that time in the society (von Raffler-Engel, 1978b).

Even though the list of problems for the study of developmental kinesics may not be longer than for the study of first language acquisition, there are two basic obstacles that make the former in some ways much more complex to investigate than the latter. In the study of children's verbal language, we know at least what their model is. The language has been described in dictionaries and grammars. We also have mechanical equipment that can analyze sounds, and we have various theories of syntax and semantics. The transcription of vocal material is fairly well standardized. In the realm of kinesics we have only a spotty knowledge of the adult system; we do not possess a kinesic inventory even for one single language. In addition, the study of videotaped material is infinitely more fatiguing than the study of audio material. In the analysis of motion on a screen, the strain on the eye is so great that the work can proceed only at a slow pace, with frequent rest periods. Mechanical equipment for filming or video analysis is extremely expensive, and computerized programs are available only in selected research centers, such as Paul Ekman's in San Francisco or Klaus Scherer's in Giessen, Germany. Last, and most important, analytical procedures for the description of body movements have not yet been fully worked out, and the established notational systems are cumbersome (Birdwhistell, 1970).

All this may explain why very few people responded to the challenge of a proposal to form a Cross-Cultural Archive for the Study of Developmental Kinesics (von Raffler-Engel, 1975). Cross-cultural research is greatly hampered by the incompatibility of video bands and cassettes around the world. The conversion of tape from one model to another can be done only in one specialized commercial establishment in New York City, at $165 per tape.

Only a cross-cultural comparison of the various developmental stages will provide insight into what is universal in the acquisition of kinesics and in the proxemic and gestural behavior between mother and child and in the communication between children of the same age or other age in other sex and same sex combinations. Having to work under such hardships and financial burdens, it is not surprising that our knowledge of the field is still extremely limited. The following is an attempt to synchronize the chronology.

MATURATION CURVE

Infancy

The human infant is sensitive to touch as soon as he is born. (There is growing evidence of this sensitivity many weeks before birth.) Obstetricians and nurses are aware of this and, like mothers, make use of the loving touch of the hand to calm the newborn (von Raffler-Engel, 1964:67). Equally, from the time of birth, the human infant reacts to the body rhythm of his caregiver. Condon and Sander (1974a, b) have shown that babies will move their limbs in unison with the articulatory rhythm of the speech addressed to them. In a recent study, Condon (1980) demonstrated that different body parts display the same rhythms seen in the body as a whole and that each culture has its peculiar body rhythm, which is thus transmitted to the child through his earliest contact with his mother, right after birth. Rhythmic enculture motion begins in utero. The sameness or difference of body rhythm rarely reaches consciousness and becomes one of the most powerful tools of subconscious group identification (von Raffler-Engel, 1979).

While the mother is cuddling her baby she also frequently chants or speaks to him, reinforcing the body rhythm peculiar to the infant's language and culture. But the significance of maternal cuddling goes beyond its function of communicating enculturation. According to Restak (1979), rocking and caressing stimulate the "pleasure pathways" of the infant brain; if a baby is deprived of such pleasurable stimuli, his brain is flooded with violent impulses, later forming the roots of violent behavior in adult life. The lack of rhythmic enculturation creates antisocial individuals. Human interaction is verbal and nonverbal, and when the nonverbal component is absent from its inception, the infant does not develop into a normal, social being.

The function of the baby's smile as regulator, both for initiating and maintaining communicative interaction, and for setting that interaction on the level of friendliness, has been widely recognized since the pioneering study by Spitz (1965) of the communicative function of the infant smile. Kagan and his group (1963) worked for many years on the reciprocal smile as a means of communicative expression. The whole facial mimicry of the infant was explored by Herzka (1978).

Bullowa's (1975) films show that within the first 2 weeks of postnatal life, there is already mutual adjustment between infant and mother. As he grows older, the infant becomes able to mesh his activity with more and more complex aspects of his mother's interactional behavior. Bullowa and her co-workers (1975) documented that even when in discomfort from an overstuffed belly and crying, the baby continues the eye contact necessary for a communicative interaction. "The film frames at half-second intervals showed the infant and father's faces oriented toward one another despite the infant's crying with his eyes closed part of the time. The father turned his head away for one second (first frame). When his gaze returned to his son's face (second frame), the baby had turned his face away, and it took another second for him to turn back and reestablish mutual gaze (fourth frame)" (Bullowa et al., 1975: 273).

In a case study, the correlation between vocal and gestural behavior in the small child was observed (von Raffler-Engel, 1964:66–70, 90, 101–102). At the end of the fourth month of life, the subject manifested a consistent sound /m:/ to initiate or confirm communicative interaction. At 4½ months, the child added the pointing gesture to define his topic, an object within visual range. At 6 months, the child added comment to his topic. When the carrier sound /m:/ was uttered with rising intonation, it had a desiderative function, and when uttered with falling intonation it functioned as an interrogative. The meaning of the pointing gesture plus the rising intonation was equivalent to *Could you please give me this particular object?* and the same gesture and the same sound with falling intonation meant *Look at this. What is it?*

The literature of child language provides many examples of the pointing gesture, but it is only in the study just cited that the association of gesture and intonation became the focus of a theory of language development. At that time (1964), the theory was largely ignored because of the prevailing trend to study language acquisition outside any strictly nonverbal factors. Fortunately, this unnatural approach to pedolinguistics is no longer practiced. In her case study, Carter (1978) further expanded on the concept of the association of gesture and intonation contour to form a consistent meaningful expression in the prelinguistic stage.

By the end of the seventh month, the subject of the case study by von Raffler-Engel (1964) had acquired the leave-taking formula *cǎ* (Italian *ciao*, 'good-bye') together with the hand-waving movement. At first he waved only his forefinger, but eventually he learned to wave the whole hand in the proper Italian fashion, with the palm showing toward the speaker. The gesture was as culture specific as the word *ciao* was language

specific. The child had passed from prespeech to speech and from prekine-
sics to kinesics.

The First Years

At 1½ years, the child observed by von Raffler-Engel (1964) had memo-
rized the sequence of hand gestures and head movements his mother was
accustomed to make when she sang a little ditty intended to console the
child when he was slightly unhappy. When the child saw his mother upset,
he would perform the whole set of gestures for her without singing the
words. He was perfectly quiet during the performance, looking sympathet-
ically at his mother while "doing" the song for her.

Foster (1979) videotaped children between the ages of 0;1 and 11;1
over a 6-month period and discovered that:

> The ability to combine gaze at mother and gaze at the object of attention within
> the same topic initiation sequence, emerges around the end of the first year and
> is used extensively from then on. A combination of gaze at mother and vocali-
> zation, i.e., directing vocalization at the conversational partner, is evident from
> 0;1 though it is little used during the first year, increasing in frequency around
> the beginning of the second year. This directed vocalization is combined with
> gesture at the beginning of the second year, the vocalization becoming verbal
> towards the end of the second year. The ability to combine action/gesture or
> gesture with both gaze at mother and at the object of attention and with vocali-
> zation emerges at the beginning of the second year.

The degree of culture specificity of the hand gestures and head movements of these children can be determined only when the cross-cultural
archive proposed at the beginning of this chapter has been established. An
example in the archive is from Japan. At 2;3, a Japanese girl knows the
kinesic rules for leave-taking. In a videotape made by F.C.C. Peng, a Japanese colleague (Peng, 1975; von Raffler-Engel, 1978b), one can see a little
girl speaking over a toy telephone. She enjoys the play conversation, bows
when greeting her imaginary partner, smiles when conversing with him,
and finally bows to say goodbye.

Empirical observation in toddlers shows clear culture specificity when
comparing the child's body movements with those of his elders. Albertino,
the 3-year-old Italian boy who was mentioned earlier for his ability to distinguish homophones by facial mimicry, showed a clear imitation of his
father's gaze, head tilt, and the musculature of his face. That the parents
readily recognized what the child meant reinforced his use of nonverbal
expressions to clarify a verbal ambiguity.

Group pictures of children are very useful in exploring the maturational curve of their kinesic development. Bullowa (1975) and Condon and
Sander (1974a, b) had documented the early development of interactional
synchrony in children. Later, however, it does seem that sometime between
the middle of their first year and the end of the third year children use the

dissonance created by interactional synchrony as an attention-getting device. To get attention, the small child will use distractive techniques. He will gear his behavior to contrast with that of the group by running around, screaming, and talking nonsense. In group pictures, one can observe that small children do not conform to the posture of the older members of the group. In conversational interaction, even when they are actively participating in the conversation, they sit differently from the older people. When a small child wants to become part of a group, he draws attention to himself by behaving in a dissynchronic manner. He wants the others to focus on him. If older children, or adults, behave in such a manner, they are said to be immature. The small child makes use of a self-centered (distractive, nonconforming) attention-getting device, whereas older children and adults adopt the other-centered (attractive, conforming) attention-getting device (von Raffler-Engel, 1974b, 1978a).

Later Years

It seems that children use different interactional strategies depending on age. The manner in which a 9-year-old draws attention to his presence is the exact opposite from that of the 3-year-old described above. A group of three children consisting of one girl, age 9, and two boys, age 12 was videotaped. The boys huddle together ignoring the girl. The girl does not like to be isolated. She observes the body posture of the boys and quite consciously adjusts her hand and leg position to conform to theirs. Eventually, she has become part of the group, and from then on the conversation proceeds in the triad (von Raffler-Engel; 1974a, 1978a).

Trying to establish a maturational curve for speech-regulatory nonverbal behavior is even more difficult than establishing a curve for referential gesticulation because the development of the nonverbal counterpart of referential kinesics has been explored to some extent, whereas speech-regulatory language is not well known even for adults. So far, all that can be ascertained is a *terminus post quem*, after which a certain type of behavior is present in the child. To determine the exact age at which it appears, an extended longitudinal survey or a cross-sectional study with a very large population would have to be done.

Concerning the concept of conversational dominance, with its social rules of who is expected to be the dominant partner and the nonverbal expressions for manifesting dominance or submission, it seems that at 8 years of age the child is fully developed. The child's mastery of the dominance relationship was apparent from a series of videotapes prepared to test various dominance configurations in the child (von Raffler-Engel, 1974a). An 8½-year-old girl is seated between her parents. The father takes a rather stiff, formal posture and is copied by the mother and the daughter. He initiates the conversation by asking questions of the daughter, to which she replies with the same type of short sentences accompanied by brief staccato up-and-down body movements.

Later on, the same child is seated opposite a younger girl, age 3;9. This time, she assumes the role her father had taken, asking questions of the smaller child in the same staccato manner, verbally and nonverbally, that her father had previously used in speaking to her. She makes no attempt to adjust her posture and movements to those of the smaller child. She looks as if she expects the smaller child to conform to her behavior.

In the third frame, the 8½-year-old sits down opposite a 9-year-old school friend. The two girls observe each other and coordinate their movements while seating themselves. The 8-year-old initiates the conversation, which proceeds on reciprocal stretches of speech of approximately the same duration.

Even younger children, by age 7, seem already to know the rules of societal dominance; they are aware of the power structure. From a study concerning the nonverbal behavior of adult minority groups in the United States (von Raffler-Engel 1974c), it became apparent that there is a definite relationship between kinesic behavior and social status. In societal bilingualism and bidialectalism, members of the minority tend to behave differently from members of the majority when associating with the out group.

A subsequent study involving second graders between the ages of 7 and 8 was conducted in Canada in 1970–1971 (von Raffler-Engel, 1973, 1976b). The kinesic behavior of bilingual French and Canadian children was observed in in-group and in out-group interaction. It seemed that bilingual Canadian children have one full kinesic system and two languages. But the two ethnic groups differ radically. In code switching, the Anglophone children maintain their own customary kinesic system, but sometimes intersperse it with exaggerated Francophone kinesics. The Francophone children do not correlate kinesics with language code switching: they correlate kinesics with ethnic group switching.

SOME RESEARCH AREAS IN KINESICS STUDY

Proxemics

Cross-cultural research aimed to determine the distance between conversation partners and the direction in which they face each other has produced interesting if inconclusive results for the study of acquisition of proxemics. The field observations and experiments conducted over the past years in research groups have shown that one cannot speak of equilibrium distance in terms of various cultures without a very narrow description of the situational and interpersonal variables involved. The kinesic development of the child cannot be researched until model behavior can be adequately described.

To state that "young children (for instance, second graders) are most aware of distance in communication in the 'closer' zones— the intimate and personal zones"—and that "their understanding of communication conventions in the social and public zones may depend on the social and public communication experiences in their elementary school years" (Wood, 1976:245) begs the question. The acquisition of language is not exclusively expériential, and it cannot be automatically assumed that the acquisition of kinesics is exclusively experiential. Preschool children have certainly seen adult interaction outside the family circle, at least in shopping centers, not to mention on television. More important, when there is no contrast, there is no differentiation. If, according to Wood (1976:239, 245), small children (birth to 2 or 3 years) always communicate in the intimate zone and children ages 3 to 7 add the personal zone, this does not mean that these zones correspond to the adult definition of such distances. If the small children have only one proxemic pattern, it is clear that they have not acquired the concept of proxemics qua concept.

According to Wood (1976), until age 7 children do not communicate beyond the personal space because they are still in the egocentric stage and have only an extremely limited understanding of socialization. Informal observations indicate, however, that children may communicate beyond the personal space before they reach age 7. It depends very much on their adult models. Moreover, the young child's alleged egocentricity is no longer agreed on by most child psychologists. There is evidence that even during the very early years a child is not necessarily exclusively egocentric (von Raffler-Engel, 1964:99). Beyond this, it is not clear why egocentricity must be associated with closer interpersonal distance. During so-called egocentric play interaction, children keep greater distances from each other. Above all, it must be clarified whether age 7 is a biological age or depends on the first year in school, the latter case implying that children who go to kindergarten or enter grade school at age 5 reach the public zone at an earlier period.

Even though one area of proxemics has been researched with a developmental curve in mind (see Jones and Aiello, 1973, and the literature reported in that article), it does not seem that the correct formulation of the problem is available yet.

Sex Identification

Although extensive literature on the development of sex identification in the child is available in psychology, the study of sex differences in the conversational behavior of the child has been barely touched. From the studies in proxemics performed in the early 1970's by Jones and Aiello (1973), it seems that among black and white fifth graders in American schools, boys have a less direct orientation than girls in face-to-face interaction.

Sex differences in conversational behavior were also apparent on videotapes of children ages 3 to 15. Looking at the children revealed that the sexes behave in different manners and that the differences increase with age. The boys were more relaxed than the girls, who kept a stiff posture while the boys leaned forward with knees spread. The girls answered questions more appropriately but did not interrupt the experimenter/story teller when they got involved and wanted clarification. When the girls disapproved they became stiffer; the boys showed bewilderment in their faces. The boys and girls differed greatly in the way they were dressed. The girls arrived at the television studio in Sunday-type clothing, whereas the boys wore neat but not formal garb. The experimenter said that she felt as if she were teaching Sunday School when she was with the girls. She gesticulated less freely with the girls than with the boys, and her posture was more rigid. The story teller's proxemics, eye contact, and haptics were not differentiated in relation to the sex of the child (von Raffler-Engel, 1978b). In the tape frames, the sexes behaved as socially expected, but to what extent the sex difference is biologically or culturally conditioned cannot be verified until a cross-cultural archive becomes available for comparison. Walters (1978) has discussed the interrelationship of innate and cultural causes in shaping the more aggressive style in posture and gesticulation common to the male when compared to the female under similar environmental conditions.

That children model their behavior on the same sex parent is an established fact in psychology, and there is no reason to believe that kinesics should not follow the same pattern. Less known is the tendency of adults to identify more closely with same sex children than with other sex children when initiating their nonverbal behavior as when describing the gesture made by a child (von Raffler-Engel and Weinstein, 1977). Men seem to have taboos in copying the body motions of female children (von Raffler-Engel and Weinstein, 1977).

The Bilingual Child

It is surprising that the kinesic behavior of bilinguals has hardly been studied. Efron's pioneering work dates from 1941. He compared the gestural system of immigrant groups depending on their degree of assimilation into the broader culture of the new country. It was not only the first study of the gesture of bilinguals and the first contrastive study in kinesics, but also the first in sociokinesics.

In a study with children in Canada in 1970–1971 (von Raffler-Engel, 1973, 1976b), the kinesic behavior of bilingual French and English Canadian children, ages 5 to 7, was observed in in-group and out-group interaction. Bilingual Canadian children seemed to have one full kinesic system and two languages. But as noted above, the two ethnic groups differed radically.

In code switching, the Anglophone children maintained their own customary kinesic system, but sometimes interspersed it with exaggerated Francophone kinesics. Overcorrectness was particularly evident among children who were not completely fluent in the French language.

The Francophone children did not correlate kinesics with language code switching. They correlated kinesics with ethnic group switching. When speaking either French or English with an Anglophone, they employed a reduced version of their own customary kinesics. When speaking English to Francophones (this occurred more frequently than outsiders might presume), they seemed more relaxed in not altering their native kinesics.

Bilingual and/or bidialectical children, in addition to the sociolinguistic rules of their own culture, learn the rules of the other culture and/or the rules for intercultural conversation. Eventually, the bicultural individual knows whether his own culture holds majority or minority status. At what precise age the child becomes aware of the social status of his group is not known. So far, from the Canadian study, only a *terminus ante quem* can be established: children of kindergarten age are already conscious of group status.

Children also know that different interactional rules apply when two cultures are of equal status and when there is a hierarchical relationship between the cultures. An equal status situation was tested on videotapes of two siblings, a 13-year-old girl and her 12-year-old brother. Both the parents were French, the father being a professor at an American university. The children spent the winter with their family and peers in the United States and the summer with their family and relatives in France. The tapes show the two siblings among themselves and with their American playmates. The analysis of the nonverbal behavior of the participants indicated that when two cultures are of equal social status, intercultural behavior allows for a certain flexibility. It seems that the kinesics of either culture is permissible at the discretion of the individual (von Raffler-Engel, 1974a).

The two pilot studies mentioned above permit the conclusion that nonverbal behavior in a bilingual setting depends primarily on the societal relationship of the interacting cultures (von Raffler-Engel, 1976b). It is therefore necessary to study the onset of the social and political awareness in the child when investigating the acquisition of bilingual and bikinesic behavior. This ramification of the problem of bikinesicism has not received sufficient attention, although the literature on cross-cultural misunderstandings due to nonverbal patterns is quite extensive. Particular attention has been devoted to the interaction between the minority schoolchild and his teacher. Freedle (1979) lists some of the difficulties arising from different social rules for eye gaze: American Indian children avoid eye gaze, although this is exactly contrary to the white teacher's expectation, because in their culture one does not look directly at people. Black children look at the teacher when they speak, which is the opposite of the white custom of looking at the conversation partner when one listens, not when one speaks.

What all the literature shows is that schoolchildren exhibit culture specific patterns of nonverbal conversational behavior. With respect to proxemics, Hall (1966:194) believes that patterns of spatial orientation are acquired before school age and that these remain stable throughout the school years (see Chapter 3). Jones and Aiello (1973) agree with Hall that the proxemic patterns are established early. They do, however, believe that some aspects of proxemics—namely, level of interpersonal distance as opposed to the axis of orientation—undergo changes in the black minority child. According to Jones and Aiello, the black child adapts to the white majority level of distance, while maintaining his subcultural axis of orientation. As far as the data can be interpreted, given that level of distance in adult blacks has not been conclusively measured, it is impossible to know whether the black children of that study assimilated the white pattern or whether they approximated more closely the adult black pattern as they grew older. The latter would then be a simple case of maturation, and we would not know what its maturational counterpart is in the white child. If one agrees with Jones and Aiello that the black children partially conform to the white pattern, it is not clear from the data whether the children change from one level of distance to another or whether they simply have become bikinesic, using the white level only at school, not at home. However, bikinesic interactional behavior has been informally observed in various groups.

In conclusion, information is available on selected aspects of kinesics acquired at an unspecified period, but sometime before school age, and hardly anything is known about nonverbal patterns the child may acquire during his school years. Although there are exceptions, the majority of researchers believe that a 7-year-old has full command of kinesics, but nobody has argued for full kinesicism in the bilingual child. The problem has not yet been well formulated.

Little is known about how the simultaneous acquisition of two kinesic codes from birth on compares to the acquisition of a second kinesic code around school age or earlier (see Chapter 11). With too few exceptions, foreign language teachers do not teach nonverbal behavior; therefore, no comparison can be made between learned kinesics and street kinesics. The acquisition of culturally different rules in elementary school is within the realm of street kinesics.

Adult Kinesic Adjustment

In his whole communicative behavior toward the child, the adult adjusts to the level, real or imagined, of the child. This largely unconscious adjustment has been observed for verbal language (von Raffler-Engel and Rea, 1978) and is quite evident for kinesics. Brazelton and his research team (1974) have extensively documented the mutual gaze between infant and caregiver, showing that in most instances eye contact is initiated by the baby.

The videotapes mentioned above for the observation of sex differences (von Raffler-Engel, 1974a) have been analyzed for the accommodation of adult gesticulation to the maturity of the child. The videotapes involved 30 children ages 3 to 15 and were produced by this author and Brenda Hopson-Hasham. Hopson-Hasham divided the children into three age groups depending on the behavior of the adult toward them:

1. *Childhood (3 to 7 years)*:   There seems to be an emphasis on keeping the attention of children from 3 to 7 years old. They have not been socialized enough to pay attention because the rules of propriety call for politeness. By the same token, children who are not overly shy and self-conscious are not uncomfortable in a formal setting, which has not yet acquired evil connotations. The adult touches younger children more frequently to involve them and keep their attention, and tries to elicit smiles and laughter (back-channeling responses). The adult speaker often cannot "illustrate" as much with very young children because he is busy trying to make them keep still; the still posture here being associated with attentiveness. In telling the story to younger children, the adult acts out the passages and changes the voice more frequently to indicate the roles of characters. The adult uses a slower phonation rate to help the young child understand the story, and has more extremes of pitch.

2. *Preadolescence (8 to 11 years)*:   When interacting with children of this age group, the speaker/adult is aware that the children have longer attention spans and are more familiar with the rules of social interaction. This age group is also more assertive and needs to let the adult know how they stand so that the speaker will not underestimate them. The speaker here needs definite feedback and back-channel cues to signal whether she is using the proper approach. There is usually more distance between the speaker and the hearers, a proxemic shift from the positions taken by the younger children, and the adult does not touch the children as frequently. The story is related in a narrative form, and there are fewer voice changes to mark characters.

3. *Adolescence (12 years and up)*:   The adult approaches this age group in an adult manner—almost as peers. The adult speaker is not alone

in adjusting to the verbal and kinesic markers in the conversation. The interactional adjustment is reciprocal. The adult seeks the approval of the teens as much if not more than they seek her approval. Gesticulations in general are more subdued, and politeness and manners are a much more important factor in the interactions. In telling the story to the teens, the adult uses language such as "cool" and "dude," and intonation contours such as he believes the teenagers will identify with. Because these teenagers must eventually retell the story to children, he gesticulates moderately, to give the hearers an example to follow when they act as speakers.

Much of the adjustment mentioned above occurs on a subconscious level. It seems that the rules of an interaction are usually taken for granted unless something goes wrong (Hopson-Hasham, 1977).

In addition to this first function, which is geared to language perception, adult adjustment serves a second function geared to language production. The adult behavior, verbal and nonverbal, is also intended to serve as a model for the child. Adult behavior demonstrates to the child what aspects of the language and culture the child is likely to be capable of performing himself. A 3-year-old is not expected to construct sentences with three or four embeddings, or to sit still for an extended period of time.

It is known that adults use a restricted number of verbal registers when conversing with children (DeStefano, 1972). The nonverbal expressions pertaining to these registers are not known, nor their increase in quantity and quality over time. The child perceives the visual and the verbal message at the same time. Even if they are not stored in the same part of the brain, they certainly are retrieved together and connected meaningfully through the brain's electrical circuits. If communicative expressions, be they verbal or visual, are stored according to function (Pribram, personal communication), it follows that referential expressions are stored by themselves, while regulatory and affective expressions are stored jointly in another part of the brain. In considering the acquisition of communicative competence, it will be necessary to determine how these expressions are transferred to different places of storage when the child gradually separates the three functions from an original global and eventually erroneous interpretation of these functions. Indeed, considerable research is still needed to clarify perception, storage, retrieval, and production of kinesics throughout the life of the individual.

CONCLUDING REMARKS

The components of the developmental kinesics paradigm are many and diverse. One could synthesize the basic components, which must be studied well and integrated into a composite developmental pattern, in the following way:

Fundamental predisposition to communicate vocally and by body
    movement
    Gradual split of vocal component into language and paralanguage
    Gradual split of movement component into kinesics and body
    language
    Distinction between regulatory and referential kinesics
Exposure to cultural model
    Handling of infant by mother and her vocalization/verbalization
    (e.g., chanting) to him
    Adjustment of the adult to the child
Psychological maturation
    Perception (with cognition)
    Production (with intent)

These and the many other components treated in this book are being studied, and the 1980's should yield real progress.

One major problem mentioned earlier but worth repetition is the nature of meaning in kinesics. Because kinesic meaning is expressed by single gestures only rarely and by gesture clusters most often, the child's production of the appropriate combination of various movements requires motor command of all the muscles involved, as well as recognition of the gestalt beyond single movements. It is conceivable that the child perceives the gestalt before he becomes aware of its component parts, and it is also possible that he is only gradually able to produce the complex structure. (This area has received scant attention in the literature; see Chapter 7.) The components listed above form a basic list from which to proceed in the research.

The decade of the 1970's saw great interest in and results concerning the areas outlined in this article. The 1980's, given cooperative work across the relevant disciplines, should provide the best paradigm within which we can make substantive contributions to developmental kinesics. One major advance, already begun but with a distance yet to go, will be the application of the paradigm, especially to the field of education, wherein our models of development are subjected to some of the most stringent forms of accountability. For this reason the model of developmental kinesics is of intrinsic interest to specialists in child development, speech pathology, language-learning disabilities, child psychology, to name only a few.

Chapter 2
ACTIONS SPEAK LOUDER THAN WORDS?

Karen F. Steckol and Richard G. Schwartz

In principle, von Raffler-Engel's argument concerning the importance of movement and action in communication and in the acquisition of communicative competence (Hymes, 1972) is accurate. However, the specific relationship between action and early communicative behavior may be somewhat more complex than von Raffler-Engel has described it.

Before examining this relationship, it is necessary to clearly distinguish between actions and movements. In any discussion of kinesics, it is important to avoid any conflation of these terms. There have been several attempts to differentiate actions from movements in terms of their hierarchical relationships (see Newell, 1978). In many instances, the distinction is straightforward in that movement may be specified in terms of kinematics (spatial and temporal patterns), whereas actions are more appropriately described by their goal (e.g., throw the ball) or end result (e.g., hopping, spinning). In such cases, an action may be described in terms of the movements that comprise it. However, this hierarchical distinction may be ambiguous for what Poulton (1957) has termed "closed skills," in which the goal involves a highly specified, essentially immutable set of movements (e.g., gymnastic routines) and for actions that involve only one identifiable movement (e.g., kicking). The goals are thus inextricably related to the movement(s) involved.

According to Newell (1978), the difference between action and movement is more unambiguously specified in terms of intentionality. Although at times intentionality is difficult to identify, Bruner (1973) has suggested some behavioral criteria (e.g., demonstrated expectancy of outcome). Specifically, actions are associated with an intentional goal, whereas movements do not typically involve an intended goal (Newell, 1978). In adults this distinction is frequently clearcut, and in fact, it often is marked linguistically. For example, we differentiate between *falling* off the side of a pool into the water, and *diving* off the side of a pool into the water.

29

However, the intentionality of the vocal or motor acts of young children is often open to question. Early in infancy, adults respond to infant acts as if they were intended, even though intentionality on the part of the infant is doubtful. Bates et al. (1975) termed this period in which infants' acts have effects on listeners but are not intentional *perlocutionary*. Subsequently, infants enter a period in which it is assumed, based on at least indirect evidence, that there is intentionality underlying motor and vocal communicative acts. This period, termed *illocutionary* (Bates et al., 1975), is the focus of the initial portion of this chapter. At this point in development, communication may largely be dependent on motor acts (e.g., pointing, reaching). It is not always easily demonstrated that these behaviors are in fact *actions* in terms of intended goals. The identifiable actions produced by children during this period are focused on. Once initial words have emerged, children are considered to have entered the *locutionary* period. The intentionality of the child's motor and vocal acts now can be more reliably demonstrated. In fact, the child's intentionality may be inferred with as much confidence as we have in making such inferences concerning adult acts. The final portion of this paper discusses some of the actions of this period.

There are two types of action of interest: 1) actions that serve some communicative function, either in isolation or in conjunction with some type of vocalization; and 2) actions that do not seem to have any communicative function, but instead serve as a means of simply acting on various aspects of the environment. The first section of this chapter examines the relationship between these two types of action during the illocutionary period of development. Then the focus shifts to the relationship between the second type of action mentioned and the early acquisition of lexical concepts. It is hoped that the discussion of these two aspects of the relationship between action and communicative development will add to proposals and points of view put forth by von Raffler-Engel.

PRELINGUISTIC GESTURAL COMMUNICATION

What seems to be neglected in von Raffler-Engel's discussion is the recent trend in the child language literature relating children's early gestural and cognitive abilities. Before a discussion of developmental kinesics can be complete, this critical body of literature must be addressed. To draw appropriate conclusions between gestural communication and performance on cognitive tasks, a review of pertinent information regarding both areas is in order.

Researchers have taken Piaget's (1954) early descriptions of sensorimotor skills and attempted to devise developmental scales that would measure these sensorimotor skills. One such measure that has received much attention in the literature is that of the ordinal scales of infant development reported by Uzgiris and Hunt (1975). This index is divided into six separate subtests of Visual Pursuit and the Permanence of Objects, Means for Obtaining Desired Environmental Events, Imitation (Vocal and Gestural), Operational Causality, Construction of Object Relations in Space, and Schemes for Relating to Objects. Each of these subtests measures a child's ability to perform on cognitive tasks through six stages of sensorimotor development.

Bates et al. (1975) borrowed Austin's (1962) classification system to demonstrate how these six stages of sensorimotor development related to communication skills. The period through sensorimotor stage IV was termed the perlocutionary communication stage. At this stage, children are not aware of the communicative intent of their signals. With cognitive attainments of stage V, the child moves into the illocutionary stage of communication. Here he demonstrates an understanding that people can perform actions, that objects can be acted on, and that object and people activities can be coordinated. Sensorimotor stage VI coincides with the locutionary stage of communicative development. Now the child is using words to stand for actions, objects, and events.

At the same time that these sensorimotor and communicative skills are developing, so too are the child's gestural abilities. In a preliminary article and later in comprehensive form (Bates et al., 1975, 1979), specific areas of nonverbal communication in children were defined. Bates and her colleagues identified a set of 10 gestures that evolved during the age span of 9½ and 12½ months of age. These gestures were "showing off," "ritualized showing off," "showing," "giving," "noncommunicative pointing," "communicative pointing," "unritualized requests," "ritualized requests," "unritualized refusals," and "ritualized refusals." After identifying and observing these gestures with 25 children, Bates et al. (1979) computed a series of correlations among the behaviors. The results suggested that showing, giving, communicative pointing, and ritualized requests form a "gestural complex" having components that are somehow related because they are good predictors of one another. Further correlations were instituted to determine the relationship between gesturing and language acquisition. Communicative pointing was found to be the best predictor of later language development.

In relating gestural abilities (i.e., communicative actions) to sensorimotor skills (i.e., noncommunicative actions), Bates et al. (1979) found that among the subtests of the Uzgiris and Hunt (1975) scales, Means-End, Imitation, and a modification of Schemes for Relating to Objects items correlated highly with and predicted gestural skills. The correlations suggested that combinatorial and symbolic play (modification of Schemes for Relating to Objects) were the best predictors of the gestural complex. The second best predictor was Means-End performance, and the third best predictor was Imitation.

The initial work of Bates et al. (1975) prompted other researchers to further delineate gestural skills in young children. Probably the most notable in this regard was the work of Sugarman-Bell (1978). She was interested in observing the gestural actions of children as they related to other people and objects in the environment. She devised a rather extensive hierarchy of gestural behaviors that were divided into three distinct categories of simple single orientations, complex single orientations, and coordinated person-object orientations. Simple single orientations were behaviors that could be directed at either a person or an object, yet there was no attempt to manipulate or control the environment. Complex single orientations were combinatorial within the person or the object classification, but no attempt to coordinate the two domains was observed. Coordinated person-object orientations were an integration of the use of objects and people in an attempt to socially interact with the environment. These three categories were ordinal and occurred between the ages of 4 and 14 months. Sugarman-Bell related simple single orientation to stage II of sensorimotor development and complex single orientations to stage IV; not until stage V of sensorimotor development did the children begin using coordinated person-object orientations.

Harding and Golinkoff (1979) found that children judged to be in stage V (mean age of 11.9 months) of sensorimotor development on causality tasks used a combination of vocalizations and communicative pointing as attention getting devices. These data would suggest that S. Foster's observation (1979) that this behavior does not emerge until the beginning of the second year, cited in Chapter 1, may be a rather conservative one. Contrary to what one might expect, Harding and Golinkoff, like Bates et al. (1979), found that communcative pointing did not decrease as vocalizations increased. Rather than replacing gestural skills with newly acquired linguistic skills, the combination of both was used to possibly "add a new dimension to the infant's ability to act on the environment" (Harding and Golinkoff, 1979:39).

Within the gestural complex proposed by Bates et al. are two specific gestural skills that emerge during stage V of sensorimotor development. These are the protodeclarative and protoimperative. The protodeclarative is defined as the child's use of an object or gesture as a means of obtaining an adult's attention. The protoimperative is defined as the child's use of an adult as a means of obtaining an object or getting an act performed.

In a study by Steckol and Leonard (1979), the relationship between two specific sensorimotor skills and the acquisition of protodeclaratives and protoimperatives was investigated. Past research had shown that Means-End and Schemes for Relating to Objects sensorimotor skills were important for the development of nonverbal and verbal communication abilities. Steckol and Leonard initiated a research design to experimentally manipulate sensorimotor abilities to observe the resultant effect on gestural development. Thirty-two infants, equally divided into four training conditions, served as subjects for the investigation. The four training conditions consisted of training on Means-End schemes, training on Relating to Objects schemes, training on Means-End and Relating to Object schemes, and no training (a control group). Training occurred over a 6-week period or until the children reached criterion. Before training, all the children were tested using the Uzgiris and Hunt (1975) scales as being in stage IV or below, and none showed evidence of protodeclarative or protoimperative usage. Results indicated that Relating to Objects training was successful. In addition to the increase in the developmental level of these schemes, the same children also displayed a significantly greater usage of performatives. One finding of this study, then, was that gestural skills could be indirectly facilitated through Relating to Objects schemes training.

The children in this study ranged in age from 0;7(20) to 0;9(7) at pretesting to 0;9(5) to 0;11(8) at posttesting. All children were trained for the 6-week time frame because none reached the dismissal criterion. All the children reached a certain level of training after which no progress was made. For example, on the Means-End training, the child was to model the examiner by using a ruler to obtain an object that was out of his reach. It was believed that the children understood what was expected of them, but they did not possess the physical coordination to succeed at the task. In fact most of the children struggled with the ruler, hitting or touching the object, but could not coordinate the actions of reaching for the object and pulling it toward them. That is, for many of the children, there seemed to be a strategy for retrieving the object. After several unsuccessful attempts, the children threw the ruler in frustration. This suggests that if the children were truly attempting to obtain the object, yet were physically incapable of doing so, the central nervous system had not matured enough to permit them to put their thoughts into actions. This hypothesis would be in agreement with von Raffler-Engel's comment that "the development of kinesics requires readiness in motor coordination, psychological intent, and knowledge of the proper form of nonverbal behavior" (page 11-12).

Before closing this section, we would like to comment briefly on von Raffler-Engel's statement that:

> What causes the perception and/or production by the child of one modality before the other remains to be explored. It is possible that the child chooses to produce one modality of an intersemiotic synonym before the other simply because he finds that modality easier to produce. It is also possible that at certain stages of his cognitive maturation, the child is more advanced kinesically than verbally, or vice versa. Ultimately, it may be that the understanding of certain particular meanings is more readily grasped when perceived through the eye than when perceived through the ears, and vice versa. The answer lies probably in a combination of all these (page 13).

Research relating to performance on cognitive tasks and communication supports what had been termed the homologue model (Bates, 1977) interpretation. This model suggested that language does not precede communication or vice versa. Instead, communication and cognition are enhanced by an underlying operative scheme common to them both. An increase in cognitive abilities passes through the underlying operative scheme and influences communication, and vice versa. With subsequent data, Bates et al. presented evidence to support a "local homology or skill specific model" (1979:128). One of their four explanations for such a relationship is based on the fact that certain cognitive skills are good predictors of communication while others are not. It would be interesting to investigate the relationship between those that are and are not good predictors and central nervous system maturation, specifically motor coordination.

ACTIONS AND LEXICAL CONCEPTS

Three aspects of the relationship between actions and early lexical acquisition are considered: 1) the type of exemplar involved (objects vs. actions), 2) the types of similarity among the exemplars of a given concept, and 3) children's performance of action exemplars and object-related actions.

Varying views concerning children's initial focus in early lexical acquisition have been expressed. Some investigators have posited that children's early words will predominantly be words for actions (Schank, 1972). Other investigators (Nelson, 1973; Benedict, 1979), however, have observed that within children's first 50 words, a far greater number of object words than action words is produced. Benedict found a similar pattern in the words children comprehended during this period, but the gap between object and action words was not as great in this domain. Additionally, Goldin-Meadow et al. (1976) have reported that children do not begin to produce verbs until sometime after they have begun to produce a number of nouns. Although these investigations provide some preliminary evidence of an early "preference" for object over action words, the role of types of exemplar in lexical acquisition has remained undefined. Specifically, it is unclear whether this apparent preference is based on the input that is received by children, on inherent differences between objects, or on children's organization of knowledge at the outset of lexical acquisition.

The second factor to be considered is the type of similarity among the exemplars of a lexical concept. This factor has arisen from two theoretical proposals concerning the nature and progression of lexical acquisition. According to Eve Clark, (1973b, 1974, 1975) children form lexical concepts and extend these concepts on the basis of shared perceptual attributes. These attributes are primarily static features such as shape, size, and texture. Alternately, Nelson, (1974) has argued that the dynamic functional relationships into which objects may enter are the primary basis for the formation of concepts. Static perceptual attributes are assumed to play an apparently minor role; they serve only as a basis for recognizing new probable instances of an already formed concept.

More recently, Nelson and her co-workers (1978) maintained the argument for the primacy of functional relations, but suggested that words may be attached to concepts at any point in their construction. A word attached to a concept at or shortly after the point of its initial formation should be applied to referents that are functionally similar. Concepts that are lexicalized well after their formation should also be based on functional similarities, but extended to perceptually similar instances. At issue here is the role of action in the acquisition of lexical concepts. These proposals are divergent in that the latter suggests that similarities in the actions that can be, and are, performed on objects are the primary basis of the formation of concepts and their lexicalization.

Clark, however, maintains that static features are the primary basis for this development. A function-based proposal concerning concept formation and lexical acquisition would predict that lexical concepts involving *objects* that are functionally similar (in terms of actions that can be or are performed on them) should be acquired more readily and more rapidly than those involving objects that are functionally dissimilar. A prediction concerning concepts involving actions can also be extrapolated. Lexical concepts involving *actions* that are functionally similar (i.e., have similar end results) should be acquired more readily and more rapidly than those involving actions that are functionally dissimilar (i.e., have different end results). The final factor in the relationship between actions and lexical acquisition is the potential influence of children's performance of actions and object-specific actions on their acquisition of the words referring to these actions and objects. Nelson (1974) speculated that children first name objects in the context of their concept-defining actions. However, observations of the language development of two children provide counterevidence to this claim (Greenfield and Smith, 1976). These children first named various objects in nonaction contexts. Given the limited amount of data, it remains unclear whether the initial naming of objects occurs in action or nonaction contexts. Furthermore, to our knowledge, children's performances of object-specific actions or actions in general have not been examined as possible facilitators of the later acquisition of objects and actions words.

Recently Schwartz and Leonard (1980) conducted an investigation that served to further explicate the roles of the various action factors in early lexical acquisition. Twelve children (1;1 to 1;3 (15) at the outset), who had not evidenced usage of more than five "true" words, were presented with 16 contrived lexical concepts over a period of approximately 5 months. Each consisted of a nonsense word and four unfamiliar exemplars that served as the referents for that word. Eight of the concepts involved four unfamiliar objects (e.g., a nose clip) on which an action was performed by the experimenter. The remaining concepts involved four unfamiliar actions performed by the experimenter on more familiar objects (e.g., pressing down on an object with an elbow or spinning an object with thumb and index finger). Within each of these groups of concepts, half involved exemplars that were functionally similar but perceptually different and half involved exemplars that were perceptually similar but functionally different.

Objects that were perceptually similar shared static attributes (i.e., shape and texture) and were functionally different in the actions that could be and were performed on them. The presentation of these concepts involved a different action on each of the exemplars. Actions that were perceptually similar involved the same direction of movement and similar body parts. These exemplars were functionally different in terms of the end result or the effect on various familiar objects.

Functionally similar objects were those on which the same actions could be and were performed (e.g., spinning by hand). In presenting these concepts the same action was performed on each of the exemplars. The objects could be perceived to differ in shape and texture, however. Functionally similar actions were actions performed on various familiar objects that had similar end results (e.g., propelling objects). These actions were perceptually different in the direction of movement and the specific body part involved.

Examinations of the children's acquisition of these words and concepts (spontaneous and elicited usage of the words to refer to their designated referents) revealed that words for objects and object concepts were acquired in greater numbers and more rapidly than action words. This contradicts the results of the recall study reported by von Raffler-Engel (1970b) in which older children were more likely to recall contrived verbs as compared with nouns and adjectives. Even under conditions of controlled input, words for objects seem to dominate early lexical acquisition.

The study also revealed that children were as likely to acquire concepts involving functional or action-based similarities among exemplars as concepts involving functional or action-based dissimilarities among exemplars. This as well as the finding above may suggest that action is less important to children in this period than investigators such as Piaget would have had us believe.

One final aspect of the data from this study suggests that actions are indeed salient to children at this point in development. However, the role of action seems to be rather specific. As was mentioned earlier, the presentation of each of the experimental exemplars involved the performance of an action on an object. After each presentation, the child was permitted to manipulate the object involved. During this time the children actually performed a large number of the actions demonstrated (at least one of the actions in 75% of the experimental action concepts; at least one of the object-specific actions for 84% of the object concepts). Further analyses indicated that although the performance of such actions did not necessarily facilitate subsequent lexical acquisition, such actions were more closely related to the acquisition of action than were object words. The number of actions performed by the children indicates their salience to the children, even though the behaviors may not be directly related to lexical acquisition.

It may be that at this point in development noncommunicative motor actions serve primarily as organizing principles and responses to language for the child, whereas objects are the central focus of cognitive organization and lexical production. This would seem to be consistent with aspects of Nelson's (1974) theoretical proposal and with recent findings reported by Benedict (1979). However, without further examination of the role of action during this period of development, this proposal will remain more within the realm of speculation than of fact.

CONCLUSION

The relationship between action and the acquisition of communicative competence is clearly more complex than is suggested by von Raffler-Engel at various points of her chapter. Although we are in basic agreement concerning the importance of studying action and, more specifically, kinesics, we believe that the establishment of such a field of study must be approached with great caution. It will not, in the long run, benefit our overall understanding of development to have another area of study that generates a flurry of research activity in isolation from other areas of development, as has sometimes happened in the field of child language (e.g., in syntax, semantics, pragmatics). Instead it seems to us that the most propitious start for the study of developmental kinesics would be with an eye toward the integration of information about the acquisition of this aspect of communicative abilities with what we have learned and are learning in other related areas.

Chapter 3
PATTERNS OF
KINESIC DEVELOPMENT

Bates L. Hoffer

Von Raffler-Engel observes (Chapter 1) that most researchers would agree that the native kinesic system is learned by age 7. This chapter looks at that claim and tests it on Ekman's body manipulators, emblems, and illustrators, as well as on some areas of developmental proxemics.

Like other chapters in this volume, this one refers to the language acquisition and development (LAD) pattern as the major pattern with which to compare the kinesic development. Age 7 appears prominently in LAD. The average age for beginning the *phonemics* of the native language is age 1 and for finishing is age 7½. Because that is the average, a percentage—possibly as high as 30% in some groups—has finished at age 5, and another segment takes until age 9. Systematic *morphemics* (formation of words such as plurals and pasts) begins at 2 and the regular patterns are usually finished by 7½. Irregular forms may be learned later, such as cactus, cacti. Basic *syntax* begins at 1½ and ends at 7½, although we now know (Chomsky, 1969) that many important syntactic features are not learned until 11 or 12 (Hoffer, 1978). Stylistic variations and so on can be learned any time. The fourth area of LAD, *vocabulary*, begins by age 1 and continues throughout life. Table 1 summarizes this information. Different aspects of kinesics may be found to develop according to any of these four patterns or to follow patterns of their own. The research is just now coming into its own and should give some clear pictures in the decade of the 1980's.

Some aspects of kinesics are treated below. The first set consists of three of Ekman's (1980) classes of nonverbal behavior: body manipulators, emblems, and illustrators; the second class falls under the heading of proxemics.

Table 1.   The language acquisition and development pattern

LAD component	Average age begin	Average age end basics	Average age end intermediate
Phonemics	1	7½	
Vocabulary	1	life	
Morphemics	2	7½	life
Syntax	1½	7½	11/12

EKMAN'S CLASSES OF NONVERBAL BEHAVIOR

Body Manipulators

"Body manipulators are movements in which one part of the body does something to another body part. Scratching the head, picking the nose, wringing the hands, licking the lips are examples" (Ekman, 1980:96). From the definition and examples, it should be clear that children need no instruction in using body manipulators. Quite the reverse. Instruction concentrates on *eliminating* culturally offensive actions that the children do naturally. The question to be researched is the average age for conscious restraint—or better yet, the *stage* of kinesic development at which self-restraint is possible. For any individual child, it is the stage, not age, that is important. The hypotheses to be tested are rather obvious. The body manipulators that are cultural "taboos," such as picking the nose in public, should be the earliest controlled because they invite the strongest negative response. Von Raffler-Engel pointed out the great diversity in culturally taboo actions.

There is another aspect of body manipulators not fully treated in Ekman's short article of 1980, and that is the culture-specific body manipulator. Although most examples seem to be "natural" motions such as scratching, some are learned motions. Although in many cultures a hard question triggers a motion of hand to head, the configuration of that gesture may be culturally conditioned. In Japan the palm goes to the back of the head, often moving down the hair on the neck, perhaps with the voicing of *saaaa*. (Many foreigners who stay in Japan a number of months acquire this gesture.) Two research questions relate to the issue of culturally conditioned body manipulators: 1) What is the inventory of such gestures? 2) At what stage is each acquired?

Emblems

Ekman says that emblems "refer to symbolic actions where the movement has a very specific verbal meaning, known to most members of a subculture or culture, and typically is employed with the intention of sending a message. The head nods 'yes' or 'no' are examples of emblems" (1980:89). Emblems are movements that substitute for words, and it is predictable that children learn emblems as they do verbal vocabulary, that is, from before age 1 throughout life, depending almost entirely on experience. At age 2;10, one of my sons learned seven signs (from American Sign Language) in a few minutes while watching a performance on signing. Six months later and today he ran through his seven-sign vocabulary given only the verbal cues. Emblems are learned quickly and well, perhaps because they are so closely tied to the vocabulary aspect of LAD.

Illustrators

Illustrators are "movements which are intimately tied to the content and / or flow of speech" (Ekman, 1980:98). Currently, eight types are distinguished in terms of how they relate to the simultaneous speech.

1. *Batons:*   Movements that accent a particular word
2. *Underliners:*   Movements that emphasize a phrase, clause, sentence, or group of sentences
3. *Ideographs:*   Movements that sketch the path or direction of thought
4. *Kinetographs:*   Movements that depict a bodily action or a nonhuman action
5. *Pictographs:*   Movements that draw the shape of the referent in the air
6. *Rhythmics:*   Movements that depict the rhythm or spacing of an event
7. *Spatials:*   Movements that depict a spatial relationship
8. *Deictics:*   Movements that point to the referent.

Checking the list against videotapes of preschool children, one can find easy and definite examples of batons and deictics, as well as fewer kinetographs (my experimenter used a rabbit's hopping motion with his hand, two fingers raised, as he told the story) and pictographs (circles in the air for balls, and so on). Spatials occur, although they may be blurred with deictics. Note that batons emphasize words, even as every child has learned contrastive stress, and that deictics, kinetographs, pictographs, and spatials make use of the visual properties of the referent. The three illustrators that are hard—perhaps impossible—to find in preschoolers do *not* refer to visual properties: rhythmics refer to time or timing, ideographs to thoughts, and underliners to more and more complicated subparts in syntax, much of which remains to be learned.

Jakobson showed us (1941/ 1968) that child language acquisition follows a general pattern that is reversed in simple aphasia and refollowed in a reacquisition. He arranged the language features in the general pattern of acquisition. Borrowing from his pioneering work, we can hypothesize a general sequence of acquisition of illustrators and test both by observation of acquisition and study of pathological loss. The hypothesized general order can be stated, using the numbers from the list of illustrators above, as 8—1—7—5—4—6—2—3, with the last three being the primary focus of future acquisition research. Perhaps underliners, which involve intermediate syntax, are not fully learned until 11/12 or even later on the average.

This section has dealt with three classes of movements that have different learning curves and involve some acquisition after age 7. The next section deals with an area of proxemics that is surely still being learned years after age 7.

PROXEMICS
The study of the use of space, especially distance and orientation, is called proxemics, following Hall's (1966) excellent foundation research. The study posits four distinct zones that separate social interactors and form levels of nonverbal communication. Briefly stated, the zones are:

The intimate zone: Our faces and bodies are only a few inches apart. Relatives and intimate friends may enter this zone, but others doing so *invade* and threaten us.
The personal zone: Friends may approach within a foot or so for conversations.
The social zone: Most social interaction occurs out to a few feet away.
The public zone: Further than a few feet away; the public zone is used for limited types of social interaction. There are touching, smelling, seeing, and language correlates of each zone.

The field of proxemics now deals in centimeters and degrees of orientation in carefully controlled experiments. What is needed in the research is some further attention to developmental proxemics.

The development of the proxemic zones, as noted by von Raffler-Engel (1976b), needs much more and more careful research. One of the most interesting recent studies is summarized below, but first a short preliminary section is necessary. In the research of Gesell et al. (1946), age 9 is interesting for our purposes in that, on the average, children begin to be conscious of any feature that marks an in group or an out group. It is a great time for "secret" clubs or scouting or other social structures that satisfy the stage of "in-grouping." Often the parents and teachers of these children accuse their opposite numbers of teaching racism at home or in the school because children who had not paid much attention to ethnicity before suddenly note differences clearly. This is a natural stage, however, and can be handled with common sense. One particular result is that the boys intensify their grouping in contrast to the girls, and vice versa. (There is some evidence that girls move through this stage a bit earlier, as they usually proceed through all the developmental stages earlier.) One potential hypothesis about proxemic development is that the boys and girls at this stage will show exaggerated distances in cross-group conversation. The research treated below does indeed support that hypothesis.

Yet another related topic can be, perhaps, integrated into the developmental picture in which age 9 or so is the beginning of a critical stage in aquiring proxemics. The evidence here is observational rather than from a controlled experiment, but it is a strong piece of evidence nontheless. Those who have attended children's mass in which the first graders sit in the first pew, the second graders next, and so on, have noted the children's behavior. As the first graders enter from the outside aisle, they pack together in the pew in such proportions that some must kneel leaning backward for lack of shoulder room, some must turn sideways because there is only room for one shoulder, and occasionally one squirts into the center aisle and must go around and enter from the open end. The effect is not unlike a family of gerbils huddling together on a chilly night. For the sixth, seventh, and especially eighth graders, however, adult spacing is evident. The regularized pattern is seen to begin halfway back, or at the fourth and fifth grade levels. It seems clear that the in-group spacing is being learned by age 9 or so, while the boy-girl conversation spacing is overlearned and must be finally learned at age 10+, as is evidenced below in the summary of Ihara's (1978) work in Japan.

Ihara did research with fourth, fifth, and sixth grade children in Japan. He gave each one 20 human silhouettes (10 male and 10 female), some paste, some standardized square pieces of cardboard, and instructions. The children were given nine situations in which people talk for 5 minutes. For each of the nine situations, the students were to paste the figures appropriately on the cardboard. The situations varied the sex of speakers and degree of familiarity (Table 2).

Male students in the fourth grade treated only strangeness as significant; female students treated strangeness as significant *and* especially so when the stranger was male. Both set minimal personal distance between female friends.

Table 2. Variance of sex of speaker and familiarity in Ihara's (1978) research

Degree of familiarity	Sex of speakers		
	M-M	M-F	F-F
Stranger	1	4	7
Acquaintance	2	5	8
Friend	3	6	9

For the fifth grade, the average distance between strangers (#1, 4, 7) jumps by over 40%. For the females with M-F stranger (#4), the distance jumps 82%, and for the males, it jumps 15%, but the figure given (5.16 cm), is the highest for males in the whole article.

For sixth grade the average distance for strangers drops 20%; for female and male students, the distance between M-F strangers drops almost 15% and 30%, respectively.

To put the results another way, the male students treated strangeness as significant in fourth grade, added sex distinction in fifth grade, and retreated to essentially the adult performance by sixth grade. Female students treated the strangeness and to a small degree the sex difference as significant in fourth grade, greatly increased both features in fifth grade, and retreated to the adult pattern in sixth grade. It would have been quite helpful to have the third grade included as a base, but the evidence is clear that conversational proxemics is being stabilized in sixth grade or approximately ages 11/12. Replications of this type of research and the many other possible ones in different cultures around the world can help us learn the human universal patterns and the culturally conditioned ones.

CONCLUSION

This chapter explores a few of the potential research areas under the rubric of developmental kinesics and suggests that the traditional wisdom of 7 as the age of kinesic maturity should be carefully reexamined. As von Raffler-Engel has noted, all aspects of kinesics need to be well studied in maturational terms.

Section II
THE NATURALNESS PRINCIPLE

A constant concern in the study of human development is the concept of *order*, the pattern or lack of pattern in the sequence of acquisition of behaviors. Children acquiring symbols are continually faced with the problem of their patterning. In language learning the early acquisition of words is soon followed by the onset of syntax, the appropriate ordering of symbols for communication. Child language researchers have sought to determine which aspects of language acquisition and structural patterning might be universal (natural) and which are language or language family specific (conventional). Similarly, developmental kinesicists study children's nonverbal movements as correlated with language development to establish the *natural* versus the *conventional* patterning. The chapters in this section explore the naturalness principle. First Robert St. Clair gives the backgrounds in Western scholarship; then I. M. Schlesinger deals with the nonverbal systems of sign language as they bear on *natural* grammar, interrelating the research with kinesics research where possible.

It is now almost two decades since Joseph Greenberg (1963) presented his research on word order at a conference on the universals of language. Having investigated the syntax of some 30 disparate language systems, Greenberg recognized interesting patterns within the typology of grammatical properties. Among stylistically neutral transitive sentences, for example, he arrived at a dominant word order which he based on statistical inferences and other forms of linguistic usage. The elements of these patterns consist of a subject (S), a verb (V), and an object (O). What is significant about the dominant pattern

Table 1. Greenberg's Word order patterns in transitive sentences

Language type	Dominant pattern	Nondominant pattern
I	VSO	VOS
II	SVO	OVS
III	SOV	OSV

of word order is the fact, as Greenberg notes, that the subject always precedes the object (Table 1). This is not the case, however, among the nondominant forms, in which the reverse order happens to occur.

The work of Greenberg on word order is also important for its treatment of language types. Among transitive sentences, for example, there are verb-initial languages (VSO), verb-medial languages (SVO), and verb-final languages (SOV). The sentence "John saw Mary" could be rendered as:

I: VSO language (Hawaiian)
'ua   'ike Ione   'i Meri
(past see John object marker + Mary)
II: SVO language (English)
John   saw   Mary
(John see + past Mary)
III: SOV language (Japanese)
John wa   Meri   wo   mimashita
(John + subject marker Mary + object market see + past)

Of particular interest to linguists have been the verb-initial (VSO) and the verb-final (SOV) word orders because they appear to form mirror-image patterns of grammatical distribution (Table 2).

In addition to sharing these interesting properties, linguists have found that languages change word order historically. This usually occurs in the direction of a verb final shifting to a verb medial or initial. Old English, for example, had features of an SOV language, whereas its contemporary counterpart is analyzed as a SVO language by some and even a VSO language by others. The same kind of transition can be found among the Romance languages in which Latin word order may be verb final, but its modern derivatives ordinarily may not. Hence, there is much speculation among linguists about the universals of

Table 2. Patterns of grammatical distribution in verb-initial (VSO) and verb-final (SOV) word orders

	VSO	SOV
Question marker	initial	final
Adjective	adj + N	N + adj
Possession	possessive + N	N + possessive
Relators	preposition + N	N + postposition
Syntax	word order	case grammar

word order (Lehmann, 1975) and the chapter by Schlesinger on natural grammar is based on this informative area of research. The findings that he reports on, word order among users of sign language, including individually created nonverbal systems, suggest an interesting dichotomy between verb-final languages and others. This dichotomy reflects, in his model, natural word orders.

	Sign language	Verbal language
Dominant	SOV	VSO
		SVO
Nondominant	OSV	VOS
		OVS

To fully understand the implications of this research and its patterns or word order, it is necessary to first look at the work of Roman Jakobson (1968/1941) on the universals of language. He developed within the theoretical framework of distinctive feature theory several aspects of language change that have immediate application to the study of the natural history of kinesic systems. They are:

1. The acquisition of features in language
2. The loss of features in aphasic speech
3. The historical change of language
4. The relationship of language typologies

Although these four areas of linguistic research were considered to be unrelated, Jakobson found in them a common theme of growth and decay. For him, language acquisition and aphasia were opposite aspects of the same process. The order in which certain elements are acquired is the mirror image of the order in which they are lost with the onset of aphasia, and reacquisition follows the original order. At the time that Jakobson developed this model, much less was known about aphasia, but what is significant about this approach is the intriguing claim that the acquisition and the loss of language are two sides of the same coin.

In addition to these developmental claims, Jakobson saw in the historical change of linguistic elements many similarities with these processes. Languages do not change in a random fashion, he argued, but in line with the same constraints of acquisition and loss that regulate psycholinguistic development. What happens historically, then, is a longitudinal expression of language change at the ontogenetic stage of growth. Finally, Jakobson saw in language typology a series of microlinguistic systems arranged in a natural order from simple to complex and from a homogeneous composition to a heterogeneous one. The stages at which these systems were arrested in the growth process reflected the same immanent or internal psycholinguistic forces operating in the acquisition, loss, and historical evolution of language systems.

What is significant about the work of Jakobson is the developmental scale of implicational values that he found across a wide range of linguistic processes. When Greenberg shared his claims on the universals of language with his colleagues in 1963, he implicitly relied on the work of Jakobson by stating his findings in terms of structural expectancies:

If a language is verb initial, it is expected to have an initial question marker (QM + VSO).
If a language is verb final, it is expected to have a final question marker (SOV + QM).

It is important to highlight certain recurrent themes within the vocabulary of motives characteristic of developmental linguistics. These words center around the use of "natural" grammars and the "evolutionary direction" of "normal" growth. In his discussion of the metaphoric foundations of developmental kinesics, St. Clair provides a social history of the concept of growth in Western scholarship, and demonstrates how this model has become the root metaphor of many contemporary fields of scholarship. It is this metaphor of growth that underlies the long tradition of scholarship associated with the writings of Roman Jakobson and his distinctive feature theory (Jakobson, et al., 1965); it is the same metaphor that underlies the typological findings of Greenberg as well as the theoretical claims of Schlesinger on the word order of sign language. If there is a common force on which developmental kinesics can be founded, it is surely this root metaphor. It unites most of the current research models of psycholinguistics, social psychology, neurolinguistics, learning disabilities, cognitive psychology, diachronic linguistics, speech pathology, and other developmental studies.

Chapter 4
THE METAPHORICAL FOUNDATIONS OF DEVELOPMENTAL KINESICS

Robert N. St. Clair

THE METAPHOR OF GROWTH

When models of science are subjected to sociohistorical analysis, they sometimes reveal rather interesting insights. One of these is the metaphor of growth. It is endemic to nearly all contemporary models of natural and social sciences and can be traced back for several millenia in Western thought. It is what Aristotle wrote about in his treatment of *physis*; and it is what St. Augustine modified in his establishment of a sacred theory of development. More recently, however, it is the model of social Darwinism in which Herbert Spencer formulated his principle of differentiation, and it is the underlying basis for the modern concept of progress that grew out of the European period of the Enlightenment.

This chapter investigates the metaphor of growth in the framework of social history and linguistic historiography. It is argued that this root metaphor remains as a tacit axiom in the language sciences of psycholinguistics, developmental kinesics, and diachronic linguistics, where it has been reintroduced at the microlevel of analysis in systematic and structural terms. By discussing the social and historical parameters of this metaphor, philosophers of science and historiographers will have a clearer idea of how this concept pervades the various levels of consciousness in their own academic professions. Furthermore, it will provide them with a better understanding of the impending anomalies in their own research paradigms if they ever wish to replace the regnant root metaphor with an alternative one. Finally, this knowledge of the metaphor of growth also provides insight into the search for "natural" processes in cognitive development and how these forces are modified or attenuated by exogenous factors inhibiting growth and sequential development.

THE ROLE OF METAPHOR IN THEORY

Metaphor, it has been argued, underlies all models of the natural and social sciences and is not limited to the writings of humanists and artists (Brown, 1978). Metaphor is, after all, an expression of something seen from a different point of view; and, as an illustrative device, it provides the basis for model building. Because all knowledge is metaphorical, the study of "root metaphors" is important for an understanding of such symbolic systems as developmental kinesics, psycholinguistics, and therapeutic interaction. This is because the root metaphor provides a fundamental image of the world and its cognitive status. It defines the parameters of how facts are to be experienced and interpreted. It highlights certain events in the field of study, while simultaneously blinding the investigator to other aspects of the research paradigm (Kuhn, 1970). Metaphors allow a system of knowledge to be perceived anew from the viewpoint of another, and this is accomplished by carrying over (*metaphora*) an element from one framework into a substantially different one, with new connotations and social expectancies being created in the process. At first, these emerging implications for reinterpreting a body of knowledge can be theoretically stimulating, but eventually this paradigm of scientific innovation will begin to seem redundant as the metaphor is elaborated further by means of empirical research. What begins as an illustrative metaphor can result in an iconic representation in which predictability is high and the potential for theoretical exploration reaches or approaches sterility. Hence, metaphors may flourish and stimulate creativity in model building, but with the passage of time, they can become iconic and theoretically redundant as models of science.

There are many root metaphors currently operating in the natural and social sciences. Some of these appeal to the machine as a model of consciousness (Sayre, 1969) in which the mind is equated with a computer (Sayre and Crosson, 1968), and the dominance of this metaphor has been acknowledged as a social force in literary scholarship (L. Marx, 1976). Others focus on the stage as a model of human behavior (Goffman, 1959) or as a scenario for sociohistorical expression (Burke, 1966). However, the most significant root metaphor is one based on the organism of growth (Nisbet, 1969), and an understanding of the relevance of this form of model building is best seen in the Greek concept of *physis*.

ARISTOTELIAN CYCLES OF GROWTH

The Greeks were fascinated by the phenomenon of growth and incorporated it into all aspects of their daily living. From the organic world around them, they created models of change, growth, and decay that have dominated Western philosophy and science. In their poetry, they frequently drew on the metamorphosis of the seed from a hard, dry, and almost lifeless form that contains inner forces of genesis and growth. It is this process of becoming that the Greeks meant when they spoke of *physis*. This word has been rendered in Latin as *natura*, but this translation is inadequate because *physis* means "to give birth to," and in the genealogical scheme of Greek cosmogony it refers to the generative power in the world. Everything in the universe has a *physis* of its own. It has its own way of growing, and the Greeks were interested in finding out just what the *physis* of each thing is. They wanted to learn about its original condition and its successive stages of development. They also were interested in external factors that may inhibit growth or enhance its emergence toward its final form (Cornford, 1952).

Aristotle viewed the process of becoming from four stages of growth (Nisbet, 1969:27–28). These have been referred to in the literature as the four causes, but they are best understood as merely four checkpoints or stages in the growth process. First, there is the material from which an entity undergoes development. This raw material in its original form is the material cause of growth. Second, there are forms or the patterns of development through which matter must go before reaching its final stage, and these are the formal causes or shapes of growth. Third, there is the mechanism of growth that keeps the process going, and this inner force provides the efficient or motor cause of development. Fourth, there is the end product or the final stage in the process of growth, which Aristotle called the final cause of *physis*.

Each of these stages of growth provided an explanation of the way things grow. Through each cycle of growth, there are stages of development that offer a natural explanation for change in the physical and the social world of the Greeks. It was this doctrine of the cycle of growth that Greek historians tried to explicate in their written descriptions of events. They were not interested in providing a chronicle of historical events, but wanted to address themselves to types of events that tend to be repeated in the natural history of human experience (Nisbet, 1969:33). What is significant about this metaphor is the concept of "natural" change. In the process of becoming, for example, a plant may be prevented from developing along its necessary stages of growth by such external or endogenous factors as bad weather conditions. This is called the "doctrine of accidents" and its importance can be found in the Aristotelian quest for natural rather than conventional or accidental growth. In a planned society, therefore, the forces that hinder the natural growth of an entity must be eliminated or subdued to permit the causes of natural growth to emerge at the proper stage of development. Hence this concern for natural change became the underlying metaphor of European scholars for generations. This is evident in the theory of natural selection espoused by Charles Darwin (1859), the natural history of society by Herbert Spencer (1876; cf., Peel, 1972), the natural history of economics by Karl Marx (1973), and other metaphors of growth that incorporate the study of natural history.

THE PARAMETERS OF THE GROWTH METAPHOR

Certain premises are characteristically associated with the metaphor of growth. These underlying assumptions can be found across a wide range of social, historical, and cultural models of epistemology, and they can be summarized as follows:

1. Change is natural
2. Change is directional
3. Change is immanent
4. Change is continuous
5. Change is necessary
6. Change proceeds from uniform causes

Many of these premises result from the Aristotelian concept of the cycles of growth. Aristotle was interested in studying change, which he found to be inherent in the biological organisms that were the basis of his own metaphor of growth. Because the metamorphosis of a seed in its material cause to a full-grown tree in its final cause is what occurs in nature, he saw no reason to doubt the inevitability of change. The directionality of change derives from his discussion of the stages of growth from simple to complex and from genesis to decay. When he wrote about the various stages of growth, he set the framework for contemporary developmental models in which human beings progress through seven stages of directional change (Sears and Feldman, 1964).

The immanence of change is frequently referred to under the rubric of inherent forces within an organism, which unleash the next stage of growth when the environmental conditions are conducive to change. In any pattern of growth in time, new structures emerge from old ones, and this change is brought about immanently by forces internal to an organism. The idea of continuity is consistent with the metaphor of growth. These changes come about very gradually without interruption. Not only is this change gradual, it is also necessary. In the transition from a material raw form to its final stage of growth, an organism must undergo several natural and necessary changes. This transition is impeded only by the doctrine of accidents, whereby exogenous factors impede the natural unfolding of a pattern of growth. Otherwise, such change is necessary and will follow from the inner forces directing the organism's development. Finally, there is the principle of uniformity, which states that nature must be consistent and uniform in its evolution. The possibility of great catastrophic events is summarily dismissed. Hence, for Darwin, change resulted from the uniform cause of natural selection.

These assumptions can be found implicitly in contemporary models of psycholinguistics and developmental kinesics. When studying the emergence of grammatical structures, for example, there is a concern for ascertaining natural forms and patterns that develop in the direction of the adult grâmmar. These changes take place spontaneously and are set off by forces inherent in the organism. When the changes come about, they are produced gradually and necessarily express a natural pattern of growth. Similarly, those who investigate the acquisition of nonverbal communication among children are also working with these underlying assumptions. The selection of children as a population for study, for example, is based on the assumption that change moves from an earlier stage of homogeneity to a later adult stage of heterogeneity. This process of differentiation is gradual and necessary. If the process happens to be interrupted, it is because of the interference in the growth process by certain exogenous environmental factors that impede its progress. The stages documented in both psycholinguistic and developmental kinesic research are stated in terms of natural history. It does not matter, for instance, if there are counterexamples, since these may have resulted from the doctrine of accidents. What does matter is that stages of growth have been documented and that these provide evidence for a model of natural growth.

THE NATURAL HISTORY OF LANGUAGE

The study of natural history was a major concern of scholars in the eighteenth century. It was an outgrowth of the metaphor of biological development that Aristotle and his fellow Greek intellectuals advocated as the basis for their own cosmogony. Aristotle was not merely interested in how change took place during the process of becoming, but he wanted to know all that he could about the various stages of development, the emerging patterns of growth, and the natural transition or the natural history of this evolutionary process. In the eighteenth century, other scholars shared this research paradigm. Charles Darwin (1859), for example, was more interested in developing a theory of natural selection than he was in propounding the basic facts of biological evolution. He saw in natural selection the innate mechanism that is responsible for the gradual change of organisms along a chain of growth. Herbert Spencer (1876) used the same metaphor of growth, but his focus was not on biological growth, rather on the natural history of societies. Similarly, Adam Smith (1776) wrote about economics, but his main concern was with the natural history of wealth. He was trying to ascertain the natural propensities of mankind, assuming that once these were known, the cycles of wealth could naturally develop in line with its destiny. Given this concern for the natural history of various disciplines during this period of Western thought, it is only natural to find that philologists were also interested in the natural history of language, and this emerged in the field of diachronic linguistics known as comparative grammar.

The vocabulary of motives in linguistic historiography of this period is insightful. Philologists spoke of languages being born, growing, and dying. They classified languages into families and saw proto forms as belonging to mother languages and derived cognates as being a part of sister languages. These languages underwent cycles of growth and followed laws of phonetic or sound change that were not only necessary and immanent, but also directional (Palmer, 1978; Pedersen, 1959). Max Müller (1864), for example, wrote about phonetic decay and looked back to the golden age of Proto-Indo-European when Sanskrit represented the adorned or perfect language from which all other cognate forms fell through the process of use. The only person to seriously challenge the established stages of development was the Danish scholar Otto Jespersen (1924). He was a strong Anglophile and argued that English was not a lesser copy of Sanskrit, but that languages became more mature as they developed. As a consequence, he saw English as a more mature form of linguistic development.

When the influence of logical positivism was felt in linguistics about the turn of the twentieth century, the concern for historical and comparative linguistics was replaced by typological studies of linguistic structures across various language systems (Palmer, 1978). Given the nature of this shift, one could assume that these typological studies meant the demise of the metaphor of growth. However, this was not the case. As Robert Nisbet (1969) has noted, this shift from macrolevel theorizing to micromodels based on coherent systems did not do away with the underlying premises of this developmental tradition.

The newer models were supposed to eliminate metaphysical assumptions and other ideological claims to linguistic epistemology, but they did not. What they did espouse was the metaphor of growth in a new disguise. Typological studies were based on the assumption that language systems change in a certain direction with the passage of time and that this change is immanent (Togeby, 1951). Even though these metaphorical extensions are subtle, they nevertheless exist. Consider, for example, the role of markedness theory in the writing of Nikolai Trubetskoy (1939), who assumed that some sound changes can occur only in one direction and not the other and that the marked forms represented later stages in the evolution of structural forms. Actually, several volumes could be written on the role of the growth metaphor in linguistic theory, and in this short chapter an overview of the evidence is sufficient to convey the notion that current synchronic models are based on the tacit metaphor of growth characteristically associated with Western scholarship.

NATURAL GRAMMAR

The historical foundations of the root metaphor of biological growth can be readily ascertained from a study of psycholinguistics (Blumenthal, 1970). It is a continuation of the nineteenth-century philologists' concern with implications of evolutionary change for a theory of natural grammar (Schleicher, 1863). With the advent of transformational grammar, psycholinguistics grew in popularity because it provided a formal means of documenting the various stages of growth from the acquisition of linguistic systems by children as they progressed on their way toward adult grammars (Greene, 1972). The concern with developmental syntax paralleled many findings from theoretical linguistics because they were different versions of the same underlying metaphor of linguistic change (Reber, 1973). It does not matter whether psycholinguists studied the forms and the functions of language acquisition in children or the more complex forms of systematic growth; their research paradigms share the same focus on emerging grammars (Bloom, 1970) and the genesis of language in children (Smith and Miller, 1966).

As in the study of natural history, it is not a question of every single case study being in accord with the model, but one of documenting the stages of growth in only the models in which it is assumed that no interference from the environment has delayed or disturbed the natural unfolding of the growth process. This concern with natural grammar has an interesting parallel in the work of Jean Piaget and his colleagues (1954). Piaget was trained as a biologist and began his study of language and cognition in children with the same underlying metaphor of growth that he had acquired in his academic training (Piaget, 1926, 1952). When he spoke of the various stages of growth from sensorimotor behavior to the more abstract functions of the young adult, he was not overly concerned with the actual ages of the children undergoing this growth process. All that mattered was that they follow the natural history of intelligence in children.

The study of how children acquire nonverbal behavior reveals the same underlying metaphor of growth. The issue among scholars is not whether children undergo the natural process of acquiring this mode of symbolic expression, but whether it is innate. The concern for a strong innate model of symbolic acquisition follows from the metaphor of growth. If change is necessary, it can be argued, there must be a motor cause or an inherent mechanism that triggers this change and allows it to develop naturally. This, in essence, is what a natural history of kinesic and psycholinguistic acquisition would need if it were to account for the acquisition of both verbal and nonverbal systems by children. However, there are some who counter this claim of innateness (Peng and von Raffler-Engel, 1978), and they base their contention on the empirical findings that do not support the innateness paradigm. They argue, in effect, that the innate model of linguistic faculty is unnecessary as a theoretical construct because most of the same stages of growth can be accounted for by other natural processes of cognitive growth (Peng, 1978).

In addition, there are some who point to other causes for what Aristotle would have explained by way of the doctrine of accidents. Robert Hutcheson (1978), for example, points to the pathological development of language in children and relates it to low body weight among pregnant teenagers and among those who are caught in the web of poverty. What is significant about this controversy is the reliance of the opposing parties on the same metaphors of growth. They differ only on whether a separate linguistic faculty is needed to account for the immanence and the necessity among children. Those who argue against the innateness position of language acquisition have enriched this controversy by providing a model of developmental kinesics with greater explanatory power. They are interested in ascertaining the various stages of cognitive growth and need not posit a special model of innate faculties to explain a derived process of development (von Raffler-Engel, 1978a).

CONCLUDING REMARKS

The metaphor of growth is intrinsically related to essentially all models of language. It can be found in the rise of diachronic linguistics during the nineteenth century, the subsequent concern for positivism and structural forms, and the psycholinguistic models that have recently appeared with the advent of generative grammar. These models all assume that there are stages of growth through which language must travel before reaching its final form. They all reflect a belief in the immanent forces within the linguistic system that are responsible for the emergence of new forms and structures of growth, and they all have a sense of necessity in the processes of change and gradual growth along the way. There is not very much that separates the root metaphor of the Greeks in Aristotle's time from the psycholinguists and the developmental kinesicists of today. They are all working from the same root metaphor and share similar views of change and growth.

Robert Nisbet (1969) has openly attacked the metaphor of growth and wishes to replace it with alternative models of cognition. This is not the time nor the place to openly address this question. What is important at this time is that scholars in the language sciences, psycholinguistics, kinesics, and other models of symbolic expression recognize that they are operating with a tacit model of epistemology that may prevent them from dealing with the various anomalies in their own research paradigms. This metaphor of growth is so dominant in Western thought that it goes virtually unnoticed as an underlying assumption on which scientific investigations take place. Hence, there is more that binds various disciplines together through this root metaphor than separates them, and the field of developmental kinesics is no exception.

Chapter 5
SIGN LANGUAGE
AND NATURAL GRAMMAR

I. M. Schlesinger

In one of his aphorisms, Goethe says: "Ein jeder, weil er spricht, glaubt auch über Sprache reden zu können." [Because everyone speaks, he also believes (himself) to be in a position to talk about language.] This belief is erroneous; in fact, we may often be too close to language to study it impartially. To gain the proper perspective, it may be profitable to study it from the vantage point of a radically different communication system. Such an opportunity is provided by research on kinesics, a new area of investigation into which von Raffler-Engel has made important inroads.

In 1967, it seemed that research on sign language would throw new light on problems of language and language development, although we could not at that point specify the areas in which sign language would be revealing, let alone formulate the relevant problems clearly.[1] At that time, very little research on sign language had been published; this area did not become fashionable until several years later—and even then our team had only a faint conception of the venture on which they were embarking. Despite our methodological blunders that perhaps unavoidably attended breaking ground in this new field, the study of sign language did enhance our understanding of language and language development. This chapter explores only one problem concerning which the investment of effort has yielded rich returns: the problem of natural grammar.

THE NOTION OF NATURAL GRAMMAR

A theme that has turned up time and again in the literature (e.g., Tylor,

[1] Our research on sign language, which is quoted extensively in this chapter, was supported by the U.S. Department of Health, Education and Welfare; Social Rehabilitation Service (Project VRA-ISR-32-67), and was carried out at the Hebrew University, Jerusalem, in cooperation with the Association of the Deaf in Israel and the Helen Keller House (I. M. Schlesinger and J. Shunary, principal investigators). The influence of Slobin's work (1976) on the present chapter should be obvious. I thank Dr. W. Kaper for his valuable comments.

1881; Jespersen, 1922; Park, 1970a; Schlesinger, 1976; Yau, 1978) is that of a natural word order. Although the world's languages differ in respect to word order employed, there is an order that in Jespersen's (1922: 356) words, "must be founded in the very nature of human thought." Specifically, Jespersen held that the subject was positioned before its verb in early languages, and some languages replaced this "natural" order only in later stages of their development by the verb-subject order. That the subject-verb order is more natural was taken for granted by Jespersen, who adduced no reasons for this being so. Before him, Tylor (1881) had written about a "natural order" in the sign language of the deaf, which was "the same among the mutes of different countries and wholly independent of the syntax which may happen to belong to the language of their speaking friends." Again, Tylor did not present any independent argument to the effect that the observed order is "natural." The claim for naturalness thus seems to boil down to a definition: the occurrence of a given order in all early languages—or in all sign languages, in the case of Tylor—seems to be deemed sufficient justification for regarding that order as natural.

However, this is not the way Jespersen and other writers thought of the natural word order concept. What they seem to have had in mind is an empirical hypothesis, although they did little to formulate it precisely or to show how it might be tested. This raises the question of what arguments—other than post hoc ones—might be adduced in support of a claim that a given word order is natural (see Greenberg, 1963).

This chapter is concerned with this methodological problem. The investigation has been prompted by the hunch that behind the statements of various writers about a natural order there lurks a notion that could turn out to be valuable for the explanation of certain phenomena. Thus, the empirical status, not just of "natural word order" but of a somewhat broader concept—for which the term *natural grammar* may be appropriate—is examined. By this is meant the features of grammar that one would tend to resort to in the absence of any external influence, such as that from the language spoken in the environment. This informal definition already shows that the concept of natural grammar is an abstraction. No one resorts to grammar in the absence of any external influence, because there is always a linguistic community exerting such an influence on the speaker. However, the grammatical features actually employed by a speaker may, under certain circumstances, be a resultant of two influences: the features he would have adopted if left to his own devices (i.e., the natural grammar), and the pressures exerted on him by the language of his speech community.

Natural grammar, then, is viewed here as a theoretical construct. This construct may be useful for the explanation of various linguistic phenomena, as will be shown later on, because it is the human propensities formalized by natural grammar that serve as the groundwork on which the structure of any particular grammar must be erected.

A caveat is in order here. The problem of natural grammar is not to be confused with that of language origins. The foregoing definition of natural grammar does not imply that this is a grammar actually employed by the speakers of any language, whether this is the putative original language of the human race or any other language. According to a widely held view, there are at present too few empirical constraints on speculations about the original language of man. Such constraints do seem to exist, however, in respect to speculations about natural grammar, and the latter might therefore be a useful construct.

Let us turn now to the question of what might count as evidence for hypotheses about natural grammar.

SOURCES OF EVIDENCE

Most languages spoken today are the product of a long process of development, and their grammars may therefore have characteristics that differ very much from those of the primordial languages they stem from. Hence, modern languages should not be consulted for specifics about natural grammar. Hypotheses about natural grammer must be based on features exhibited by languages in their earliest stages of development. Fortunately, some such languages are extant: most sign languages in current use have only a relatively short history. Presumably, therefore, their grammars are very similar to those they had in their formative stages, and reflect the natural tendencies of those who took part in their formation. Some sign languages are even known to have existed for less than a single lifetime: there are reports of sign languages invented by isolated deaf individuals living in speaking communities (Kuschel, 1973; Macleod, 1973). Material is also available on the spontaneous signing of 2- to 4-year-old deaf children who have had no experience of conventional sign languages (Goldin-Meadow, 1975).

Some spoken languages, too, have only a relatively short history. Pidgins originated in the need to simplify an existing language (notably, English or Portuguese) so that they could serve as minimal languages for contact between speakers of different linguistic communities. The simplifications may reflect certain natural tendencies; hence these languages may furnish valuable clues to natural grammar.

In the absence of written records of the earliest stages of most currently spoken languages, linguists have attempted reconstruction of these stages (see, e.g., Van Coetsen and Kufner, 1972, on Proto-German, and Lehmann, 1974, on Proto-Indo-European). A consideration of grammatical features in which these reconstructed languages differ from their later offshoots may throw additional light on natural grammar.

Not only the early stages in the phylogeny of languages but also the early ontogenetic stages may furnish us with material relevant to natural grammar. Although the language of the young child very soon shows the influence of the grammar of the native language, one may often observe for a brief period certain peculiarities not accounted for by adult grammar, which may reflect the child's natural tendencies and thus give us some pointers to natural grammar.

These natural tendencies are overlaid in adult language by the rules of the vernacular. They can be brought to the fore, however, in the psychological laboratory. Whenever a language has two alternative ways of expression, we may predict that the one corresponding to natural grammar will be processed more easily. Hypotheses about natural grammar can therefore sometimes be validated experimentally.

It is suggested, then, that the empirical study of natural grammar is made possible by a consideration of evidence from a variety of sources: sign languages, pidgins, reconstructions of earlier forms of existing languages, child language (both verbal and nonverbal aspects), and experimental findings on language processing. The greater the convergence of data from all these sources on a given feature, the more confidence we may have that a genuine characteristic of natural grammar has been revealed. Usually it will not be difficult to find an intuitively plausible explanation for the correspondence of such a characteristic to a natural tendency. At any rate, one should not accept psychological post hoc explanations in advancing a hypothesis regarding natural grammar.

Previous writers have been content with some rather cavalier remarks on the natural order of words, based usually on a single source, rather than on the convergence of evidence from several sources. The notion of natural grammar deserves a more serious treatment, not because it has already been shown to be a useful construct, but because there is no way of evaluating its usefulness without investing effort in its investigation.

Among the sources deserving consideration mentioned above, there are only some that are discussed here: sign language, child language, and experiments on language processing. Findings from these areas are quoted and data from the other sources are mentioned only to some extent.[2] If only for this reason, the conclusions arrived at must be regarded as merely tentative. Three problems of natural grammar are considered:

1. The expression of relations by means of the sequence of clauses and words
2. Negative characteristics of natural grammar (i.e., grammatical devices found in some languages, which natural grammar presumably lacks)
3. The categories expressed in natural grammar

---

[2] The various papers on sign language often fail to specify the size of the corpus on which the conclusions are based, and occasionally one may suspect that the description is based on no more than the general impression gained by the writer. In the following, all these papers are quoted indiscriminately; reports are not distinguished according to their reliability because usually such judgments cannot be made with any degree of confidence.

The final section discusses some implications of natural grammar for research on the ontogenesis and phylogenesis of language.

ORDER OF EVENTS

When Julius Caesar summed up one of his military exploits saying *veni, vidi, vici,* he followed the order of events recounted: I came, saw, and was victorious. The tendency of language to follow the temporal order of events referred to has been discussed by Jakobson (1965), who saw in it a manifestation of the iconicity of language. Thus he observed that in all languages the unmarked construction puts the conditional clause before the conclusion in accordance with the order of events.

Spoken languages, however, do not invariably follow the rule of putting first things first. In English, for instance, one can say *We went home after it started raining.* In the Israeli sign language, by contrast, this translates into two simple sentences in the order corresponding to the order of events (Namir and Schlesinger, 1978:119–120). The same is true of American Sign Language (Cogen, 1977). Tervoort (1961) also states that chronological order of events is one of the determinants of sign order, and Hansen (1975) reports that in what he calls the "original" Danish sign language, the cause is stated before the effect. However, the opposite order—effect before cause—was observed in the German sign language by Tylor (1881: 251). This may possibly have been due to the influence of spoken German (*x* because *y*), although no sign for BECAUSE introduces the cause in the signed sentence.

So much for the evidence from sign language. Let us look now at converging evidence from other sources. In a study of nursery school children, Clark (1973a) found a developmental sequence: children's utterances at first follow the temporal order of events. This tendency may also be manifested in children's errors, as that of a child presented with the beginning of a sentence *A man fell down in the road because* . . . who completed this by mentioning the succeeding event: *he broke his leg* (Piaget, 1928:17). Katz and Brent (1968) found an increase with age of the preference for conjoined sentences preserving the order of events (e.g., preference of *John studied hard and he did well in school* over *John did well in school and he studied hard*). Adults have also been found to prefer descriptions in which events are mentioned in the order of their occurrence (Clark and Clark, 1968).

It may be concluded tentatively, therefore, that natural grammar includes the tendency to adhere to the temporal order of events. Notwithstanding this tendency, however, the grammars of many languages permit complex sentences in which the order of mention does not match the sequence of events referred to. In English, the subordinate clause can be placed either before or after the main clause. Thus one can say not only

> After the rain began, we went indoors

but also

> We went indoors after the rain began.

Both constructions are permissible, because they conform to the rules for subordination in English, which apply not only to temporal clauses but to clauses of all sorts. We may ask, however, why the second type of construction, which presumably runs counter to our natural tendency to mirror the order of events, should be resorted to at all. After all, a sentence may be stylistically unacceptable even though it is not ungrammatical, but this obviously does not apply in the case above.

The answer seems to be that our natural tendency to adhere to the course of events in speaking may be overriden by other tendencies. The two sample sentences, for instance, differ in focus. Thus, as an answer to the question *When did you go indoors?* the second sentence is more natural than the first. That is, the need to provide the right focus may overrule the tendency to recount events in the order of their occurrence. When no considerations conflict with this tendency, the first type of sentence is in fact preferred, as indicated by Clark and Clark (1968).

There is a lesson to be drawn from this, which is applied in later sections. The actual grammar of a language, and even the actual stylistic preferences, are the result of an interplay of conflicting tendencies. Hence there is no reason to expect any single feature of natural grammar to have been grafted on the grammar or stylistics of, say, English as a rule without exceptions. This is of course precisely what makes the construct of natural grammar difficult to investigate.

Adherence to the temporal order of events is a principle that can be expressed by complex sentences as well as by paratactic constructions (as it is, for instance, in the Israeli sign language). As far as natural grammar is concerned, we have no grounds yet for crediting it with complex sentences, nor with sentences of any particular structure, for that matter. In the following we deal with principles of natural grammar that unlike the order-of-events principle, pertain to relations between constituents of a single clause.

MODIFICATION

One clause in a sentence may be dependent on another, and a given word in a clause may be dependent on another word and modify it. Thus an adjective is dependent on the noun it modifies. Next we attempt to determine whether there is any preferred ordering of the modifying and modified elements in natural grammar.

Adjectives and Nouns

Consider first the position of the adjective relative to that of the noun it modifies. Two different orders are found in the languages of the world. Some, like English, position the adjective before the noun—we will call this the AN order—whereas others, like Hebrew, adopt the NA order. Is either one of these alternatives more "natural"?

NA Order in Sign Languages   Some evidence concerning the natural order may be obtained from sign languages of the deaf. Sign languages employed in different countries differ among themselves in many details (and are in some cases even mutually incomprehensible), but one of the features that seems to be common to practically all of them is the NA order.[3] This order has been reported for the sign languages used by the deaf in Germany (Tylor, 1881), Russia (Geylman, 1964; Leont'yev, 1969), and Israel (Namir and Schlesinger, 1978), and by Hansen (1975) for the "original" sign language of Denmark, employed by deaf children there. Furthermore, it has been reported for the American Indian sign language (Mallery, 1879–1880; West, 1960; Mallery, however, found this order to be common but not obligatory; see also Kroeber, 1958) and for a monastic sign language (Hutt, 1968). Because in some of the countries mentioned here the spoken language observes an AN order, the ubiquitous NA order in sign languages cannot be put down to the influence of spoken language.

It is legitimate, however, to turn to the influence of spoken language as an explanation for isolated exceptions to observed regularities. Take the case of American Sign Language, which has a relatively long history, having been used by the deaf in the United States since 1816 (at least; see Woodward, 1978), and has been very much influenced by English. In this sign language, both AN and NA constructions seem to be permitted (McCall, 1965), and presumably the presence of the former is attributable to the influence of English.

In addition to institutionalized sign languages, which have already developed to a greater or lesser extent, there are incipient sign languages that have not yet had a chance to develop and to change much, thus are particularly valuable for the investigation of natural grammar. We have a report of a sign language invented by a single deaf man living in a small English village where he has spent life (Macleod, 1973). Billy (this is the name given to him by Macleod) is averred to have "certainly no knowledge of the structure of the English language" (1973:72), and to communicate

---

[3] It is debatable whether the terms "noun" and "adjective" are applicable to sign languages at all, since these languages do not have morphologically distinguishable parts of speech (see Cohen et al., 1977:23–24; Namir and Schlesinger, 1978). But for the sake of convenience, signs translatable by an adjective are referred to as adjectives, and for other parts of speech are designated similarly.

with the hearing, he has invented his own sign language. In his signing, Macleod reports (1973:78) "[a] nominal invariably precedes any adjective specifying it, and the adjectives are never separated from the nominal by any other sign." Billy, then, employs the NA order, which is contrary to the English word order.

It is interesting to note in this connection that Washoe, the famous chimpanzee who learned American Sign Language from tutors who were more conversant with English and therefore used the AN order in signing, spontaneously signed *flower red* (Howard Gardner, personal communication, December 1970).

The NA order in signing has been explained as being in accord with natural tendencies (Wundt, 1904; Kroeber, 1958). The noun denotes an object or person that can easily be conceived of by itself; in this the noun is unlike the modifying adjective. The sign BLACK by itself, for instance, conveys little information about the communication: indefinitely many things may be black, and *black* said of an object refers to a quality different from *black* said of a person, and both again differ from *black* in *black night*. It helps to know the subject of the communication from the start; hence it is more "natural" to mention the object or the person first.

If some spoken languages nevertheless have an AN order, this is presumably a result of diachronic processes in the course of which they have moved away from the pristine, natural word order. Thus, according to Lehmann (1974), the AN order is a concomitant of the object-verb order: the verb and its object form a unit that resists interruption (by, e.g., a modifying adjective of the object), hence adjectives were preposed in early object-verb languages.

Conflicting data from spoken languages, then, do not constitute evidence against this putative principle of natural grammar. On the other hand, it might be argued that evidence for such a principle that is based only on sign language is insufficient. Conceivably, there may be something in the nature of sign languages that causes them to have an NA order, unlike many spoken languages. For instance, the pictorial quality of sign languages may make it necessary to establish a context, to form a picture of what it is that one refers to, before elaborating on it by modifying adjectives, as suggested by Bühler (1934:334). Another factor, (mentioned by Stern and Stern, 1928:222; Kroeber, 1958) is rate of presentation: the question of which information is presented first may be of less moment in speech, which is typically faster than signing (by a one word—one sign comparison; see Namir and Schlesinger, 1978:103). Assuming these explanations of the difference between spoken and sign languages in word order to be valid, their implication for the hypothesis that the NA order is a principle of natural grammar is equivocal. There seem to be two possibilities:

1.   The hypothesis is true, but since the tendency to use the NA order is

weaker for spoken languages, it often is not revealed in their grammars because of other, conflicting influences (e.g., those suggested by Lehmann; see above).

2. There is a tendency to use the NA order *only* for sign languages. This means that we are not entitled to ascribe this order to natural grammar *tout court*; at best it may be ascribed to the natural grammar of sign languages (if such a construct is of any interest).

In brief, the fact that sign languages do employ the NA order is not sufficient corroboration for our hypothesis. We should look for converging evidence from other sources, as suggested above in the section "Sources of Evidence."

Converging Evidence   In a paired-associate learning experiment, Lambert and Paivio (1956) found noun-adjective pairs easier to learn than adjective-noun pairs. If it is assumed that while learning, subjects tried to combine the noun with the adjective into a meaningful construction, this result is predicted by the explanation given above for the preference of the NA order. In the experiment cited, however, there were fewer errors in the recall of adjective-noun pairs.

There is not much evidence from child language concerning the preferability of the NA order. Apparently, children learn readily whatever order is prescribed by their native language. Children's errors, however, may give a clue to the preferred order. Reviewing research in the acquisition of Hungarian, MacWhinney (1976:406) reports that although word-order errors were few, "[i]n a couple of reported cases, children failed to put the adjective before the noun it modifies." This is in accord with our hypothesis, but before accepting errors of children learning Hungarian as definitely corroborating evidence, one should make sure that in NA languages the reverse error does *not* occur. To my knowledge, no reports show this.

The converging evidence cited so far seems to be very meager. Our case for the NA order rests mainly on evidence from sign languages. Now, the psychological explanation given for the NA order in sign language would gain credence if it could be shown to predict other phenomena correctly. Modification by a qualifying adjective is after all only one kind of modification, and the explanation of why the noun should precede the adjective by which it is modified should be expected to hold for other kinds as well. Evidence from other types of modification is considered next.

Adverbs and Verbs

If the noun, because of its greater informativeness, tends to precede the adjective, the verb should be expected to precede the adverb by which it is modified. This is indeed the order reported for sign languages used by the deaf in Germany (Wundt, 1904) and Russia (Leont'yev, 1969). For the Israeli sign language we found this rule to hold only for adverbs of manner, but not for temporal and locational adverbs[4] (Namir and Schlesinger, 1978), and in American Sign Language (which, as pointed out above, has been influenced by English) no fixed order seems to hold (McCall, 1965).[5]

For the relative position of verb and adverb, then, the evidence is rather weak.

Negation

A rationale similar to that advanced for the NA order would seem to apply to the ordering of the word or sign expressing negation relative to the negated element. The sign for NO or NOT indeed comes after the sign to which it pertains, in the Russian sign language (Geylman, 1964), the French sign language (Woodward, 1978), the early German sign language (Kainz, 1960), and Indian sign language (Kroeber, 1958; West, 1960). For the Israeli sign language, however, we found the opposite order (Namir and Schlesinger, 1978), and the same seems to hold for American Sign Language (McCall, 1965). In both these sign languages the prepositioning of NO may result from the influence of spoken language. Billy, the man who invented his own sign language, put the negating sign either initially or finally, or both (Macleod, 1973:78).

Several writers have noted the tendency of children to put *no* after the negated element, in contravention of the regular order of the language they learn (Jespersen, 1922:136; Sully, 1924:173–174). MacWhinney (1976:406), reviewing findings on children learning Hungarian, writes that among the few errors of word order, there were two in which "the negative failed to precede the word it negates." Stern and Stern (1928:223–224) report that negation is usually postposed, but occasionally preposed, by children learning German. Preposition of negation may in this case have been attributable to the influence of adult language (as has been argued above for the exceptions found in sign languages). Another possibility is that *no* is uttered first because of the special urgency felt by the speaker on the specific occasion of the utterance. This may also apply to the cases in which Billy signed the negation initially.

Main and Subordinate Clauses

Just as the adjective is dependent on the noun and the adverb on the verb, the subordinate clause of a sentence is dependent on its main clause. In a sense, it may also be said to modify the main clause. Our hypothesis of a tendency to position the modified element before the one modifying it

---

[4] Presumably, by signing first the time and the place at which an event took place, a sort of context is provided. These counterexamples therefore seem not to weigh heavily; consider that no similar argument can be made concerning manner adverbs.

[5] Adverbs of manner are mostly not signed separately but are expressed as modulations of the verb signs (Fischer, 1973; Namir and Schlesinger, 1978; Warren, 1978).

therefore predicts the main clause—subordinate clause order for natural grammar.

This statement may need some clarification. No claim is being made here that natural grammar has complex sentences with main and subordinate clauses. Such a way of putting it is ill advised, in the first place, because it intimates that natural grammar is the grammar of some actual language. There is of course no such natural grammar language, extant or extinct; "natural grammar" is merely a collective name of certain tendencies. Furthermore, constructions with subordinate clauses are actually a somewhat later development; as Kiparsky (1976:101) put it: "A well-traveled one-way street in historical syntax leads from coordination to the subordination of sentences." In speaking of a main clause-subordinate clause sequence in natural grammar, therefore, the claim is merely made that *if* a sentence has a main clause and a subordinate clause, there will be a tendency to position the former before the latter.

Now, regarding this tendency, there is little evidence from sign languages. Sign language prefers paratactic constructions, and according to Thompson (1977) American Sign Language—which is one of the most developed sign languages—has no subordination at all (a claim that has been debated by Liddell, 1978, on the basis of a detailed analysis of non-manual features). In Israeli sign language, the expression of what is said, thought, known, agreed to, and understood, is put after the signs for SAY, THINK, KNOW, AGREE, UNDERSTAND, and so on (Namir and Schlesinger, 1978), and this seems to correspond to a main clause–object clause order.

In spoken language, the main clause-subordinate clause order has been found easier to recall than the reverse order (Clark and Clark, 1968), and seems also to be preferred in the construction of sentences (Jarvella, 1972). Superiority of the main clause-subordinate clause order in the comprehension of sentences was found by Holmes (1973), who used the technique of "rapid serial visual representation" to increase overall task difficulty, and by Bever (reported in Fodor, et al., 1974:357) by means of self-ratings of comprehension.

Ellipsis

Certain findings on the acceptability of elliptic constructions reported by Greenbaum and Meyer (1979) are also relevant here, although they do not involve modification. The explanation given above for the preference of the NA order has a parallel in their explanation for the difficulty of sentences in which "the realized item follows the ellipted item," for example,

Fred wrote a book and edited a magazine

in which an item is ellipted in the second clause, is preferred to

I wrote, and he sent the letter,

in which an item is ellipted in the first clause. In the second sentence, they argue, "a greater strain is imposed on short-term memory, since speakers have to wait in suspense for the realized item before they can supply the ellipsis."

Evaluation of the Evidence

Evidence has been reviewed for the hypothesis that in natural grammar the modified element precedes the one that modifies it. For the non-adjective order, the hypothesis seems to be well supported by data on sign languages, but other sources afford only little evidence. The main clause—subordinate clause order, on the other hand, seems to be preferred in adult spoken language, but little converging evidence for it was found in other sources. The evidence pertaining to adverbs and negation, again, seems to point in the direction of our hypothesis, but is not very clearcut.

In evaluating the evidence we should first of all be clear about the import of negative findings in this area. When an order hypothesized for natural grammar fails to be found, this is usually not particularly damaging to the hypothesis, because the notion of natural grammar does not imply that its principles are manifested in every language system (sign language, child language, etc.). There may be various conflicting tendencies at work that override those of natural grammar. In sign languages and child language, the influence of spoken language may win out over natural tendencies, and intralinguistic processes may obliterate the effect of natural grammar on spoken language. By contrast, any regularity in a language system that runs counter to these conflicting tendencies is in need of explanation, and it is such regularities that may provide evidence for principles of natural grammar.

Because it is in the very nature of hypotheses pertaining to natural grammar, then, that they cannot be easily invalidated by counterevidence, it is all the more important to refrain from accepting any such hypothesis before a considerable body of positive evidence has been amassed. Preferably, as has been pointed out before, this evidence should come from a number of sources. In the present case, the convergence of evidence may be deemed sufficient for the tentative acceptance of the modified-modifier hypothesis.

Another hypothesis about the relative position in natural grammar is discussed below.

SUBJECT, OBJECT, AND VERB

Several possible reasons come to mind for Jespersen's (1922:356) view, quoted above, that it is "in the very nature of human thought" that the subject precedes its verb. First, verbs often describe actions that are more transient phenomena than the concrete objects or persons often denoted by the subject noun. Concreteness has been mentioned as one of the determinants of word order in the earliest utterances of the child (Stern and Stern 1928:222). Related to this is the observation that verbs often have a much less definite meaning than most nouns. Thus the meaning of the English verb *run*, differs with the subject it is predicated of. Compare: *the chicken runs, the train runs, the road runs through the village, the fire runs through the street* (Schlesinger, in press, Section 6.3).[6] We may expect a tendency for the word that is concrete and stable in meaning to precede that which depends on it for its meaning; that is, the subject will tend to precede its verb.

Similar considerations may lead us to hypothesize that in natural grammar the object precedes the verb. This leaves two candidate word orders for natural grammar: SOV and OSV (where S, O, and V stand for subject, object, and verb, respectively). For two reasons we will put our bet on SOV. First, the object and verb together belong to the predicate, and second, it seems to be more natural to mention first what it is that is being talked about, which, typically, (though not always) is the subject. In this connection it is of interest that in most spoken languages S precedes O (Greenberg, 1963). All this makes the OSV order a less likely candidate for natural grammer than SOV. We therefore look next at the evidence for the SOV order.

Sign Languages

The SOV order has been reported for sign languages of the deaf in Germany (Wundt, 1904), Russia (Leont'yev, 1969), and China (Yau, 1978), and also for the American Indian sign language (Mallery, 1879–1880).

In some sign languages, however, divergent orders are found. To discuss these, the claim for an SOV order is broken into three subclaims: SV (i.e., S appears before V), OV, and SO; each is examined in its turn.

SV: Besides the sign languages of Germany, Russia, and China, and the American Indian sign language, mentioned above, the SV order seems to be adhered to in American Sign Language (McCall, 1965; Fischer, 1975; Friedman, 1976; the latter found occasional repetitions of the subject: SVS; see however, Edge and Herrmann, 1977:141), and in that of Marseilles (Sallogoïty, 1975). In a filmed corpus of the Israeli sign language we found only few exceptions to the SV order (Namir and Schlesinger, 1978), and in a previous study (Schlesinger, 1971a) none was found. Kroeber (1958) states that subject-predicate is the

---

[6] A related fact is that several English verbs do not translate as one single sign in sign language. An example of such a "covariant" sign (Cohen et al. 1977:18) is CARRY, the form of which depends on the thing said to be carried (a handbag, a basket, a baby, a tray, etc.).

"probable" order in American Indian sign language. Washabaugh (in press) has described the "rather immature" sign language of Providence Island, which is used by only about 20 deaf people and seems to have but a short history. In the utterances quoted by him, the SV order is usually employed, but there are some exceptions. Last, Billy, the deaf man who invented a sign language of his own, has been reported to form sentences that "are almost always of the 'subject-predicate' type, with a nominal in initial position followed immediately by a verbal phrase" (Macleod, 1973:78).

A discordant note comes from Goldin-Meadow's (1980: Section IVc), study of the spontaneous sign language of young deaf children without previous experience of a conventional sign language, in which examples of VS as well as SV were found.

OV: As mentioned, the German, Russian, Chinese, and American Indian (see also Kroeber, 1958) sign languages put the object before the verb, and the same is apparently true of the sign language of Providence Island (Washabaugh, in press). On the other hand, in a filmed corpus of the Israeli sign language VO as well as OV was observed; in the sign language of Marseilles both SVO and OSV occur (Sallogoïty, 1975); and the SVO order has been reported to be adhered to "frequently" in the French-Canadian sign language (Mayberry, 1978:362). Furthermore, although Fischer (1975) claims that American Sign Language is basically an SVO language, Friedman (1976) finds that, in addition, SOV, OV, SVOV (e.g., PACK CLOTHES PACK), and OSV may be used (see also Edge and Herrmann, 1977). In the spontaneous signing of deaf children 2 to 4 years old, examples of both OV and VO have been reported (Goldin-Meadow, 1980: Section IVc).

Since the predominant word order in Hebrew and English is SVO, the observed cases of VO in the Israeli and American sign languages may be attributable to the influence of spoken language. In fact, there is some indication that the tendency of Israeli signers to use the VO order increases with knowledge of Hebrew (Namir and Schlesinger, 1978:117). Such an explanation, however, seems inapplicable to the OSV constructions in the sign language of Marseilles or to the spontaneous signing of young deaf children.

SO: The prediction of an SO order is upheld by the four above-mentioned sign languages that have an SOV order. Contrariwise, the sign language of Marseilles with its OSV constructions, the "original" Danish sign language, in which O is "often" put before S (Hansen, 1975), and American Sign Language, which according to Friedman (1976) admits OSV, refute the prediction, and so does the Urubú sign language, which has an OS order (Kakamasu, 1968). For the sign language of Providence Island, too, OS constructions are reported (Washabaugh, in press). For the Israeli sign language we have obtained a filmed corpus of spontaneous signing (Namir and Schlesinger, 1978) and data from two experiments on sign order (Schlesinger, 1971a; Namir and Schlesinger, 1978), and each of these sources there is a preponderance of SO and only a small minority of cases of OS (OSV in the spontaneous signing).

There are thus exceptions in several sign languages to the predicted SOV order, and not all of these can be explained as being results of the influence of the spoken language. The problem of exceptions and converging evidence from other sources are presented below.

Child Language

Verb final order has been reported for the earliest child utterances in several native languages. Children learning German, in which the SVO order is predominant in declarative sentences (in the present and past tense), have been observed to place the verb in final position (Park, 1970a; Miller, 1975) Russian is an inflected language with a relatively free word order, but the SVO order is more frequent in adult speech. The finding of Jakobson (1963:269) that the SVO order is also adhered to in child language may be put down to the influence of adult speech. However, Slobin (1966) quotes an observation on Gvozdev's son, whose Russian utterances were SOV, in contrast to the predominant adult word order. Likewise, among the children learning Finnish (another language with relatively free word order) studied by M. Bowerman (1973), one adhered at first to an SOV order.

On the other hand, there are some conflicting data. Bates (1976: Chapter 6) reports that in the earliest utterances of some children learning Italian (an SVO language), the subject tends to appear in final position. Slobin (1978) found that in Turkish, which has a free word order, O often precedes S in adult speech, but still more frequently in children's early utterances. Slobin rejects the thesis that SOV is in some sense more natural. If this were the case, he argues, we should expect it to be more difficult to learn a language with a different order, but in fact no differences in ease of acquisition between languages have been found.

Early Languages

Jespersen (1922:356), according to whom the subject-verb order is the "natural" one, writes that after the earliest period of unstable word order, there developed "a growing tendency to place the subject first." It has been claimed that Proto-Indo-European is an OV language, and a shift to VO has occurred in some languages developing out of it (Lehmann, 1974; see also the recent discussion of Givon, 1979).

The Adjacency Principle

Although the data reviewed above seem to provide some support for the SOV order hypothesized for natural grammar, there is, as we have seen, also a significant number of contradictory findings. These cannot be dismissed out of hand, and we turn now to a discussion of various ways in which one might want to deal with such exceptions. We first explore the possibility that the SOV rule proposed for natural grammar is too stringent. Instead of ascribing fixed positions to S, O, and V, one should perhaps make the much weaker claim that natural grammar adheres to what one might call the *adjacency principle*. This principle states that the hierarchical structure underlying a sentence is kept intact; no claim is made regarding the order of elements within a constituent of the hierarchy.

The adjacency principle has been supported in a cross-linguistic study by Wexler et al. (1975). These authors hypothesized that the universal deep structure includes the hierarchical structure Determiner (numeral (adjective, noun))—for instance: the (two (old men))—and that although the order of elements between each pair of parentheses is free to vary, the bracketing itself should be left intact. Thus the following word orders might be found in languages of the world:

> the two men old
> the men old two
> two old men the

but not

> the old two men
> two the old men
> two old the men

because the latter disrupt the hierarchy. Only eight out of the 24 possible permutations are thus predicted to occur. In fact, all but one of the 218 languages included in the sample of Wexler et al. (1975) observed this hierarchical structure constraint.

A similar principle has been invoked by Lehmann (1974:16) in his work on Proto-Indo-European. He claims that the adjective, genitive, and relative constructions modifying the noun will take up the position, relative to the noun, opposite to that of the verb; that is, they are normally preposed in OV languages and postponed in VO languages. Thus O and V constitute a unit that is not to be interrupted.

In Billy's invented sign language "the adjectives are never separated from the nominal by any other sign. Equally, the subject nominal phrase is never separated from the verb" (Macleod, 1973:78). In these respects, then, the deaf man's signing conformed to the adjacency principle.

It might be suggested, therefore, that rather than following a fixed SOV order, natural grammar is merely subject to the adjacency principle, which would imply that the following hierarchy is to remain intact: S(OV). Accordingly, permissible orders would be SVO, SOV, VOS, and OVS, but not OSV and VSO, which disrupt the hierarchy (see Namir and Schlesinger, 1978, where this proposal has been made for the Israeli sign language). It seems, however, that the adjacency principle hardly accounts for the data any better than does the hypothesis of a fixed SOV order. As stated above, OSV constructions, which are ruled out by the adjacency principle, occasionally occur in the sign languages of Israel, the United States, and Marseilles. The evidence for the adjacency principle in child language is discussed in Schlesinger (in press, Section 8.3), and there, too, exceptions sometimes occur. In a study of Turkish-speaking children, a considerable proportion of OSV and VSO constructions were found both in the speech of children and in that of adults directed to children (Slobin, 1978). Making less rigid requirements on natural grammar by adopting the weaker adjacency principle therefore does help us much to eliminate exceptions.

The last remark should not be taken to mean that the adjacency principle fails to hold for natural grammar. Presumably, the principle is in fact part of natural grammar, as is strongly suggested by the findings of Wexler et al. (1975), quoted above. But in accounting for exceptions, no advantage is gained by retreating from the SOV hypothesis to the adjacency principle. The problem of exceptions to the SOV order must be dealt with differently. One possibility, to be explored presently, is to adopt an alternative to the SOV hypothesis.

TOPIC AND COMMENT

A variety of languages have topic-comment structures. As the following examples show, the topic is not necessarily identical with the sentence subject (sentences translated literally by Li and Thompson, 1976; topics italicized):

> *This field*, the rice is very good.   (Lahu)
> *School*, I was busy.   (Japanese)
> *That house*, fortunately it didn't snow last year.   (Mandarin)
> *That tree*, the leaves are big.   (Mandarin)
> *Fish*, red snapper is delicious.

The closest English equivalent to the last example would be *As for fish, red snapper is delicious*. The topic "sets a spatial, temporal or individual framework within which the main predicate holds" (Chafe, 1976:50). According to Li and Thompson (1976), it is always sentence initial (see the examples above).

In the examples given in the preceding section of SOV constructions prevalent in sign languages and child language, what has been construed as subject may, in fact, have been the topic. On the other hand, in the exceptions where O preceded S, O may have been the topic of the sentence. (Of course, this would have to be checked on in a respectable sample of cases.) In what Li and Thompson call "topic-prominent" languages, the verb has final position, and this would be in accord with the verb-final constructions prevalent in sign languages and in some of the samples of child language.

Perhaps, therefore, we should hypothesize that natural grammar has a topic-comment structure rather than an SOV structure. There may be a natural tendency for the speaker to set up a "framework," in Chafe's terms, "within which the main predication holds," and accordingly he puts the topic first. Li and Thompson (1976:484) suggest that "subjects are essentially grammaticalized topics." Givon (1979) has also argued for the ontogenetic and phylogenetic priority of the topic-comment word order. If natural grammar has a topic-comment structure, we may expect the child to start out with a penchant for topic-comment constructions, which under the influence of adult language give way to subject-predicate constructions in some languages; there are others, like Lahu and Japanese, that are "topic-prominent."

Early Languages

That natural grammar has a topic-comment structure seems also to be suggested by the development of Indo-European Languages. According to Lehmann (1976), Proto-Indo-European had a topic-comment structure, and in its offshoots the subject-predicate structure subsequently developed. I do not know whether a similar development can be shown to have taken place in other language families, but should this turn out to be the case, the claim for a topic-comment structure in natural grammar would gain considerable support. It is of interest in this connection that certain dialects of Black English have topic-comment structures (see studies cited in Chambers, 1973). Presumably, Black English is a language at a less developed stage (some writers view it as a creole), and it may accordingly provide information on natural grammar.

Sign Languages

American Sign Language has been claimed to have a topic-comment structure (Friedman, 1976; see also Edge and Herrmann, 1977; Ingram, 1978); but it seems that further investigtion is needed to find out whether this language uses topic-comment structures to the exclusion of subject-predicate structures. The sign language used in Providence Island has also been reported to have a topic-comment structure (Washabaugh, in press).

Child Language

Turning to child language, we note von Raffler-Engel's (1970a) observation that the child's two-word utterances have a topic-comment structure, since the first position can be taken up by either the agent or the patient. According to Bruner (1968), the topic-comment distinction is rooted in the child's prelinguistic motor behavior.

The following developmental course has been charted by Gruber (1967). In the first stage, the topic is left unexpressed and only the comment appears in the utterance.[7] Next, both topic and comment are expressed, and eventually this topic-comment structure gives way to adult subject-predicate constructions. Gruber gave examples of topic-comment constructions from the corpus of one child between the ages 2;2 and 2;5 (e.g., *Car, it broken*, and *Those other, put them*),[8] and adduced several arguments to the effect that utterances that seem to have a subject-predicate structure actually have an underlying topic-comment structure. Examining Gruber's thesis, Brown (1973) found these arguments not to be compelling and the examples too few to warrant a rejection of the customary subject-predicate analysis of early utterances.

Yau (1978) found examples of topic-comment constructions in the speech of children at ages 2;6 to 4;2 (e.g., *une voiture, un monsieur qui pousse la voiture*). It seems, however, that the specific situation in which his data were obtained (the children were given pictures and asked to describe them) was conducive to the deployment of just these structures: when seeing a picture, one first tends to point out one of the figures appearing in it (e.g., *une* voiture).

Finally, Bates (1976:69) observed that several Italian-speaking children often put the subject in final position, and attributed this to the tendency to mention the comment before the topic. Although this may be true, it should be realized that by assuming that the topic can occur not only in initial but also in final position, the hypothesis that child language has a topic-comment structure becomes even more difficult to validate empirically. Bates and MacWhinney (1979), and Givon (1979), however, have reviewed several findings that they interpret as showing that the topic-comment distinction may precede the development of the subject concept.

The available data do not seem to provide compelling evidence for including the topic-comment structure into natural grammar instead of the

---

[7] Similar observations have been made by several investigators. For the one-word stage, Greenfield and Smith (1976) claim that the word expresses that element which is most informative. MacWhinney (1976) has reviewed research on Hungarian child language, showing that new (as opposed to given) information is coded in one-word utterances. Likewise, Weisenburger (1976) finds that in early multiword utterances, redundant information is more likely to be omitted.

[8] Gruber includes examples in which the alleged topic is in final position, which does not accord with Li and Thompson's (1976) view that the topic is always sentence initial. But conceivably the later-appearing topic is tacked onto the comment originating in the previous period; see Goldin-Meadow (1975) for an analogous conjecture concerning other relations.

SOV structure. Despite the many exceptions encountered, the SOV structure seems on the whole to be better substantiated. Another way of approaching the problem of these exceptions is explained below.

SITUATIONAL AND AFFECTIVE FACTORS

In spoken languages, the unmarked order of words may be changed in accordance with various factors operative at the time an utterance is made. *Ice cream I like!* is not an unlikely exclamation, although it diverges from the regular structure of English declarative sentences.

Writing about German sign language, Wundt (1904) observed that when there is a strong wish, the usual sign order, SOV, may be abandoned (e.g., WATER DRINK I). We have seen already that contrary to our hypothesis about natural grammar, the negating element is occasionally preposed by children and by Billy, the inventor of an idiosyncratic sign language. Conceivably, in these cases effective factors led to the primacy of the negation. Other alleged determinants of word order suggested for child language are "focus, saliency, or relative importance" (Bloom, 1973:53). For an experimental investigation of some of these factors, see Osgood and Bock (1977).

Many of the exceptions to the hypothesized rule of natural grammar may perhaps be put down to such momentary factors as these. It might be objected that if such escape clauses are admitted, there is no way of testing any hypothesized rule. However, the factors resorted to here as an explanation have not been made up for the purpose of defending these hypotheses; rather, they are needed anyhow to account for phenomena in spoken language. Affect, focus, and saliency are factors that enter into the construction of all utterances, and there is no reason for them not to be operative in child language and sign languages as well. The objection thus loses most of its force. Natural grammar presumably includes all these momentary factors. It is not made up of rules without exceptions any more than spoken languages are; rather, it is the playground of conflicting tendencies.

The foregoing may be relevant to what has been called the "formless period" (Jespersen, 1922:134–135) observed, which occurs in the language development of at least some children, that is, a stage at which word order is completely or almost completely free (see Braine, 1971; Bloom et al., 1975:39). The observed haphazard word order cannot be assumed to be simply random; presumably it results from one, or the interplay of several, momentary factors of the kind mentioned above. Likewise, the "groping pattern," in which word order is not fixed yet (Braine, 1976), is not necessarily the outcome of the child's search after the adult pattern. Instead the child may at that stage be still at the mercy of tendencies deriving from factors such as saliency.

The lack of a fixed word order was also a characteristic of languages at their earliest stages, according to Jespersen (1922:356; see also p. 372), who argued that this is "what we should naturally expect from primitive man, whose thoughts and words are most likely to have come to him rushing helter-skelter in wild confusion." The "helter-skelter" is the result of those conflicting tendencies originating in various situational and affective factors that influence us all. The difference between us and Jespersen's primitive is that we have been trained by the grammar of our language to bridle the verbal expression of our thoughts—somewhat.

REPETITIVENESS

Before children master adult language structure, their utterances exhibit much repetitiveness. The following is a typical example (Braine, 1971:16):

> Stevie gun. Tommy, Stevie gun. Tommy give gun.
> Gun. Tommy gun. Tommy, give Stevie gun.

Since the child at that stage still lacks most inflections, function words, and even a fixed word order, such repetitiveness may introduce the redundancy necessary for communication to succeed (von Raffler-Engel, 1970a:281; 1970b:30).

Repetitiveness is also found in the signing of the deaf. An excerpt from the Israeli sign language, in which grammatical relations are not reliably coded (Schlesinger 1971a; Namir and Schlesinger, 1978) runs as follows:

> . . . week money loan debt loan loan much. First-of-month already-pay-all that's-it. Week coming membership-fee cash-down exactly . . . Elections soon before-long. Five-months five soon five-months elections new. Who membership-fee no? (Cohen et al. 1977. 29–30)

A similar tendency is found in American Sign Language (Fischer, 1976; see Namir and Schlesinger, 1978:100, for an example), and in the creole spoken in Hawaii (Fischer, 1978).

The word or sign standing for the negative is sometimes particularly likely to be repeated. Bellugi (1971:105) noted that in early child language the sentence may taken on a "negative coloring" (as in *He's not doing nothing but standing still*). Jespersen (1922:186) quoted an example of a triple negative in a sentence found in the corpus of isolated twins. In the invented sign language of Billy, the negative sign appeared in both initial and final positions; the same was true for interrogatives (Macleod, 1973:78). Repetition of the negative is also found in Afrikaans (a simplified dialect of Dutch that originated in the second half of the seventeenth century as a contact language; see Kainz, 1960:691), in Bantu languages, and in Old English (Jespersen, 1922:186).

The evidence presented above entitles us to regard repetitiveness tentatively as a characteristic of natural grammar. Not much repetitiveness is left in most well-developed spoken languages, presumably because the introduction of grammatical devices did away with the need for redundancy. At times, however, a nervous or scatterbrained speaker may fall back on repetitions to get his meaning across.

ABSENCE OF INFLECTIONS AND PARTS OF SPEECH

Lack of Inflections

We now come to some negative properties of natural grammar. It is well known that early child speech lacks most inflections and function words, a trait that has led to its description as "telegraphic" (Brown and Fraser, 1963). Lack of inflections is also found in sign languages (Namir and Schlesinger, 1978:99–100)[9], and in pidgins (Slobin, 1977a). The lack of inflections in Afrikaans (Kainz, 1960) is probably the property that has earned this simplified language the Dutch appellation "baby Hollands." We may hypothesize, therefore, that the main syntactical device of natural grammar is word order, not inflections. In fact, even children learning inflected languages, in which word order is relatively free, often adhere to a fixed word order (Slobin, 1973; see also subsection of "Subject, Object, and Verb" entitled "Child Language," above).

Lack of Parts of Speech

Another property sign languages have in common with child language is the absence of fixed parts of speech. Thus a single sign may stand for both EAT and FOOD, for SEW and TAILOR (Stokoe, et al., 1965; Cohen et al., 1977:23–24; Namir and Schlesinger, 1978:98–99).[10] Likewise, in the early stages of language acquisition, children often confuse parts of speech, and errors like the following occur:

---

[9] Sign languages do exhibit certain inflection-like phonemena. These are modulations of the verb (Namir and Schlesinger, 1978:102–103, 131–132; Warren, 1978; Bellugi and Klima, 1979; Poizner and Bellugi, in press), usually denoting aspect, not the grammatical relations expressed by affixes. Sign languages have no indigenous affixes.

[10] Feldman et al. (1978), who studied the spontaneous sign language of deaf children who were not exposed to any formal sign language, found that nouns were indicated by pointing, whereas verbs were characterized by gestures. This distinction is obviously dictated by the nature of the entities referred to, and one would hardly credit these children with having a part-of-speech distinction in their grammatical inventory. Remember that the parts-of-speech classification of a language does not correspond to any semantic classification. A distinction between nouns and related verbs in American Sign Language has been observed by Supalla and Newport (1978). It remains to be seen whether a similar phenomenon can be found in other sign languages, or whether this is a peculiar development of American sign language, which has had a much longer history than most others.

Louding plane (Carlson and Anisfeld, 1969)
It's still soring (Carlson and Anisfeld, 1960)
Piece it (Wundt, 1904:282)
Allgone sticky (Braine, 1973)

Such examples are found among the utterances of children learning English, German (Schlesinger, in press, Section 8.1), and Polish (Smoczyńska, 1979).

Once a language has established parts of speech, a word belonging to one such class may subsequently begin to do duty in another class. Examples of such functional shifts are common in English, where verbs are used as nouns (e.g., to catch—a catch), and vice versa (a tailor—to tailor). In Afrikaans, functional shift seems to be the rule (Kainz, 1960:685).

Children learn the distinction between parts of speech in the course of acquiring the grammar of their language (see Schlesinger, in press, Section 8.1, for a discussion). We may tentatively conclude therefore that natural grammar has no parts of speech.

CATEGORIES EXPRESSED IN NATURAL GRAMMAR

We now come to the third and last issue. What are the semantic categories expressed in natural grammar? Are any such categories obligatively and universally expressed?

Slobin (1976:209) has proposed a distinction between salient or basic categories of perception, which will be encoded in all languages, and those "resting on more complex cognitive processes." To the former he assigns certain aspects of the action (e.g., duration, repetition), and he shows that aspect takes precedence over tense in child language, language contact situations, historical development of languages, pidgins, and creoles—and possibly, we may add, in sign languages (see Fischer, 1973, 1978; Warren, 1978). There seems to be some evidence, therefore that natural grammar evinces preferences for some relations over others, but clearly more study on the problem is needed.

Another suggestion due to Slobin (1976) is that there is a universal core of categories that must be expressed by all languages of the world. This core would belong accordingly to natural grammar. As long as the categories that are hypothesized to belong to this core are not specified, it will obviously be difficult to refute the claim that there exists such a core. However, it seems even now that its existence is very doubtful (cf. also Schlesinger, 1977a). Semantic categories that one might hold, on a priori grounds, to be a requisite of every language may turn out on further examination not to be universal.

As a case in point, consider the subject and the object—or the agent and the patient. One might be tempted to think that the distinction between these categories must be universal. How, one might reason, could a language possibly function if it lacks any means to convey the distinction between, for example, *dog bites man* and *man bites dog*? The fact of the matter is, however, that not all languages make this distinction.

In our experiments we found that the Israeli sign language has no grammatical devices for distinguishing between agent and patient. (There are only some statistical tendencies of sign order; see "Subject, Verb and Object," above. When signers were asked to describe to one another one of several pictures differing in the identify of the agent and the patient, they were signally unsuccessful: a very high proportion of messages were not understood (Schlesinger, 1971a; Namir and Schlesinger, 1978). If this language is nevertheless a perfectly suitable means of communication in everyday life, it is because there is usually enough context built around an utterance to render it unambiguous. In our experiments, by contrast, there were no situational cues, and since the language lacked grammatical devices to fall back on, our subjects failed to make themselves understood.

This peculiarity of the Israeli sign language is not shared by American Sign Language, which has been considerably influenced by spoken language. Bode (1974) obtained a high proportion of correctly understood messages in American Sign Language in a replication of our experiments, and Liddell (quoted in Supalla and Newport, 1978:92; see also Edge and Herrmann, 1977) described the grammatical devices of that language for distinguishing between subject and object. On the other hand, the sign language used on Providence Island is like the Israeli sign language in that it lacks such devices (Washabaugh, 1979, in press).

These counterexamples to a putative linguistic universal have important theoretical implications (see Schlesinger, 1971a, 1977b, Section 5c; Namir and Schlesinger, 1978). There have been some attempts to salvage the universal, particularly on the part of believers in a rich language-specific base of universal principles. One move, due to Wasow (1973), was to stipulate that any language that is not spoken is ipso facto not included in the claim of universality. The absence of the oral-auditory dimension, according to Wasow (1973:51), "may well affect language in other ways which are not obviously connected."[11] To wit, classical Chinese, allegedly not a spoken language, also does not distinguish between subject and object, whereas all the large number of spoken languages studied (at the time of Wasow's writing) do make such a distinction. The moral thus seems to be: don't count your universals before they are patched.

---

[11] Not obviously, indeed. One might well ask why sign languages should not have seized on the alleged universal innate principles or structures expressed in spoken language, since these are already available. According to some researchers, sign language even does not have a different hemispheric localization (Kimura, 1976; Neville and Bellugi, 1978; see, however, Poizner and Lane, 1979, and Poizner et al., 1979). See also Namir and Schlesinger (1978:109–110).

The patching has not been successful, however, for there is also a spoken language, Lisu, that has no syntactic means of distinguishing between subject and object (Li and Thompson, 1976).

NATURAL GRAMMAR: USE OF THE CONSTRUCT

It is clear by now how one might go about investigating natural grammar. Some characteristics of natural grammar have begun to emerge, but obviously only a beginning has been made, and much further work needs to be done, based on a greater amount of data. Some of the proposals made here may have to be discarded and others may have to be qualified. Further characteristics of natural grammar will probably be revealed that have not even been mentioned here.[12] What should be evident already at this stage, however, is that one cannot expect to defend simplistic statements about *the* natural order of words in a "natural-grammar sentence" and the semantic relations expressed in it. Natural grammar is a more abstract concept; as we have argued, it should be viewed as a set of often conflicting tendencies.

These tendencies may be expected to express themselves often in incipient and immature linguistic systems, such as child language, sign language, and pidgins. Often, but not necessarily always, it is here that the main methodological problem in investigating natural grammar lies, because usually one has to reckon with the possibility that a tendency of natural grammar has been overridden by the influence of a more developed linguistic system that has already moved away from natural grammar, or by momentary factors (saliency, affect, etc.). Hypotheses about natural grammar are thereby rendered relatively invulnerable, and this is why one should be careful about accepting them. Hence our insistence in this chapter on the need of finding converging evidence from various sources for any putative principle of natural grammar. Moreover, such positive evidence from a given linguistic system should not be explainable as the result of the influence of another, more developed system.

Uncertain and laborious as such investigations of natural grammar are, they seem to be eminently worthwhile. Natural grammar plays a crucial role both in the phylogenesis and the ontogenesis of language. In theorizing about the early stages in the development of languages, one has to take into account the tendencies of natural grammar, and their interactions with various linguistic processes. In connection with the latter, some in-

---

[12] For example, there may be certain natural tendencies at work in the expression of the plural (see Jakobson, 1965; Namir and Schlesinger, 1978:127) and of temporal concepts (see Namir and Schlesinger, 1978:127), and reduplication may turn out to be one of the devices employed by natural grammar (see Kainz, 1960:680, 688, 690; Fischer 1973). Furthermore, Osgood and Tanz (in press) have obtained evidence concerning the relative "naturalness" of different structures expressing both the direct and indirect object, and Osgood and Bock (1977) have argued that the "figure" tends to be mentioned before the "ground" (e.g., *a ball on the plate* rather than *a plate holding a ball*).

triguing proposals have been made by Slobin (1976). Natural grammar and the grammar of a full-blown language at an advanced stage of its development may thus be viewed as two poles of a process, with the principles found at the natural grammar pole becoming crystallized, and in part possibly transmuted, in the course of development into fixed syntactic rules.

Likewise, the development of language in the child should be viewed as an interaction between the child's natural grammar and the rules of adult language. In some interactions there may be a conflict in which the adult rules ultimately prevail. But in the grammar of the child at a particular stage of development, natural grammar may make itself felt. This has some methodological implications for research in child language, which have so far not been heeded sufficiently by writers on the subject. The reasoning here is similar to that employed in inferring from characteristics of sign languages or child language to those of natural grammar. Just as the presence or absence of these characteristics does not constitute evidence either for or against a hypothesis about natural grammar unless the possible influence of the more developed language of the environment is considered, so the child's following or disregarding any rule of adult grammar does not in itself show that he has learned or failed to learn this rule; natural grammar has a role to play.

To illustrate this, suppose that simple declarative sentences of a language follow a SV rule (i.e., the agent is placed before its action) and that in the corpus of a child learning this language, the agent + action pattern is followed consistently. In previous analyses of child language such consistency has usually been taken as evidence that the syntactic rule of the vernacular has been learned by the child. Such a conclusion disregards the fact that the agent + action pattern may be part of natural grammar (as shown in the section "Subject, Object and Verb," above). Perhaps, then, the child is merely following a tendency existing independently of the adult model (but possibly strengthened by it). This alternative interpretation could make all the difference in studying the determinants of the sequence in which the syntactic expressions of various relations are acquired.

Suppose, on the other hand, that adult language follows the opposite order, action + agent, and that in the child's corpus both action + agent and agent + action constructions appear. Can this be taken to show that the child still uses a random "order" and has not yet learned the adult rule? Not necessarily: considerable learning may have taken place, and the unstable pattern of the child's utterances may be the result of a conflict between the natural grammar pattern, which is presumably agent + action, and the adult pattern.

The idea of natural grammar (or natural word order, as it is sometimes called) has been around for a long time. It has been talked about and occasionally resorted to as an explanatory standby, but very little has been done to investigate it systematically. No wonder, then, that it has yielded few theoretical benefits. It is time therefore to begin taking natural grammar seriously. Let's talk less about this old acquaintance of ours and try to get to know him more.

Section III
COGNITIVE KINESICS

There is a growing trend in the literature of human information processing to place many related disciplines under the rubric of cognitive sciences. This trend is dominated by the research paradigm of cognitive psychology, but it has immediate applications for experimental psycholinguistics, clinical neurolinguistics, the psychology of reading, artificial intelligence models, learning disabilities research, speech pathology, visual thinking, and other fields. The chapters in this book, moreover, suggest that the emerging paradigm of developmental kinesics is consonant with this research. However, to differentiate fully the implications of kinesics as a cognitive science, we have designated this aspect of the research under the rubric of cognitive kinesics.

Cognitive kinesics is based on research into learning development, as exemplified by Feuerstein in the chapter that begins this section, and consists of at least the two complementary parts treated in the two chapters that follow: the growth and maturation of perception (Engquist) and of performance (van der Geest). Much of the research to date has been from the area of cognitive psychology, which—as opposed to behavioral output research, usually with adults—is developing a paradigm for human information processing. Most models rely heavily on verbal models and definitions. Those studies must be complemented with work on the processing of nonverbal information.

One basic area investigated by cognitive kinesicists is the development of the perception of behavior within a symbolic system of communication. Although at times it seems that some of these basic components are structurally unrelated, it usually turns out they are merely variations on a theme. This concept of how structures participate in a complementary framework is known in linguistics a "emics."

The term was coined by Kenneth Pike (1947) to capture the notion that the sounds of human language (phonetics) are structured into patterns of verbal behavior (phonemics). For example, in English whether we use a trilled /r/ or a flapped /r/ or a retroflex /r/, the meaning of the word (emics) is not changed, although the difference in physical production (etics) is obvious. In Spanish the etics are structured differently. The trilled /r/ (spelled "rr") and the flapped /r/ (spelled "r") are "emic" because they differentiate words, such as /pero/ but and /perro/ dog.

This contrast of unstructured (etic) versus structured (emic) information has been adopted by scholars from other fields, but its most significant use for developmental kinesics can be found in the writing of Birdwhistell (1952), who found eye behavior, gesture, proxemics, and other forms of nonverbal behavior to be structured in some systems of communication as variations on a theme. Rather than treating them as disparate phenomena, he saw them as different expressions of the same underlying concept. Hence, as noted by French and Dorfman in the Introduction, he speaks about *kinemes*, or basic units of nonverbal behavior, and their complementary expressions of a theme, *allokines*. For example, in communication we may emphasize a word with vocal stress, with a baton gesture, with an eye roll, or in other ways. Because all have the same meaning addition, they are allokines.

The concept of etic/emic structuring of human behavior is an important and promising one among social scientists. Linguistics who have limited themselves to language as recorded on tape or paper have not been able to study the full range of allokines that are necessary in the full study of human communication. The consequent distortion of the study of communicative competence is still with us in the inability of followers of certain schools of linguistics to perceive the constraints on the validity of their results. This distortion can be rectified through the use of the full paradigm of human behavioral studies as recommended throughout this book.

It is indeed fortunate that those active in developmental kinesics studies have had access to more than one model of human information processing; not only are they aware of the vast research on verbal studies from psycholinguistics, but also they have been much involved in cognitive psychology models by virtue of attention to research in comprehensive developmental studies. Furthermore, they are always being made aware of the "doctrine of accidents," wherein pathological systems emerge in areas of mental retardation, language learning disabilities, neurolinguistics, and speech pathology. For this reason, the concept of cognitive kinesics is not only part of a rich tradition of scholarship and experimental research, but it also promises to enhance the growing field of cognitive sciences. This awareness of the rich tradition of scholarship is particularly strong among scholars outside the United States, and we have much to gain by close attention to their contributions.

Chapter 6
MEDIATED LEARNING EXPERIENCE IN THE ACQUISITION OF KINESICS

*Reuven Feuerstein**

Developmental kinesics is an integral part of a wider system of developmental phenomena that can be studied under the specific concept of mediated learning experience. One of the components of mediated learning experience, imitation, is probably the royal road leading toward the establishment of kinesics as a nonverbal communicational modality. Neither the general meaning of kinesics for communication nor the specific content transmitted through kinesic communicational patterns is the major concern of this chapter. Rather, we explore the formative significance of the acquisition of kinesics, its role in producing in the individual modalities of interaction with the environment, and how this affects the ontogeny of learning in the organism. That is, we are mainly concerned with the differential capacity of individuals to become modified through experience by making use of both formal and informal opportunities for learning. It is the contention of the author that much of what are usually considered to be innate and stable characteristics of individual intelligence can best be understood as the differential capacity for learning. In turn, the differential capacity for learning can be ascribed to particular characteristics of certain interactions between the individual and the environment, specifically referred to by us as mediated learning experience, which according to the theory of cognitive modifiability is considered to be the proximal determinant of differential cognitive development (see Feuerstein et al., 1980; Feuerstein, 1979; Feuerstein and Rand, 1975). The child/environment interaction leading to the acquisition of kinesics represents a special case of mediated learning experience, and it is therefore of interest to us to explore

---

* Reuven Feuerstein is Professor at Bar Ilan University, Ramat Gan, Israel; Director of the Hadassah-WIZO Canada Research Institute, Jerusalem; Director of Youth Aliyah Child Guidance Clinic, Jerusalem; and Adjunct Professor, Peabody College, Vanderbilt University.

tein

impact of the acquisition of kinesics on the development of lifiability in the individual.

KINESIC COMMUNICATIONAL PATTERNS

It is assumed here that kinesic communicational patterns reflect culturally determined behaviors, that inasmuch as kinesic patterns transcend universal traits, they are *acquired*, primarily through observational learning and imitation, and that their acquisition involves a strong mediated learning component. By definition, the acquired dimensions of kinesics are the products of interactions between the organism—as defined by its structural, physiological, and temperamental characteristics—and its sociocultural environment. Certain aspects of kinesic communicational patterns surely have universal traits and sources. Innate components of kinesics such as emotional mimicry are determined by the common neurophysiological structure of the animal world in general, and the human in particular. These innate and structural components set the limits and the orientation of the acquired components of kinesics, and to some extent form a common basis for communication across cultures, and even across species. However, these innate components of mimicry and kinesics can be modified, reduced, or even wiped out of the behavioral repertoire of the individual by acquired components that have their basis in culturally determined behaviors.

Kinesic patterns that are basically motoric and iconic for the expressive and receptive aspects of communication, respectively, cannot be conceived except as the products of exposure to models of behavior. To elicit a specific imitative behavior, this exposure must be characterized by certain levels of intensity and frequency as they interact with certain characteristics of the observer/imitator. In brief, all these determinants combine to produce in the observer/imitator a unit of behavior more or less similar to that emitted by the model; therefore, acquired kinesics can be considered to be the direct product of imitation. The specific conditions under which exposure to a model will effectively establish imitative behavior must be investigated and described by scientists more directly involved in the study of developmental kinesics (see Chapter 1). For the purposes of this chapter, however, kinesics is of interest because both its establishment and its development in the organism seem to be affected by the learning capacity of the individual and to affect this capacity, as well. This reciprocal effect contributes to the individual's increasing accessibility to various modalities of exposure to stimuli, and in consequence, to the resultant enhanced modifiability of his cognitive functions in the direction of higher levels of adaptability. Therefore, we deal very little with the content dimensions of kinesics. We focus on remarks concerned mainly with the process leading to the development and the establishment of kinesic communicational patterns, and with the more general impact of this process on the structure of the organism's adaptive behavioral repertoire. To discuss the meaning of imitative behavior leading to the development of kinesics and its effects on the modifiability of the individual, we must first describe the nature of mediated learning experience (MLE), of which imitation represents a particular case.

COGNITIVE MODIFIABILITY THEORY

Differential cognitive development and correspondent changes in the organism are attributed in this theoretical framework to two modalities of the interaction between the organism and its environment. The first modality, and the most pervasive one, is direct exposure to stimuli. The organism, relative to its psychophysical, neurophysiological, and maturational characteristics, is constantly being modified (i.e., learning through direct exposure stimuli). Of course, in addition to the nature of the organism, the changes occurring in the organism will depend on some characteristics of the stimuli such as their novelty, intensity, and frequency, their meaning in combination with the organism's past experience, and the degree to which they respond to immediate and vital needs. Certainly direct exposure learning is most powerful during early childhood, when the naive organism is strongly impressed with the primal nature of impinging stimuli. However, effects of direct exposure learning continue throughout life to the extent that a stimulus brings to and impresses on the individual a new or altered perspective, or to the extent that redundancy, itself, of a given stimulus affects and modifies the organism. Direct exposure to stimuli certainly may affect a wide range of behavior. However, the occurrence of such changes, their amplitude, and their degrees of permanency are functions of both the nature of the behavior and the characteristics of the organism.

Direct exposure to stimuli, however, does not suffice to explain either the entire range of changes occurring in human cognitive structure that lead to the development of higher mental processes, or the extent of the organism's plasticity that serves to enhance adaptation to discontinuities in the environment. Furthermore, direct-exposure learning alone certainly cannot explain differential cognitive development, especially with respect to differences in learning capacity and in the potential for cognitive modifiability. Realization of this end calls for a second modality of organism/environment interaction by help of which learning capacity is developed. The second modality to which we refer is mediated learning experience. In MLE the learning organism is not being exposed directly to the stimuli; rather, an interposing, mediating adult is organizing and transforming the random stimuli impinging on the organism. As the initiated and intentioned adult selects, groups, orders, and frames certain stimuli, he is mediating to the learning child, and introducing meaningful changes both in the stimuli and in the learner with respect to the learner's perception of the stimuli, and regarding his attitude toward them. Through MLE the learner acquires an attitude toward the stimuli that would not be engendered by their sheer registration. This attitude is marked by an active search for stimuli according to their general meaning and the specific need systems that through mediation come to be present in the learning organism. The mediating process affects the learning organism in the following three areas:

1. MLE provides the individual with areas of interaction and mastery that would be inaccessible to him were they not offered by the mediating adult. The existence of these areas in the repertoire of the individual are contingent on the processes of mediation. Consider, for example, the relationship of the learner to past events that have not been experienced directly, or to events requiring a representational modality of experience. These situations require mental activities relating to objects and events that are temporally and spatially inaccessible to direct perceptual sensorial activity, and these can become available to the individual only through MLE or through the inferential activity of the learner himself. The meaning of these areas of interaction surpasses the mediated content, producing in the organism a readiness to relate to information that is not directly accessible to him. The establishment in the individual's repertoire of events that have not been directly experienced but have been learned about through the experience of others, enriches the individual with modalities of perception that to a certain extent resemble a sixth sense.

2. The mediating process provides the individual with active modalities of interaction with the world. Through MLE, the learning individual acquires and develops autonomous modalities of actively transforming, grouping, scheduling, linking, and relating objects and events otherwise disparate; and the individual actively selects certain stimuli while ignoring, eliminating, or delaying the appearance of others in favor of a specific purpose responding to an adaptive need.

3. The MLE meaningfully affects the nature and structure of the need system, expanding the limits established by the biologically oriented requirements to those transcending into the sphere of specifically human needs and human motivational structure. Thus human motivation, with its differential manifestations, is largely a product of MLE, which endows the organism with needs of types that cannot be accounted for by the sheer biological basis of existence, and cannot be considered to be the sheer epiphenomenon of the maturational unfolding processes of the organism.

The relationship between MLE and the direct-exposure type of learning can be formulated as follows: the more efficient the exposure to MLE, the greater the individual's capacity to become modified through direct exposure to stimuli. Individuals who for one reason or another have not been exposed to MLE are marked by the syndrome of cultural deprivation, which manifests itself mainly by reduced and limited modifiability when confronted by direct exposure to stimuli. Such an individual's capacity to benefit from life experience, from formal and informal modalities of learning, may be severely stunted because the individual experiences each event to which he is exposed as an episodic condition with very little relationship to what has preceded it or is to follow from it. The nature of such a person's experiences is essentially task bound, and generalization may be arduous, perhaps occurring infrequently; in certain cases it may be totally absent.

Thus exposure to models of behavior can have very different effects on the observer according to the individual's capacity to benefit from them—a capacity that in cognitive modifiability theory is held to be proximally determined by the amount and nature of experienced mediation. It is important to realize that the occurrence of MLE is not contingent on either the language through which the mediational process is taking place or the content at hand around which the mediational process happens to be revolving. MLE can be considered to be a universal process taking place whenever and wherever cultural transmission is ensured by various agents, especially the nuclear family, with its primary love objects and caregivers.

In all cases involving mediational processes, MLE will increase the capacity of the organism to become modified through direct exposure, ultimately enhancing the organism's capacity to adapt to situations becoming less familiar, more novel, and more complex. The adaptation of the culturally deprived person may not be conspicuously deficient as long as the individual remains in a relatively uniform, familiar, and stable environment. However, adaptation will become difficult if the individual suddenly is confronted with the need to change, when modifying himself is the sole way to adapt to a situation that is discontinuous and new. Under these conditions the organism's limited modifiability will become a source of inadequate functioning, conflict, and stress.

Role of MLE in Cultural Deprivation

The reasons for inadequate MLE resulting in cultural deprivation can be grouped into two broad categories.

The first and most pervasive category consists of organisms that simply are not provided with MLE by the environment and its socializing agents. For example, poverty may hamper the capacity of the parents to mediate to the child because the priorities of the need system within the family are restricted to elementary requirements for physical survival. Other reasons for the failure of the environment to provide the child with MLE may involve the obstruction of transmissional processes in a society that has ceased to strive for continuation of its existence as a group and a culture, thus discouraging the nucleal agents from transmitting their own past and values to the next generation. This situation is especially typical of oppressed and disadvantaged cultural minorities that are confronted with a dominant and advantaged culture. On the other hand, certain culturally determined phenomena such as that referred to as "counterculture" may be characterized by a volitional and purposeful obstruction of the transmissional process as a way to avoid any inculcation of dominant cultural values on either the minority group members or their children. The syndrome of cultural deprivation produced by any of these etiological determinants will manifest itself in inadequate adaptational processes due to reduced modifiability of the individual.

The second category of determinants leading to lack of MLE groups inherent conditions of the organism that at certain points in the development of the individual can produce effective barriers to mediational attempts being made by the environment. Thus some endogenous heredogenetic conditions affecting the tonus, vitality, openness, and sensitivity of the organism to mediation may result in limiting the amount and quality of MLE experienced by the individual. Barriers to mediation that may be produced by conditions of organicity, neurophysiological states, emotional disturbance, and communicational disorders, if not bypassed by appropriate changes in the intensity, nature, and / or modality of the mediational process, will leave the individual bereft of the learning sets, attitudes, and appropriate need systems necessary to render him modifiable and adaptable.

MLE is strongly linked to the processes of cultural transmission from one generation to the other. Therefore if MLE is lacking, either because of endogenous conditions of the organism or as a result of environmental exogenous factors, the syndrome of cultural deprivation will be produced. The theory of cognitive modifiability, including the concept of MLE, does not conceive of growth and development to result solely from the maturational processes, nor does it consider development to be sufficiently explained by the organism-environment interaction as it is conceived by the stimulus-response (S-R) theories, or even by the stimulus-organism-response (S-O-R) theory of Piaget, even though in the latter theoretical framework the organism is considered to interact actively with the environment through processes of assimilation and accommodation, which Piaget believed to represent the dynamic principles of growth and development of both innate and acquired schemata.

Conversely, cognitive modifiability theory considers the development of human cognitive functioning to depend on the presence of a human mediator (H), interposing himself between the S and the O (S-H-O-R), who is marked by an intention to transmit to the child his past, his cultural values, his patterns of behavior, and his communicational modalities as ways to strengthen ties with the child and to produce code systems that will help to establish reciprocal relationships. The mediator is motivated in his interaction with the child by need systems that transcend the elementary, immediate, biological, and rhythmic needs in meaningful and significant ways. Thus the motivation for cultural transmission is oriented less toward the biophysical survival of the individual than toward ensuring the cultural continuity of the group. This transcendence mediates to the child systems of needs that become increasingly wider, spreading over activities and feelings that are not the direct outcomes of nor the sole substitutes for the elementary schemata or elementary need systems of the organism. In this sense MLE represents a modality that adds the cultural dimension to the determinants of development, the significance of which lies not only in offering the organism a content repertoire that would be inaccessible to him were it not for the mediating process, but it also creates the *learning instrumentation* necessary for more adequate, efficient use of the first and more pervasive modality of direct-exposure learning.

MLE and the Child

MLE describes mediating agent–child interactions involving the two criteria of intentionality and transcendence. It starts at a very early point in the life of the child with the mother, as the primary love object and caregiver, having the most prominent role in offering the child mediational processes. Mediation is already occurring in the processes of selection and filtering of stimuli impinging on the child from the very first moment after birth. In the process of selection of stimuli (wherein certain stimuli are being made available to the child through the mediator, who is simultaneously preventing other stimuli from being allowed to reach the child), personal and culturally determined preferences, or both, are reflected corresponding to needs perceived by the caregiving person. This intention to filter out or provide certain stimuli can be a conscious act on the part of the mediator, but this is not necessary. It may reflect the collective representations and intentions of the culture to which the mediator belongs. The impact of this process of selection will be felt not only in the content of the repertoire of stimuli to which a child will be exposed, but even more important, it will ultimately result in an increased capacity of the individual himself to become involved in such processes of filtering, focusing, and selecting the relevant from the irrelevant on the basis of preferences, purposes, values, and needs that have been mediated to him or will emerge later in life.

Very early in the life of the child, the mediating mother makes herself available for a wide and varied range of transactions and interactions such as establishing gazing behavior, smiling, and other modalities of nonverbal communication. The availability of the mother's face for prolonged and intensive comtemplation will enhance imitative behavior. The constancy of the mother as a caregiving object is important above and beyond its affective emotional meaning in that growing familiarity with the mother's face will strengthen the child's capacity to observe and will induce in him the propensity to search for transformations. Furthermore, these transformations, which become perceptible only when the constant state has been established and registered, will with time become linked to certain events that have preceded them and will engender anticipations for what may follow, thus producing in the child the antecedents of causal relationships.

In the course of development of the individual, the MLE, which becomes more and more pervasive, will take on a variety of forms, will come to be elicited by different contexts and life experiences, and will also encompass a larger variety of languages of mediation. Of course, the emergence of verbal language will give the mediational process an important boost, making conceptualized, verbal, internalized types of behavior central. However, the efficiency of the preverbal mediational process lies in its ability to produce in the child the prerequisites for learning that ultimately will enable him to make efficient use of whatever direct exposure offers him in terms of stimuli, perceived objects, and experienced events.

Another group of nonverbal interactions possessing the quality of MLE is the scheduling of the appearance of certain stimuli and events along with temporal and spatial dimensions: *here*, not *there; now*, not *then*, will produce in the child the antecedents of temporal and spatial orientation that are the crossroads of experience. Making certain stimuli repeatedly available, while eliminating others, strongly enhances the ordering of events into sequences of before and after, the grouping of stimuli and events that are temporally apart (by bringing them together through reevocation, or by dividing and distinguishing among stimuli otherwise related), the generation of meaning, and the consequent emergence of certain types of motivation toward corresponding behaviors. Thus, for example, repeatedly handing back to the child an object that he keeps throwing down in his exercise of the newly acquired schema of letting things fall will endow this behavior with a meaning and will encourage the child to continue to exercise this schema as a circular reaction.

Among nonverbal mediated interactions, we count imitation as one of the most powerful determinants of cognitive growth. Imitation can be the product of direct exposure to stimuli in the sense that sheer observation of the incidental presence of a model may produce it. However, it is the contention of the author that both the capacity to imitate through incidental observation (direct-exposure modality) and the efficiency of the imitative process are determined by the amount and nature of MLE. At a very early point in the life of the child the mediator exposes himself as a model for imitation. He not only makes himself available to the child, but does it in a way calculated to produce optimum conditions for imitation to occur (e.g., by placing himself in the optimal range of sight of the child, which is known to be critical for the perceptual activity of the neonate).

The model for imitation does not present the gesture to be imitated accidentally or in a random way, but rather as a volitional, intentioned act repeated as often as necessary to elicit the desired behavior. Furthermore, the model's natural behavior may undergo very deep transformations when it is oriented by the intention to become imitated by the observer. This intention will affect the rhythm of the performed act, the saliency of certain parts, the amplitude, and the general tonus in which the performance takes place. The mediating caregiver will make sure that the child can register the modeled behavior by placing himself in the optimal visual angle, or by pursuing the child's elusive eye. Once the desired behavior has been elicited, both child and mediator will adjust each to the other, to repeat the imitated act, demonstrating that intentionality can be ascribed not only to the adult mediator, but also to the mediated child at a very early stage in his development.

Thus imitation as an instrument for learning and for the acquisition of new patterns of behavior is established and consolidated through mediational processes, is thereby rendered efficient, and ultimately becomes a very pervasive mode of interacting with the world. The acquisition of kinesics, no less than the acquisition of verbal language, is contingent on the amount and nature of the imitative behavior made available to the child by this intentional interaction.

Mediated Imitation

Mediated imitation differs, then, from direct-exposure imitation in that conditions for imitation become optimal when the events to be imitated are products of an intention aimed at producing more meaningful and lasting changes in the behavioral structure of the child than would be necessary to the performance of the immediate situation or task that has elicited the imitative act. Once intention is animating the model and later also the imitator, the focusing behavior, the amount and nature of perceptual investment, the disposition of the organism to respond as manifested by its vigilance and alertness, all will converge not only to render the imitative act possible, but also to establish and enhance modalities for further and more elaborate processes of modifiability (i.e., learning in general, and imitation in particular).

Early Modalities of Imitation   Literature on imitation reveals a disparity of views and tends to generate a feeling of insufficiency regarding our present data concerning the issues of whether, when, and how the imitative process starts (see Zazzo, 1962; Parton, 1976; Bower, 1977; Meltzoff and Moore, 1977; Yando, et al., 1978). The major research questions have revolved around the contention (now rigorously substantiated) that imitation does indeed occur at a very early point in the life of the neonate. This was denied, even on the level of observation, until lately. René Zazzo, the well-known French psychologist, described neonate imitation, but feeling unable to account for it, given the incompatibility of neonate imitation with the accepted incompetence of the infant in cognitive, motor, and volitional areas of functioning, came close to denying what he himself so accurately observed (Zazzo, 1962). Denying the existence of something because it cannot be explained by extant theories finds its best expression in the interpretation given by Abravanel et al. (1976) for the observed imitation of tongue protrusion in infancy. Because a person cannot see his own tongue, the use of the tongue in inducing infant imitation had been considered impossible. Abravanel et al. ventured that the relative flatness of a baby's nose may allow the baby to see its own protruding tongue, thus fulfilling the traditional requirements for imitation. Thus is a newly established fact reconciled with a contradicting theory!

The remarkable phenomenon of neonate imitation, albeit not fully explained, powerfully affects the child's behavior. At the neonate stage, much of the learning process must be equated with imitation. We suspect that many of the child's imitative behaviors are not registered by the adult because they are embedded within the great wealth of involuntary mimicry of the child's face and the reflective nature of his motoricity. Thus the imitative acts become lost like words in a string of undifferentiated syllables. However, it is our contention that imitations leading to more autonomous and independent types of behavior are related to very fine adjustments in the child's behavior that lead to the formation of elements necessary for the acquisition and production of complex behaviors. In this respect the repertoire of kinesic behaviors formed by the innate, universal, biologically and anatomically determined gestures and movements, and those produced through the interaction with models resulting in imitative behavior, all converge in producing the components from which nonverbal and verbal communicational patterns will gradually emerge.

Observing the infant imitating the behavior of protruding the tongue or the lips, or the lateral widening of the mouth, one is struck by the fact that as early as the first week of life the neonate starts to produce very fine peribuccal movements that precede the imitated act that will more or less conform to the act of the model. This may be interpreted as evidence that even at this stage of development the imitative process is constructed by the child and is not an all-or-nothing, spontaneously emitted response.

Furthermore, one must keep in mind that the imitation process is not always successfully performed, and that the imitated act is almost never identical with the action of the model. The imitation of a given act will certainly depend on the presence in the child's repertoire of technique needed to reproduce an act, as well as the child's accessibility to the specific act. Efforts to make a child imitate behaviors for which he lacks the necessary technique will of necessity result in more generalized global types of response, differing from the modeled act relative to the degree of the child's technical insufficiency. However, observing that the imitating child engages in a process of constructing the movement to be imitated, even one that is available to him (e.g., protruding the tongue or lips, or blinking the eyes), one realizes that the imitating child cannot just draw on available technique. Rather, the child must actively build the modeled act anew by involving himself in a preliminary trial-and-error process, only the end state of which is the reproduction of the modeled act. As the child continues to be exposed to and to perform the modeled act, the preliminary trial-and-error stages of the imitative process become progressively reduced, and the imitative behavior appears more rapidly and more spontaneously as the act of imitation is repeated.

The early stages of imitation lay the foundation for crucial expressive movements that will characterize the individual throughout life unless other new and more potent determinants of behavior produce changes in previous patterns. If, in addition to its aspect of direct-exposure observation, imitation bears the nature of a mediated learning experience, the learning capacity of the child is affected in consequence, and correspondingly, the child's level of modifiability is affected, too. According to this theoretical framework, these early stages of imitative behavior, elementary as they are, not only lay the foundation for the kinesic modality of communication but also, because of the strong mediated learning component involved in their acquisition, begin to establish a wide range of learning prerequisites in the organism.

Later Modalities of Imitation   The elementary modality of imitation, which continues throughout life, is paralleled by another modality of imitation that begins to appear at a somewhat later stage of development and is marked by increasing consciousness, intentionality, selectiveness, and preference. The initial, largely involuntary manifestations of neonate imitation that tend to resemble a reflex become increasingly inhibited, to the extent that by the age of even 4 to 5 months attempts to immediately elicit an earlier established imitative response are met with resistance, in certain cases with the child becoming plainly angry with the model or avoiding his view. The author recalls an interaction with a 3½-month-old baby who burst out laughing when he saw the author repeatedly protruding his tongue, as if to say, "Look! An old man doing silly things!"

It is as if the maturational process, in bringing about a greater integration of the central nervous system and the related development of voluntary control over different parts of the body, produces a barrier in the child that obstructs the involuntary reflexive types of behavior, a barrier that tends to inhibit the reflexive peripheral motor and immediate echopraxic type of imitative response. Concomitantly, it is as if the development of higher levels of cognitive functioning involving intentionality, selectiveness, and preference reinforce this internal barrier inhibiting peripheral motor and immediate imitative responses in favor of reinforcing the development of the more representational and transformed act. Thus the organism is enabled to defer imitative responses by mentally internalizing the behavior without having to actually perform it, to be retrieved at will at a later moment or in the absence of the model. It is as if the inhibition of the reflexive imitative behavior produces the codification of the observed behaviors in very much the same way as thought is often a codified internalization of vocalized language.

Although this barrier, which is established concurrently with the greater capacity of the organism to control and inhibit diffused motoricity, may well be strengthened by the growing representational capacity of the child, including the capacity to reevoke mnemonic acts; the barrier itself may also be, if not the origin, at least a powerful source of enhancement of the representational modality of imitation. The reflexive involuntary modality, however, does not totally disappear. Instead, it begins to take on discrete and cryptic forms that may affect, in certain cases very meaningfully, some of the most basic and elementary subconscious behaviors of the individual. The degree of awareness that accompanies our kinesic patterns established through the more involuntary modalities of imitation is relatively limited, and not always can one reproduce at will the kinesic gestures that are performed spontaneously in one's natural way of communication. Micromovements manifesting these discrete and cryptic forms of involuntary imitative processes often effect changes in the physiognomy of the imitator that result in the well-known similarity phenomenon observable in individuals exposed to each other for prolonged periods. Of course, for such discrete processes of imitation to occur, a strong relationship must exist between the model and the observer.

Conditions for producing elementary imitative behavior in the child at the primarily involuntary stage are contingent on the behavior of the model, the degree of familiarity the child has with the model, the nature of the affective emotional relationship that can be established between the model and the child, certain temporal and spatial characteristics of the modeled act, its frequency, its amplitude, and the relatedness of the observed act to existing behavioral patterns. The more complex internalized and deferred modality of imitation that will develop is more an intentional, volitional, representational, and purposeful act, with the imitation being in certain cases only a means to accomplish a goal set forth by the imitator. The dynamics of imitation at this latter stage are linked to certain types of motivation relevant to those described by Yando et al. (1978).

The greater involvement of voluntary processes such as selection, enabling the child to purposefully avoid certain models for imitation and actively seek others, will make the imitative action contingent on a variety of behavioral determinants, too. Lack of a positive relationship, for example, can negatively affect the occurrence of imitation simply because the prospective imitator may tend to avoid the presence of the prospective model, and thereby reduce exposure. In addition, the child's capacity to use MLE will depend on the neurophysiological integrity of the organism, as well as on the presence of models to which the child will choose to be exposed as sources of observational and imitative learning.

The hypothesis that increased modifiability is a product of MLE is based on the concept that MLE produces and consolidates in the child the prerequisites of certain behaviors that, in turn, render him more sensitive and more efficient in the autonomous use of subsequent nonmediated opportunities for learning. The child whose imitative behavior is part of a MLE will be involved in using focusing behavior to follow the succession of events unfolding in front of him.

MLE and the Disturbed Child

MLE, by its very nature, endows the individual with repertoires of interactions that in becoming established, continue to increase both the individual's readiness to learn from others and his accessibility to such instruction. The more or less peculiar forms of motor behavior and kinesics of the emotionally disturbed child and, even more, the autistic child, can be explained by the child's lack of readiness to become involved in a process of MLE through which the imitative processes, among others, are enhanced, facilitated, and given meaning. Some emotionally disturbed children, and autistic children particularly, almost always display not only an extreme and systematic avoidance of gaze and eye contact with meaningful caregivers, but even outright avoidance reactions to the exposure. Diffused attention and elusive perception do not permit sufficient duration, amplitude, and frequency of observation of the act to be imitated, and these in combination with certain avoidance reactions, lead to a very limited amount of imitative behavior. The result is the great poverty of culturally determined patterns of kinesic communication that is so typical of disturbed and autistic children, rendering their behavior in general and their kinesics in particular so atypical and alien to the culture to which they belong. It is in this sense that lack of MLE produces the syndrome of cultural deprivation, for not only have certain contents of behavior failed to be transmitted to the child, but the prerequisites for becoming increasingly modified through direct exposure to stimuli, in this instance to models for imitation, have not been established.

The bizarre appearance of many of those who strike us as deviant, such as the organic, and even more so the autistic child, has at least one basic cause: the individuals' repertoires of kinesic expression are very often reduced to the biologically and anatomically determined gestures in combination with idiosyncrasies of the respective deviant condition that have not been sufficiently modified by the culturally transmitted patterns of kinesic behaviors. It is the very discrete modalities of kinesics, strange and unfamiliar to the normal observer, that render the emotionally disturbed, autistic, and in certain cases the organic child, conspicuous, bizarre, misunderstood, and therefore alien to the community. Such children have been directly exposed to models of imitation, but because of their incapacity to accept the mediated forms of imitation in the way they have been presented to them, their propensity to use and become modified by means of direct exposure is meaningfully limited. In these cases, lack of MLE as a function of an internal barrier produced by a condition of the child, will manifest itself in a deficient kinesic repertoire. Even more important, however, this lack will determine deficient development of cognitive processes, thereby rendering the child an inadequate learner in general, relatively incapable of becoming modified in encounters with life events.

The theory of cognitive modifiability not only considers the conditions produced by lack of MLE to be preventable through instructing parents on how to use their interactions with their children as means to mediate to them the world, but also considers these conditions to be accessible to meaningful and structural change through focused and systematic intervention. Today more than ever, preventive and remedial measures for lack of MLE are needed because the cultural discontinuity of our time is such that in many circles, the natural tendency of parents to transmit their own cultural values to their children has been dwarfed, with mediation having become a low priority in parent/child interactions, in consequence. This holds true even among parents from advantaged social classes, even among children of normal development; and disadvantaged parents often relinquish even the aspiration to engage in behavior involving MLE.

Both prevention and remediation must view MLE as a natural interactive process, and must consider the sociological, anthropological, and psychological reasons for lack of it in instituting MLE as a volitional, conscious action—the purpose of which will be to increase the child's adaptability, in addition to expanding his affective, motivational incentives, and bringing to him the sense of belonging that MLE confers on the individual. Furthermore, whenever MLE is not penetrating the system of the child because barriers produced by his own condition are obstructing mediational attempts, the major task of the preventive and remedial measures will be to circumvent these barriers by varying the intensity, modality, and content of MLE according to the specific condition.

The major approach developed by the author and his colleagues to remediate the ill effects of inadequate MLE at the relatively later stages of adolescence is to provide the learner with phase-specific MLE substitutes, structured to correct the deficiencies, while developing the functions that could not be established earlier because of the inadequacy of MLE. Toward this end, diagnosis as a way to locate areas of strength and weakness in the functioning of an individual is a crucial step, followed by direct intervention focused on the areas of functioning that have been most affected by lack of MLE. The theory of cognitive modifiability has engendered both the learning potential assessment device (LPAD), as a dynamic approach to evaluating the cognitive modifiability of the retarded performing individual, and, based on insights gained from use of the LPAD, the instrumental enrichment (IE) program of intervention, the major aim of which is to sensitize the organism, rendering the individual more efficient in the use of direct-exposure learning for adaptation to new and more complex stimuli (see Feuerstein et al., 1979, 1980).

SUMMARY

The acquisition of kinesics, representing a culturally transmitted way of communicating with the human environment, can be studied from the double-aspect view of learning. That is, learning occurs both through the direct exposure to models of imitation and through the modality of MLE, in which the imitative process is produced by an intentioned, volitional act on the part of the model, aimed at goals transcending the immediacy of the act and the immediacy of the need that has elicited it. Direct-exposure learning will be meaningfully enhanced if the organism has been sensitized by the MLE. Inadequate MLE in the area of imitation, and in other areas of interaction, will produce the syndrome of cultural deprivation and may impoverish not only the repertoire of culturally determined kinesic patterns, but also the general capacity of the individual to imitate at will and to become modified.

The syndrome of cultural deprivation is marked by a series of deficient cognitive functions that have been conceptualized as belonging to the three phases of the mental act: *input*, involving the processes of gathering data necessary for the solution of a problem at hand; *elaboration*, including the capacity to conceive and define the problem; and *output*, describing expressive behavior (see Feuerstein et al., 1979, 1980). Deficiencies in one or more of these areas render the cognitive functioning of the respective individual inadequate, producing a corresponding inadaptability of the organism, especially when confronted with conditions requiring autoplastic changes. The study of kinesics and of the modalities through which they are acquired is of interest, therefore, not only for the investigation of communicational modalities of individuals, but also for research into the ontogeny of learning as it leads to differential cognitive development in human beings.

ACKNOWLEDGMENTS

The author expresses his gratitude to his colleagues, Professors Mildred B. Hoffman, Yaacov Rand, David Krasilowsky, and Dr. Jacob Colthof, whose remarks were helpful in preparing this chapter. Special thanks are expressed to Meira Olson, who, under rather difficult conditions, assisted in producing this paper. The gratitude of the author also goes to the Hadassah-WIZO Canada Research Institute, the Besner Foundation, and the Deitcher Center, which have provided the framework within which the author has been able to produce.

Chapter 7
THE DEVELOPMENT OF BEHAVIOR PERCEPTION

Gretchen Engquist-Seidenberg

Nonlanguage behavior involves several functions: the portrayal of affective response, the regulation of verbal behavior, and the referential supplement to language (von Raffler-Engel, Chapter 1; Mehrabian, 1968). Moreover, behavior or action also accomplishes goals. As young children learn that a smile gesture may enhance social interaction, that a frown from another can denote sadness or disapproval, so too they learn that someone stirring a pot in the kitchen can produce nourishment. Insofar as day-to-day existence as well as social interaction is determined not only by what we or others say but by what we do with purposeful behavior, the science of behavior production, comprehension, and perception is relatively underemphasized. The investigation of behavior production has been restricted by the complexities of disentwining motor development from purposeful action and by the preponderance of learning theories as explanatory concepts. Although it is a critical component of nonlanguage behavior, production was neglected in the studies discussed in this chapter.

DEVELOPMENT OF BEHAVIOR PERCEPTION

The development of behavior perception and comprehension and, for that matter, the same processes in adults, are subjects that until recently fell through the cracks in contemporary social science, although both have long been the focus of philosophical treatments. The field of study most closely related is that of person perception in psychology. Person perception refers to the processes by which we come to know other people, their behavior, their intentions, beliefs, and characteristics. Tagiuri (1954:397) argued that this label was most unsatisfactory because "one is dealing not really with perception but, instead, with complex cognitive processes." If nothing else, Tagiuri's comment reflects the interests of the field, which has been more concerned with social cognition than with person perception in that the work has focused on inference processes leading up to and including final trait attribution.

The implicit assumption in this focus of the person perception field is that the input—perceived behavior—is constant across observers (see Jones and Davis, 1965; Kelley, 1967). Unfortunately, this assumption is founded on two nearly ancient views of general perceptual processes: 1) that the perceiver is a passive receptacle for incoming information, and 2) that perception and cognition are inherently separable processes. Neither view is widely accepted (Neisser, 1976; Miller and Johnson-Laird, 1976).

The consequences of these views for a developmental theory of behavior perception are significant. First, they suggest that separate study of behavior perception as opposed to perceptual development generally is not required. All perception results from the development of sensory capability. Perceptual differences, developmentally or otherwise, are a consequence of either this sensory capability or attention to an event or stimuli. Second, this view implies that given adequate sensory ability, observed differences in interpretation of behavior as a function of age reflect in large measure differences in the assignment of inference rules to the event.

If we accept alternative assumptions about the nature of perception, namely, that the perceiver is an active information seeker and that this active perception is directed by or at least inseparable from cognition, the study of behavior perception becomes not only interesting but crucial. The suggestion is that the perceiver actively participates in the organization of observed behavior and thus actively controls the information gained from that behavior. Furthermore, some perceivers may be better than others at controlling this information gain.

Such a view is consistent with Heider's (1958) definition of the person perception process as the organization into meaningful units of a continuous stream of information from another's behavior. This organization, in Heider's formulation (1958:27) is both perceptual and cognitive:

> The distinction between perception and cognition is being drawn less and less sharply doubtless because there are so many gradual transitions between the extreme cases of the most direct and immediate forms of perception on the one hand, and the most indirect interpretations on the other. . . . In ordinary discourse one is likely to speak of inference or diagnosis rather than of perception when the construction of the percept on the basis of the raw material is itself given to awareness; yet upon analysis, a data pattern may be found in both rational inference and perception which is used in the construction of apparent reality.

Neisser (1976) identified three different points of view on perceptual processes in psychology, and argued that they may be unified by treating them as part of a "perceptual cycle" of information search, processing, and hypothesis testing:

At each moment the perceiver is constructing anticipations of certain kinds of information, that enable him to accept it as it becomes available. Often he must actively explore the optic array to make it available. . . . These explorations are directed by . . . anticipatory schemata, which are plans for perceptual action as well as readinesses for particular information which, once picked up, modifies original schema. Thus modified, it directs further exploration and becomes ready for more information. (Neisser, 1976:20–21)

Both Neisser (1976) and Piaget (1954), who accepted the notion that perception is directed by schemata of some sort, suggested that early in development these perceptual-cognitive schemata are general and impre-cise, becoming differentiated with age. Through a process of accommoda-tion, in Piaget's terms, or perceptual cycling, in Neisser's, a schema be-comes particular and precise, but this takes time. It is only with active exploration and contact with the environment that the infant or child can modify the original schema by developing a readiness for new types of information and thereby improving his or her skills as a perceiver.

This view raises important questions concerning the nature of the schemata for behavior perception, as well as the possibility of significant differences in development.

STUDY OF BEHAVIOR PERCEPTION

Dimensions of Movement

Recent research on the perception of behavior among adults has yielded more and more consistent evidence that actions are comprehended by the discrimination of successive "points of definition" in the behavior stream rather than by the interpretation of continuous chunks of movement (Newtson and Engquist, 1975; Newtson et al. 1977). Fundamental to this point of view is a distinction between action/behavior and movement. Al-though long familiar philosophical treatments of action (Schwayder, 1965), perceptual psychology has only recently begun to appreciate this distinction (see Miller and Johnson-Laird, 1976). The relation between perceived action and movement can be illustrated by an analogy between actions in movement and words in sound. Words are composed of sound, as actions are composed of movement. Just as some sounds are not words, so some movements are not meaningful actions. Similarly, as some dimen-sions of sound in words are readily discriminable (e.g., pitch, rate, accent) yet do not define the words, so some aspects of movement in actions may also be readily discriminable without being basic to the comprehension of actions.

This is not to say, in certain contexts, that such dimensions of move-ment cannot be important to the interpretation of actions. Paralinguistic cues certainly exist in speech, and in some contexts are of critical importance to its interpretation. Some dimensions of movement may contain the information that defines the basic meaning of action, and others may serve as modifying cues for that interpretation. The point is simply that assertions about the stimulus bases of perceived behavior require empirical support; as in speech, some dimensions of the stimulus may be fundamental to behavior perception, and others may not.

If, as suggested, only some dimensions of movement are basic to the meaning of action, an efficient perceiver need only extract those points. Evidence from a series of studies using a simple procedure proposed by Newtson (1973) supports just such an extraction process. Interestingly, Newtson's original purpose was to develop a technique that could be used to identify boundaries of Barker-type units or the division of the behavior stream rather than to extract certain information (Barker, 1963). Observers are provided with a continuous event recorder and are instructed to press the button when they judge that one meaningful action has ended and the next one begun. Results suggest that the stimulus points identified by perceivers using this technique do not simply represent action boundaries; rather, the points themselves have distinctive properties that are critical for the definition of action. For convenience, the points in behavior consistently identified by perceivers are termed "breakpoints," and all others "nonbreakpoints."

Breakpoints

Breakpoints are distinctive, first, in that they are strongly related to the meaning of action, whereas other parts of behavior, nonbreakpoints, are not. Inspection of a series of still breakpoints from a particular action sequence, for example, conveys a near-comic strip quality in that they seem to summarize the sequence very well. Nonbreakpoints, on the other hand, are much more ambiguous.

Beyond such anecdotal evidence, however, Newtson and Engquist (1976) clearly demonstrated this breakpoint-meaning relationship. Eight 15- to 30-second filmed action sequences were prepared and marked by 20 subjects for purposes of obtaining consensus breakpoints and nonbreakpoints. Three consecutive points of each type were identified, extracted, and mounted as slides. Triads of successive breakpoint and nonbreakpoint slides were then presented to subjects in correct order and in incorrect order, and subjects were asked to: 1) describe the action depicted; 2) judge the ordering of presentation; and 3) rate the degree to which the slides portrayed an understandable, or intelligible, action.

Action descriptions based on breakpoint slides were significantly more accurate than those based on nonbreakpoints; ordering of breakpoints was judged with 80% accuracy, as opposed to 42% for nonbreakpoints; and breakpoint triads were rated as significantly more intelligible than nonbreakpoint triads. In fact, breakpoint triads were rated as high on intelligibility as the entire continuous sequences from which they were drawn.

Newston and Engquist (1976) also found breakpoints to be more salient in memory, perhaps as a consequence of their relationship to meaning. Subjects were shown a series of short films and tested for recognition memory. The recognition test consisted of breakpoint and nonbreakpoint intervals extracted from the films and mounted as slides as above. Slides were drawn from both the set of films viewed and from similar films employing the same actors in the same settings. Half the subjects in this experiment marked the films using the button-press procedure while viewing the slides, and half watched the films normally. Results indicated that breakpoints were better recognized than nonbreakpoints and that no differences between the groups could be attributed to marking with the button-press procedure. The latter result was particularly encouraging because it indicates that the technique is relatively free of interference with normal processes of observation.

Results of these studies support the view that behavior is perceived by adults through the discrimination and/or selection of successive points of definition—breakpoints—in the behavior stream. The finding that breakpoints contain more information about action than nonbreakpoints also implies that behavior, as a stimulus, varies considerably from moment to moment in the availability of information for its interpretation. Two important issues are raised by these data. One concerns the objective basis for the discrimination of breakpoints, and the other concerns the role of the perceiver in such a perceptual process.

Whatever the *objective* basis of the stimulus, it is highly variable within the behavior stream because more of it exists at breakpoints than at nonbreakpoints. This is consistent with Newtson and Engquist's (1976) initial assumption that movement and actions are related as sound and words are related, with only some dimensions critical for action definition. One possibility is that actions are defined by "distinctive states" assumed by the actor, which are meaningful in and of themselves. Breakpoints themselves, in this view, would define actions not because of some property of movement per se, but because the actor passed through a distinctive posture or state. The most distinctive characteristic of ongoing behavior, however, is change over time. Hence a second and more likely interpretation is that actions are defined by the changes depicted by successive breakpoints. That is, the distinctiveness of breakpoints would be attributable to a distinctive change that has occurred, rather than a distinctive state.

The issue is, in a sense, whether breakpoints are selected by the perceiver according to an absolute or a relative property of the stimulus. According to a "meaningful state" interpretation, stimulus points are marked as breakpoints because they have an absolute property for the perceiver, that is, their meaning is independent of previous meaningful stimulus points. According to a "meaningful change" interpretation, breakpoints, in and of themselves, are not distinguishable from other stimulus points; their distinctiveness results entirely from their contrast with the point selected by the perceiver as the previous breakpoint.

These two hypotheses on the nature of the stimulus basis of breakpoints were tested in Newtson et al. (1977). Seven diverse behavior sequences were analyzed using the Eshkol-Wachman movement notation (Eshkol, 1973). This notation system, first developed to permit choreographers to write dance scores, has been adapted to ethological studies of animals to render precise descriptions of sequences of behavior (Golani, 1973). Coding is achieved by specifying the position of the body in three-dimensional space at successive predetermined intervals. Codings of static body position at different points may thus be compared, and the difference between the codings taken as an index of difference in body position. When such comparisons are made between positions at points successive in time, the index of position difference constitutes a measure of position change, or movement. For human movement, the system requires codings of 17 different features of body position.

Comparison of codings at breakpoints and nonbreakpoints revealed no differences in absolute state or posture across sequences. The "distinctive change" hypothesis, however, was supported in that successive breakpoint pairs contained a higher average degree of change than did successive nonbreakpoint pairs matched for separation in time. This result was consistent across the seven behavior sequences. Newtson et al. (1977) also examined feature codings for breakpoint and nonbreakpoint intervals within individual sequences. In each case, breakpoints were associated not only with high magnitude change, but also with changes in a set of specific body features. Furthermore, the set of features associated with breakpoints differed significantly from sequence to sequence. The latter finding suggests that perceivers may be highly selective in choosing feature changes to employ for organization of a given episode of behavior.

Whatever the stimulus basis of breakpoints, perception of action depends on its discrimination in the behavior stream. This does not mean, however, that perception must be exhaustive with respect to that property. That is, the presence of change per se may be a necessary but not sufficient condition for perceived action. Results of Newtson et al. (1977), for example, suggest the importance of contextual relevance of feature changes in breakpoint selection. The issue, however, is really one of the perceiver's contribution to or control over the perceptual process. Perceivers, for example, may vary in their vigilance for such points of definition, in their skill in identifying such points in a given activity, and in selectivity or use of available points according to expectancy or set and according to perceptual-cognitive development.

Newtson et al. (1976) present evidence that the process of breakpoint selection can be characterized as a skill. In this study, subjects were presented with skilled and unskilled performances by archers, and they provided both marking data and ratings of those performances. On the basis of these ratings, accurate and inaccurate observers were identified and their marking patterns compared. Results showed that accurate observers chose points of definition in the behavior stream different from those chosen by inaccurate observers. It is not clear from this result alone whether the choice was casually related to accuracy. A followup study, however, confirmed the relationship. Breakpoints identified by both groups were extracted as slides and presented to a second group of subjects. On the basis of the slides alone, these subjects were asked to rate each archer's performance. They were able to do accurate rating only when they were presented with breakpoints identified by accurate observers.

Taken together, results of the research project just described have far-reaching implications on the nature and process of behavior perception. First, it is suggested that actions are defined on a point-to-point basis, not by continuous movement per se. Discrimination of these successive points of definition, furthermore, is dependent on the objective change patterns, including both magnitude and contextual relevance of feature changes. Results of several studies, however, suggest that the perceptual process is not exhaustive with respect to change. Rather, consistent with the initial assumptions of active perception and the inseparability of perception and cognition, perceivers vary in selection of stimulus points for action definition according to skill, which is a clearcut perceiver factor, and according to ongoing plans. The process of behavior perception, then, is more one of active, selective interaction with present stimulus information than one of passive reception and interpretation.

Of central importance for a theory of behavior perception is the mechanism by which perceivers select information. Newtson (1976) suggested a feature composition or processing mechanism whereby the perceiver composes certain stimulus configurations or action-relevant features and defines actions according to changes in these elements, and when suitable information is picked up (i.e., at a breakpoint), the search is modified, in that the information becomes, in part, a basis for discrimination of the next action (i.e., each breakpoint becomes a reference point for discrimination of the next). Evidence cited above that perceiver skill affects breakpoint selection is consistent with Neisser's (1976) notion of direction of the process by an anticipatory schema.

DEVELOPMENT OF BEHAVIOR PERCEPTION IN CHILDREN

Just as the unskilled perceiver fails to select necessary feature information, so too does selection of information in behavior perception vary according to perceptual cognition development. Early studies by Livesley and Bromley (1973) and Rosenberg and Sedlak (1972) *indirectly* suggested developmental changes in person perception. Evidence presented by Livesley and Bromley (1973), in fact, suggests that critical changes in the perception of people and their behavior occur around 7 or 8 years of age. That is, children before age 7 describe people in terms of highly observable, surface cues—for example, "He is tall and has two brothers a bicycle and lives on my street." After age 7, however, descriptions are couched more in terms of abstract qualities such as values, beliefs, and traits.

Rosenberg and Sedlak (1972) presented evidence suggesting developmental changes in the perception of personality as well. Children of various ages were asked to judge which of a series of traits (good/bad, smart/stupid) went together or tended to appear in the same person. Judgments of these trait relationships, commonly referred to as implicit personality theories, differed significantly as a function of age. In general, younger children viewed more of the traits as related to each other in terms of some global notion of good/bad. With increasing age, trait dimensions became more differentiated; for example, older children considered smart/stupid to be different from good/bad, whereas the younger children did not. Rosenberg and Sedlak did not pinpoint a specific age for these changes in the perception of personality; that critical changes do occur, however, is consistent with the evidence of Livesley and Bromley (1973).

Neither of these studies, however, assesses perception directly; instead, both depend on the language mediator. It may be that these observed changes reflect differences in the processes of behavior perception, that is, in the way actions are defined for perceivers of different ages or in the meaningfulness of behavior, per se. Young children may not, for example, perceive behavior on a point-to-point basis, or they may use some criterion other than "distinctive change" for selecting breakpoints.

Selective Looking

As a preliminary step, Engquist (1977), using a variation of the Neisser and Becklin (1975) selective looking paradigm, examined the sensitivity of 6, 8, and 12 year olds to breakpoints identified by adult perceivers. This paradigm, a visual analogue to the dichotic listening task, was originally formulated to test the notion of the active direction of perception rather passive reception by presenting adult perceivers with two optionally superimposed events. Subjects are asked to follow one episode, tracking specific actions using a button-press procedure, while ignoring the other. Neisser and Becklin reasoned that if perception were not a cognitively directed process, adults would not be able to successfully disentangle the superimposed display to attend to one episode while ignoring the other. If selective looking necessitated a peripheral mechanism to filter out irrelevant material, long practice would be required to develop one for this novel task. The results suggested that adults had no difficulty in selectively following one episode rather than the other and that odd or unusual events in the to-be-ignored episode were simply not noticed.

If the conclusion of Neisser and Becklin is correct—that central cognitive control, anticipatory schema, enables the selectivity found in their study—one would expect selectivity to depend on the level of cognitive development. If the feature-defining schema were unclear or defined conflicting features for monitoring, selectivity would deteriorate.

Developmental studies of selective abilities involving other tasks, and one dealing directly with ongoing behavior, suggest that selectivity increases with age and that feature emphasis varies as well.

For example, Hagen (1967) assessed children's memory for relevant versus incidental information. Children in the first through seventh grades were shown a series of pictures depicting pairs of objects (e.g., an animal and a household object). Their task was to learn only the sequence of animals. Information concerning the household object was, therefore, irrelevant. After assessing performance on the primary task, Hagen asked the children if they remembered which household object appeared with each animal. Results showed that older children consistently remembered more of the relevant information than younger children, and that memory for irrelevant information, although not consistently related to age, decreased significantly between fifth and seventh grades.

Analogous investigations report similar findings for relevant materials, but findings on irrelevant materials are conflicting (Odom, 1972). It appears that the latter process depends on a number of factors other than age. Odom (1972), for example, found that young children remember more incidental information when it is highly salient than when it is not. Similarly, Druker and Hagen (1969) reported effects of spatial location. It seems to be easier to ignore irrelevant stimuli when they are separated in space from the relevant. These data, rather than calling into question the development of selectivity, support it. Both factors, salience and spatial location, are properties of the stimulus. If ability to ignore irrelevant information depends on them, selectivity must be undeveloped.

The developmental trends are somewhat stronger in work on children's search strategies. As in the memory work, the abilities to ignore the irrelevant and to select out the relevant are both taken as indices of selectivity. Lehman (1972), for example, gave children (kindergarten through sixth grade) a matching task involving objects that differed in shape and texture. Only one of the variables was relevant for making the match, so the other could be ignored. Search strategy was assessed by filming each child's hand movements and categorizing them as relevant or irrelevant. If the distinguishing feature was texture, for example, movements outlining the objects were considered irrelevant. The distinguishing feature remained constant over trials. Lehman found that the older children were much better than the younger children at confining their search to the distinguishing feature. When the children were told in advance what feature was relevant, the performance of all groups improved significantly, but the age trend in ignoring the irrelevant feature persisted. The search patterns of younger children, however, were affected by the particular feature. The younger children were better at ignoring shape than texture, presumably because the latter is more salient for them.

Selective Listening

Selective listening, the ability to track one message and ignore the other, has also been studied in children. In principle, this task is analogous to Neisser's dichotic condition. That is, in the typical experiment, each channel (ear or eye) receives different auditory or visual input. In the former case, subjects are asked to repeat one message as it is given. Selective abilities are assessed in terms of accuracy of repetition and number of intrusions from the to-be-ignored message. Maccoby (1967), for example, studied selective listening in kindergarten, second, and fourth graders. Results showed that both accuracy in tracking and number of intrusions were significantly related to age, with the former increasing and the latter decreasing developmentally. Maccoby also reported several other factors related to performance in this task. Hearing the to-be-ignored message in advance interferes with performance at all ages.

The Engquist (1977) study assessed selective looking developmentally, expecting increasing selection with age. Recall, however, that Engquist's purpose was also to examine sensitivity to adult-identified structure in behavior breakpoints. Building on the selective-looking paradigm by manipulating the relationship between the superimposed events accomplished this end. Findings for other selective perception tasks suggest that interference from nonattended sources often depends on this relationship (Stroop, 1935; Lewis, 1970; Dyer, 1973; Willows, 1974). In general, results of these studies suggest that increasing the semantic overlap between stimuli in attended and nonattended episodes increases interference. Selective listening, for example, is more difficult when the to-be-ignored message contains contextually relevant material (Lewis, 1970), or when it is the identical message delayed in time (Triesman, 1964). The finding, based on Newtson's work, that actions are perceived on a point-to-point basis through the discrimination of breakpoints, provides a method for semantic overlap of behavior episodes. Since all parts of behavior are not involved in action definition, perception requires only intermittent sampling of the stimulus. For interference to occur, therefore, meaningful material must be available when sampling occurs.

Overlap

Engquist reasoned that performance on the selective-looking task with ongoing behavioral stimuli should vary according to the temporal relationship between the breakpoints in the two sequences. If breakpoints were overlapped in the two episodes, potentially meaningful information from the to-be-ignored episode could interfere. Where breakpoints were not overlapped, or were intermittent, meaningful information would not be available for interference.

However, interference under overlapping conditions would be more severe in the Engquist developmental study only to the extent that children use or are sensitive to the points and features that adults use to organize behavior.

Engquist (1977), then, attempted to examine the development of selective behavior perception in visually and semantically overlapped fields. Subjects from four age groups (6, 8, and 12 years, and adults) viewed two optically superimposed behavior sequences under film conditions with overlapping or intermittent breakpoint structure. The prepared behavior episodes were relatively simple events: one showed a teacher writing numbers and letters on a blackboard, the other portrayed a woman working with plants.

Both were pretested to ensure that breakpoints, the points of definition used by adult perceivers in a pretest group, occurred at corresponding points in time. The two sequences, furthermore, were constructed using the Eshkol-Wachman movement notation to ensure overlapping objective changes. That is, when a change occurred in one sequence, a change of equal magnitude, involving the same body features, occurred in the other. Structure, then, was defined both objectively and subjectively. The same sequences were used for the intermittent condition by altering the starting time of one sequence. Subjects were instructed to follow only one of the sequences under the two latter conditions and to ignore the other. Three measures of selectivity: 1) a perceptual measure (the ability to track the occurrence of specific actions in one episode using a button-press tracking procedure) and two cognitive interference measures, 2) recall of events in both the to-be-followed and to-be-ignored episodes; and 3) recognition of events for both episodes.

Results indicated, consistent with Neisser and Becklin's (1975) findings, that adult subjects had little difficulty in tracking a single film episode within a superimposed display, either intermittent or overlapping. Adult performance under all conditions was nearly perfect, subjects making an average of 1.98 total tracking errors for each film presentation. These ceiling effects suggest that adults monitor behavior guided by extremely specific feature sets, in Newtson's terms, or by anticipatory schemata including well-defined properties of the to-be-perceived event.

The ceiling effect was thus not unexpected. In discussing his own results, Neisser commented, "The naturalness of the task and the lack of interference from the other episode are remarkable. One does not see the irrelevant game. . . . although one has a sense that something else is there" (1976:86).

Consistent with previous research on selective perception in children, comparison across age groups indicated that in general, selective perception of ongoing behavior improves with age on all three measures. The youngest subjects (6 year olds) showed no evidence of selective looking on either tracking or cognitive measures under superimposed conditions. Eight year olds showed somewhat more selectivity, but only in the intermittent condition. The performance of 12 year olds paralleled adult data on the perceptual tracking measure, but showed less selectivity on cognitive recall and recognition measures.

The data for 8-year-old subjects confirmed the sensitivity of this age group to the adult-identified perceptual structure in that increasing the semantic overlap between two superimposed behavioral episodes interferes with selective perception. Both recognition and recall measures provided supportive evidence for these interference effects. 8-year-old subjects recalled significantly less of episodes of both types when films overlapped than for either baseline or intermittent film conditions. Recognition scores for 8-year-old subjects again support the overlap versus intermittent difference in that only the latter showed a superior score for the to-be-followed episode. Performance under overlapping conditions resembled that of the youngest children, who showed no selective processing.

For the other age groups, to-be-followed recognition scores were consistently higher for superimposed films. Selectivity in behavior perception, as indicated by better recognition for the to-be-followed event than for the to-be-ignored event, did not appear for semantically overlapped films. Total errors in tracking performance for 8-year-old subjects did not produce differences corresponding to those found for either cognitive measure. Tracking misses as opposed to inappropriate intrusions on the button-press measure, however, were consistent with the cognitive findings.

The lack of clear differences for the tracking measure is inconclusive with respect to overlapping versus intermittent film conditions. Perceivers under overlapping conditions may monitor either event and still yield an accurate tracking record. This is true even for 8 year olds, where cognitive measures produced the hypothesized differences. Several aspects of the tracking data did suggest, however, that the distinction between overlapping and intermittent film conditions was real and that subjects aged 8 and younger were affected by the manipulation of breakpoint structure. First, differences were found for two age levels in the types of tracking error made for overlapping and intermittent films. Six year olds, although making an equal number of total tracking errors for the two superimposed versions, made significantly more intrusion-type errors for intermittent films and more miss errors for overlapping films. The latter effect was also found for 8-year-old subjects. These findings must reflect sensitivity of these age groups to meaning-defining breakpoints in the to-be-ignored episode.

Perceptual Differences Between Children and Adults

The developmental progression found in Engquist's study fits in well with Livesley and Bromley's (1973) findings that until 7–8 years old, children differ from adults in their perception of other people. In the present study, the overlapping versus intermittent distinction, which is based on adult-defined points of definition, produced a difference only at this 8-year-old level. One interpretation is that during the period between 8 and 12 years, anticipatory schemata or monitored features sets become more specific, most likely including a context component. The result would be that even under overlapping conditions, a behavior episode would preserve its integrity for these selective perceivers. Until 7 or 8, however, not only would selectivity be undeveloped, but also perception of behavior would differ fundamentally from the adult process. If this is true, then, the overlapping versus intermittent distinction would not be meaningful for 6 year olds because they would not use adult points of definition in defining action. Thus it is suggested that because the information in the to-be-ignored episode must be meaningful to cause added interference under overlapping conditions, this information was not meaningful for the 6 year olds in the present study.

How, then, might behavior perception differ between young children and adults? First, the absence of selectivity in Engquist's data and for other tasks implies that young children may have difficulty in selective feature monitoring. Without such feature selection, the process would depend more on surface stimulus properties than on action meaning. That is, children may simply monitor the behavior stream for change and, regardless of the kind of change, perceive action whenever a certain magnitude is exceeded. Perception of behavior, then, would be based solely on the objective patterns of change in the stimulus and the child's vigilance in monitoring. Such a model is consistent with the large number of tracking *intrusions* made by the 6-year-old group. Seventy percent of these intrusions corresponded to points of great change in the to-be-ignored episode. Most of the remaining intrusions corresponded to points of high magnitude change in the to-be-followed episode that did not involve one of the points of definition.

However, evidence from a recent study by Newtson et al., (1980) suggests that actual discrimination in the behavior stream of adults used breakpoints appears earlier. Newtson et al. replicated with children 5, 8, and 10 years old and concurrently with adults two of the studies from the Newtson and Engquist paper (1976) discussed earlier. The first study examined recognition memory for breakpoints versus nonbreakpoints identified by adult perceivers, which were extracted from a filmed behavior sequence and mounted as slides. Newtson et al. found that recognition memory for nonbreakpoints across age levels. However, the absolute level of recognition accuracy increased significantly developmentally. In interpreting this latter result, which implies that the ability to discriminate breakpoints improves with age, the investigators suggested that it may reflect the increasing convergence over age to the breakpoints used by adults. That is, younger children discriminate some breakpoints as points of definition in the behavior stream, but they do not use them all in defining behavior, with the number of nonused points decreasing overtime.

In a second study, Newtson et al. (1980) assessed the ability of children aged 5, 8, and 10 to utilize breakpoint information when such points were extracted and mounted as slides. Recall that previously (Newtson and Engquist, 1976), adult subjects were able to more accurately describe the continuous event and correctly judge the presentation order of triads of breakpoints as opposed to nonbreakpoint slides. The younger subjects in the more recent study were asked simply, "Are the slides in the right order to tell a story?" Results indicated that order of presentation for breakpoint slides was more accurately judged than for nonbreakpoints at all age levels.

A second analysis of the stimulus set—the breakpoint and nonbreakpoint triad sets—seems to clarify the discrepancy between these data and Engquist (1977). Using the Eshkol-Wachman movement notation, Newtson et al. (1980) calculated the degree of feature change between slides in breakpoint and nonbreakpoint slide sets, making separate lists for the correct and incorrect presentation orders. Results indicted that overall degree of change did not differ significantly between breakpoints and nonbreakpoint slides, regardless of order. Corrections between change indices and recognition accuracy, however, suggested substantial differences in the underlying strategies for order judgments by age level. For the youngest children, accuracy of judgment correlated 0.98 for breakpoint items and 0.90 for nonbreakpoints with degree of change in the triad set. A significant correlation was also found for 8 year olds, but only for nonbreakpoint slide sets. No correlations between amount of item change and accurate order judgment were found for 10 year olds and adults.

Thus 5 year olds, although able to discriminate breakpoints at least according to their recognition data, do not use the mean-defining information available to them for judgments of logical order. Instead, they seem to use a degree-of-change criterion for such judgments. This result parallels differences in the type of tracking error found for younger children (age 6) versus the cognitive interference found for 8 year olds by Engquist (1977). Both may reflect the absence of cognitive structures or schemata that permit selective feature perception.

CONCLUSION

It has been suggested that the study of nonlanguage behavior must include an examination of the perception of purposeful action not only in its relation to discourse or social interaction but as it conveys meaning of what others do. The series of studies discussed here emphasize the importance of behavior perception because it may be a mediator for developmental differences found in traditional person perception areas.

These studies are preliminary at best. They do not integrate the various functions of nonlanguage behavior into a single theory of development; nevertheless, it is admitted that gestures and affective signals as well as kinesic regulation of discourse can and do alter the perception of action. Such studies also fail to address the issues of production or the perception of social interaction. Nevertheless they do provide a paradigm and a theoretical orientation that is amenable to the consideration of these issues. Development of production, for example, could be examined using child actors and actresses, or social interaction could be studied by filming multiple person sequences. Examination of the breakpoints for such episodes may shed considerable light on those issues. Moreover, the notation of feature change and its measurement could be adjusted to accommodate gestures and facial characteristics. Such issues await further research.

Chapter 8
THE DEVELOPMENT
OF COMMUNICATION
Some
Nonverbal Aspects

Ton van der Geest

In discussions on the acquisition and development of language, there is generally a sharp distinction between the acquisition of mere linguistic facility and such nonlinguistic but communicative phenomena as contextual dependency, interactional capability, and speech style, and last but not least the nonverbal aspects of language use. Recently Greenfield (1978) and Dore (1979) discussed the acquisition of language. Greenfield's position is essentially that in the one-word stage, children construct complex messages because they combine the single word with nonverbal elements such as gesture, action, object, and intonation. Greenfield is not talking about linguistic structures but about "the meaning relation between the single words and cognitive representations of real world events." One might deduce, furthermore, as Dore does, that Greenfield accepts that the child's event representations somehow account for the emergence of words and utterances. She claims finally that there is a single cognitive organization underlying both linguistic and nonlinguistic modes of expression and understanding.

Dore (1979) has refused to accept this "single organization" hypothesis because it has no analytic or empirical support: "arguments and / or evidence are needed." In his opinion one needs a guiding hypothesis intermediate between the excesses of the strong innatist language acquisition device (LAD) and the additive single cognitive source view on the other. In contrast with Greenfield, Dore does not accept semantic representations of a predicate-argument structure. He does not attribute to the child different abstract representations for the same sentence (as a linguistic type) on the basis of different (nonlinguistic but communicative) behaviors. Linguistically single words with different communicative intents are pragmatically not linguistically distinct according to Dore.

Both positions are legitimate starting points for research. Dore puts the perhaps rather artificial question of how to describe "linguistically" what is going on in the acquisition of linguistic structure, but this may stimulate interest according to Feyerabend's principle that counterintuitive theories are generally highly productive. Greenfield investigates how linguistic and nonlinguistic modes of expression and understanding constitute communicative units and how the process develops in each developmental stage. This author feels (see, e.g., van der Geest, 1970, 1975, 1978a) more affinity for a position similar to that taken by Greenfield, because: 1) Dore's standpoint abstracts from reality, in which linguistic structure always (except for linguistic studies) occurs in complete integration with and dependency on context, action, and other than linguistic communicational modes of expression; and 2) Dore's separation between acquisition (initial realization of a structure) and development (expansion and proliferation of the structures) seems arbitrary and artificial because children (at the beginning and later) and adults do similar kinds of things when communicating before and after the acquisition of a new phenomenon, but afterward it is as an alternative to the newly acquired structure.

Another point that may illustrate the present discussion concerns the problem of whether a human sign language may be considered to be strictly a language in the linguistic sense. Whether one answers this question positively (Schlesinger, 1971a; Stokoe, 1972; Bellugi and Fischer, 1972) or negatively (Wasow, 1973; Tervoort, 1974) depends on the metaquestion, namely, whether one strictly subdivides between linguistic and nonlinguistic modes of expression—that is, whether one accepts the independent nature of linguistics as propagated by Chomsky. Wasow, for example, accepting contextual dependency as a criterion for deciding this question, assumes that the sign language of the deaf, but also old written Chinese and the language of chimpanzees, are contextually dependent and cannot therefore be regarded as natural languages. According to Wasow it is in verbal behavior that language is contextually independent to a large extent. Actually, however, he fails to observe that verbal behavior is generally rather contextually dependent. Only the linguist's constructs, like "sentences," are context independent to a certain extent (but: substitution, anaphora, deixis, contrastive stress in but-phrases, equideletion, pronominalization, definite vs. indefinite, etc.). This way one abstracts from context, rather than demonstrating that language is contextually independent. If our concern, however, is with the utterances of a natural human language (as in the case of old written Chinese, sign language, or child language), we can demonstrate that the context is a necessary condition for correct interpretations in almost all cases, and that the judgment of the context by the speaker must be accepted if his utterances are to be described validly.

The Greenfield-Dore discussion and the linguistic-nonlinguistic controversy lead automatically to the methodological issue of rich interpretation, as introduced in child language study by Bloom (1970) and worked out by others (e.g., Antinucci and Parisi, 1973; Slobin, 1973; van der Geest, 1975; and Greenfield and Smith, 1976). The development of this phenomenon in the study of child language can be described as follows:

1. One initially described syntactically what was present at the verbal level, and accidentally (Menyuk, 1969) some nonverbal aspects were taken into account.
2. Since 1968 two alternatives developed in the rich interpretation assumption. The first alternative describes semantically what is present at the verbal level (one needs contextual knowledge to deliver a semantic interpretation: e.g., Schlesinger, 1971b; R. Brown, 1973). The second one describes syntactically (Bloom, 1970) or semantically (Antinucci and Parisi, 1973; van der Geest, 1975) the meaning of the child's utterance on the basis of context, accompanying behavior, or whatever (independently of whether it is realized at the verbal level), thereafter defining what is realized in speech, and finally what kinds of process we have to assume to exist to be able to connect the semantic description with its syntactic realization.

That Brown was not placed into the same category as, for example, Bloom, is not so much because of his theoretical opinion: as far as the differences between the two distinct rich interpretation methods are concerned, he discusses the work of Bloom positively and that of Schlesinger negatively. The problem is that Brown presents the "Adam-I" data as an inventory of the semantic relations that are explicitly present at the verbal level. For example, verb, action, object (VAO) with declaratives is assumed to exist, but VAO with interogatives is not in the list; *like it* is taken as VO, not as AVO, the only reading that would make sense. Such a description seems to represent a decision to accept case grammar as far as it can be demonstrated to exist with word order and other surface phenomena.

In many other places in his book, Brown demonstrates his ambivalence with respect to the legitimacy of taking into account something that is not expressed verbally. Discussing his observation of the generic verb that was taken as illustrative by Slobin (1973) for the rich interpretation, he mentions that at stage 1 this generic verb is usually understood by the parents as an imperative, as a past, and so on. Furthermore, he adds, parents expand the child's generic forms in this way, and "I [Brown], as a student of the transcript and not a parent, find that the context of the child's utterance usually suggests one of the four modulations described." This careful utterance (1973: 317–318) is completed in note 17, in which he states that Slobin's interpretation "may well be correct," and "What is lacking, of course, is evidence beyond context and other than mature expression, which nevertheless demonstrates that the child has the intentions."

In my opinion we must go a little further: we do not need a descriptively valid theory of sentential constructs, but a communicational integrative model of speech production and perception in which the different modes of communicative expression are represented integratively, and one way or another in correspondence with how things happen in actual communication. As mentioned above, many communicative and nonlinguistic aspects that optionally occur in adult communication are mandatory in the speech of children developing their communicative competence. It is of primary interest for the researcher of the development of communication skills to detect these phenomena, to learn how they develop, and to identify the processes involved.

In sketching the outlines of a model of communication from the standpoint of the speaker, I consider the expressive aspects of communication only, because I restrict myself almost exclusively to the child's communicative development as it appears from his communicative acts. Of course almost all statements have their implications for a model of the hearer.

The second section demonstrates the impact of the first for the field of communicative development, emphasizing the role that intonation, stress, gesturing, and context play in this respect. Most ideas discussed here are dealt with more extensively elsewhere (van der Geest, 1975).

DESCRIPTION OF
COMMUNICATIVE COMPETENCE OF THE SPEAKER

It is very difficult—if not impossible—to describe a complete model of communication in which all aspects are dealt with sufficiently, given the innumerable different aspects involved. It is useful, therefore, to restrict ourselves to some more or less clearly defined subareas of communication. We neglect the receptive aspects of communication, the interactive aspects, such as those that can be indicated with terms like "turn taking" or "turn giving," and finally the human relational aspects of communication. Instead we concentrate on the so-called speech act with its illocutive, referential, and formal (in this case linguistic and nonlinguistic) aspects. At the content level of the communicative act, I distinguish (in contrast with speech act theory) not only between illocution and propositional reference; I also accept a so-called attentional or attitudinal component that accounts for the speaker's standpoint within the conversation with respect to the state of affairs as described in the referential component. In this component the different points of view leading to different choices of communicative form (e.g., active vs. passive, differences in sentential stress, different tenses, modalities, ellipses) can be dealt with. The referential component here is nothing more than propositional structure with a predicate-argument description of variables and their relations plus a specificational part. The consequences of such an analysis is that the referential component represents only the abstract but empty frame of relationships (propositional structure) that exists between the semantic elements that are named in the specification part of the description (van der Geest, 1975: 119-125). This referential structure is affected by the attentional aspect because it operates on the referential structure by putting some aspects in the foreground and others in the background, by adding some attributions that do not qualify the state of affairs in the proposition but only specify the speaker's attitude to that state of affairs and so on. The correspondence between the referential and attitudinal aspects of the communicative act lies in their conceptual actualization in the mind of the speaker regardless of whether he wants to communicate them, and as such they constitute a cognitive unity.

On the other hand the attentional aspect may indirectly—but not necessarily—contribute to the illocutive value of the communicative act. In the illocutive or intentional component the wish to communicate is presupposed. The referential and attentional content is the information to be transferred; the intentional aspect, however, deals with the communicative ends. As mentioned above, the attentional and the illocutive aspects may also constitute a unity insofar as both are speaker oriented, and insofar as the speaker's attention may lead to consequences for the hearer's reaction. In analyses on the basis of conversational postulates and in the description of indirect speech acts, such attentional aspects often have illocutive value. Both aspects are, for example, treated in one part of the structure in a case grammar presentation: the modality part of the structure. That this is, properly speaking, false may be demonstrated by the following observations:

(1) I want an apple / I would like to have an apple.
(2) I want to be rich / I would like to have one million dollars.

Although we may interpret example 1 such that the speaker informs us only about his wishes, the addressee will take this desiderative auxiliary at least in certain situations because it is meant by the speaker as a signal for a request and, if there are no severe grounds for refusal, the addressee will give the speaker an apple or permit him to take one. Although the structures of examples 1 and 2 are linguistically identical, example 2 will not be taken as a request, nor is it intended to be a request by the speaker.

This short discussion indicates that the desiderative auxiliary, as one of many other phenomena of the attentional component, is semantic at the propositional-referential level insofar as it is a subpart of the information—for example, that a wish is expressed—and intentional or illocutive, insofar as it often functions as the syntactic bearer of the intentional aspect of the utterance (see, e.g., von Raffler-Engel, 1968, with respect to this topic) and insofar as it often leads to problems in the description of child language at the pragmatic level, as I have demonstrated (van der Geest, 1977).

Before going into more detail with respect to a model of communicative competence of the speaker, some nonverbal phenomena are introduced. The phenomena are relevant for the tripartition of the content level of the communicative act, the distinction between linguistic and nonlinguistic, and the developmental processes that are discussed later. These phenomena are: 1) focus, presupposition, comment, and presupposedly given; 2) sentential stress and ellipsis; 3) intonation; 4) communicative functions.

Focus, Presupposition, Comment
To determine whether a sentence like

(3)   Shut the door!

is appropriate to the context in which it is produced, at least the following conditions must be met.

1. The addressee must understand English.
2. The speaker is entitled to give an order to the addressee, either because of a hierarchical relationship or because of an emergency situation.
3. The addressee can be presupposed to be able to shut doors.
4. There is a door that the addressee can identify as the door referred to by the speaker.
5. That door is open.

It is necessary here to introduce the notions of focus and presupposition. "Focus" is the essential part of the "comment," which is understood to be the new information of the sentence. "Presuppositions" are taken here to mean conditions that must be satisfied for the proper use of a sentence. Furthermore, it is assumed that if a statement is denied, its presuppositions are not denied. Presuppositions can be of quite different levels. There are, for example, pragmatic conditions in the world (see item 5 in the list above), conditions that ought to be met by the addressee (see items 3 and 4), conditions describing the speaker's beliefs (see item 2), also directions given to the addressee (see item 1).

In producing such imperative sentences as example 3, the conditions 1–5 are presupposed. If one of these conditions is not met, the consequence of example 3 is that it is an "unhappy" utterance in Austin's (1962) terminology (and unacceptable in terms of communicative competence).

Psychologically one can say that the discussed aspects are derived from the shared knowledge of speaker and hearer, the latter's knowledge as conceived by the speaker. They are furthermore determined to a large extent by the attentional component of our speech act model. The same holds for the term "(presupposedly) given" that is used with reference to the part of the information that is given in the context of the conversation or that can be supposed to be known from the side of the hearer, irrespectively of whether·it is uttered. Consider, for example,

(4)   The door!

In this sentence, as used in the same context, not only conditions 1–5 are presupposed but also:

6.   The addressee must be able to identify the activity that he is required to carry out with respect to the door.

Because of their different presuppositions, one could maintain that examples 3 and 4 are not synonymous. This is the reason that an eventual deletion or omission transformation that derives example 4 from example 3 would change the meaning of 3 unless this meaning shift is accounted for in the (semantic) deep structure description of both sentences.

In other contexts the speaker's semantic intent and the hearer's optimal interpretation might be *mind the fresh painted door*, *the door opens*, *the door should be opened*, or *the door is falling*. Therefore, example 4 is taken as a type is a sentence with more than one interpretation. This will have its consequences for the linguistic treatment of such utterances. It implies that presuppositions must be accounted for in a grammar that claims communicative validity, and also that nonlinguistic aspects, for example, occurring at the contextual and interpretive level, play a necessary part if we want to describe real things and not the constructs that only exist in the linguist's mind.

Stress

The analysis of the distinction between focus and presupposition is closely related to the analysis of sentential stress, as may become evident from

(5)   John HIT Peter.
(6)   John DID hit Peter.

In example 5 it is presupposed that John did something to Peter, and in example 6 it is presupposed that someone else has assumed that John did not hit Peter.

For the demonstration of focus, however, there are more possibilities. In example 5 one's attention is drawn to the action *hit*, as opposed to another action as presupposed by the hearer, to the fact that the action happened in the past rather than in the present, or to the fact that John was actively engaged in, not passively subjected to, the activity of hitting. See, for example,

(7)   John WASn't hit by Peter, but John HIT Peter.

In example 6, however, the hearer's attention is drawn only to the truth value of the proposition:

(8)   It is TRUE that John hit Peter.

It has been suggested (van der Geest, 1975) that there are many observations implying that the nuclear stress rule (NSR) is insufficient not only in Chomsky and Halle (1968), in which it is stated that the primary stress is placed on the rightmost of the elements already having primary stress within a major constituent (S, NP, and VP), but also in Bresnan (1971), according to which the stress patterns of certain syntactically complex sentences reflect those of the simple sentences within them in deep structure. The NSR is insufficient for dealing with such phenomena, not only because it is restricted to the so-called neutral sentence, but also because differences in stress coincide with differences in meaning and because the choice of focus, which apparently is related to primary stress in the sentence realization, is assigned not only to lexical elements in the string but also to tense, voice, the truth value of the proposition, and specific semantic aspects of a word. To illustrate this latter point, consider:

(9)   John KOCHT geen bloemen maar hij VERkocht ze.
        (John didn't BUY flowers but he SOLD them.)

In example 9 and its translation it is not the transfer of flowers from an X to a Y for money that is denied, but only the direction in which the transfer took place.

Sentential stress, which is closely related to the speaker's attention, and is to be considered nonverbal, can also be regarded as an argument to reject the linguistic approach and to accept the integrative communicational model.

Ellipsis

The problem of ellipsis is closely connected with the aspects just discussed. Linguistics is almost exclusively concerned with the so-called well-formed sentences, that is, sentences that on the surface consist of at least a subject and a main verb or predicate. It can be questioned, however, whether these sentences are representative of what actually happens in appropriate language use at all. If one observes actual performance, one will notice that large parts of the well-formed sentences are generally omitted, because they are redundant in the context in which the utterance is spoken:

(10) A pint of bitter, please.
(11) (gestural deixis with) Dutch painting.
(12) (showing the cigarette box) Smoke?
(13) Really?
(14) Into the longboat with him.

Bodily behavior like pointing and context can actually have a supporting and (or) substituting function in these cases. It can be demonstrated (van der Geest, 1975) that in contrast with Shopen (1972), a semantically based description is able to deal with the problem of ellipsis. Ellipsis is more relevant if one realizes that language users (e.g., raters in observational studies) have excellent intuitive knowledge of what parts of an utterance may in fact be omitted under certain circumstances.

The problems of ellipsis and of stress are also relevant in the description of language acquisition because children's speech is telegraphic; that is, children's utterances are fragmented, and the understressed parts of the adult variant are generally omitted.

Intonation and Tone of Voice

As is argued by Hymes (1971), one has to be concerned with explaining the possibility of a choice of alternatives suitable within a particular style of speech. This proposition incorporates the necessity of explaining the eventual differences in meaning of the alternative utterances. Taking intonation into account, one can expand the set of alternative utterances to a very high degree. The following utterances are spoken by a police officer to one of his sergeants:

(15) Go to the house of Mrs. Watson. I will . . . .
(16) You go to the house of Mrs. Watson! I will . . . .
(17) You go to the house of Mrs. Watson? I will . . . .
(18) Would you go to the (. . .), then I will . . . .
(19) If you go to (. . .), then I will . . . .

In all utterance, probably an order is expressed. Only the intonations and tones of voice are different. A special tone of voice makes some interpretation of a sentence mandatory. Consider example 20:

(20) I've a lot of work to do.

Here this phenomenon may support the interpretation that the speaker has not only a declarative intention but also a more imperative one, namely, "don't bother me."

A question sentence, for example:

(21) Where do you come from?

does not have the intention of a question when spoken with a threatening tone of voice. Its intention is actually "I require you to tell me. . . ." A last illustration could be drawn from a typical parent-to-child register.

> (22)   Thank you mommy!
> (23)   Bye bye, daddy!

in which a specific tone of voice occurred that mandatorily led to the following interpretation "I want you to say: 'Thank you mommy' or 'Bye bye, daddy.' "

Mimicry

Another possible way of expressing the speaker's intention is mimicry. On the one hand it can be doubted whether mimicry has a status completely independent of the other means of nonverbal intentional expression; on the other it cannot be denied that mimicry has a supporting function. Although this supporting function is of secondary interest in a normal dialogue, it is sometimes essential—for example, in educational situations, in a parent-child interaction in the earliest stages of the child's language development, and in communication with the deaf.

It is clear that the relation between mimicry and the other aspects of language use needs a systematic comparison. Although many studies have been written on both subjects separately, such a systematic comparative analysis is not known to me. For that reason I restrict myself to some general and very hypothetical remarks:

1.   It seems to me that mimicry, like intonation and tone of voice, can be used contrastively with the information presented at the verbal level.
2.   It is difficult to imagine that the information presented by intonation and tone of voice on the one hand and by mimicry on the other could be contradictory.
3.   It seems reasonable, therefore, to suggest that these types of information generally support each other.
4.   Like intonation, mimicry is redundant in normal speech situations if the information to be expressed does not contrast with that of the verbal level.
5.   Like tone of voice, mimicry is relevant not only for the expression of the speaker's intention but also for that of the speaker's judgments of reality. Examples can be taken from almost all novelists and writers, for example:

> (24)   "Reagan will be our next president," Carter said, *scornfully laughing* at the beginning of his campaign.

6.   Most of the time mimicry is subordinated to intonation and tone of voice.

7. Mimicry seems to be of special interest in language acquisition; in the language acquisition of the deaf, it takes over some of the functions of intonation and tone of voice.
8. Like intonation, tone of voice, and other nonverbal means, mimicry is of more substantial interest if there exists channel discrepancy between linguistic and nonlinguistic means of expression, in the sense that the latter ones are decisive for the interpretation.

Gesture

Although gesture is not limited to the realization of intentional features of the "total communication," it is dealt with briefly here because it has some essential aspects in common with mimicry. Insofar as gesturing concerns the speaker's intention, it supports intonation and tone of voice most of the time. Sometimes it is used contrastively with the information presented at the verbal level. This is the case, for example, if one says to the addressee "I did it because of you," while signing MONEY to the other people present. In that case the gesture is decisive for the interpretation.

In the child's communication, gesturing is relevant for all levels of communication; for example, pointing behavior for the expression of the state of affairs, turning away the head to indicate the negative of "I want to eat some more," grasping behavior to indicate a desire to have something, and stretching the arms to ask to be lifted out of bed.

Gesture not only supports the speech act, but also takes over some of its functions. There is, for example, an interesting group of elliptical sentences with accompanying bodily behavior:

> May I (use the phone)?
> May I (have a cigarette)?
> (Do you want) a cigar?
> (Do you want me to use the) phone?

in which certain obligatory parts can be omitted only if context and gesture substitute the meaning. These and other observations led me (van der Geest, 1975) to the following generalization:

> All contextually and nonverbally given parts of a communicative act can either be deleted, be realized unstressed, or be replaced by pronouns and other substitutes.

From this generalization and its underlying observations it may seem that the diverse nonlinguistic and linguistic aspects play an integrative part in the production and understanding of a communicative act. They influence each other to a large extent and can be understood only in mutual dependency. It is, therefore, nothing more than fictitious to assume that linguistic aspects can be dealt with systematically without taking notice of the nonlinguistic but communicative aspects of the communicative act. A valid communicative model has to account for the integral part that the nonverbal aspects play in communication and has to formulate the restrictions on this type of behavior, if there are any. Furthermore, the interrelations of the visual and the auditory channel should be formulated. The following questions are relevant, for example:

1. Does the operation of one of the channels precede the operation of the other? For example, does the gesture precede the spoken word chronologically, psychologically in the preplanning of the utterance, and (or) developmentally?
2. Does the output of the gesture production channel cover other elements than the given or understressed parts of the sentence?

To start with the second question, it seems that gesture is restricted to the new part of the information transferred, but not to the stressed part of the utterance. For example, contrast *(This is) a book* with *May I (have some candy)*. In the first case an understressed but new part is omitted. In the second, however, it is the stressed part. Furthermore, I cannot find any example in which a given part is expressed through the visual channel. In the cases just cited it seems highly redundant to point at the book or the candy box when these items are already given in the immediate discourse. If this observation is true, one may hypothesize that gesturing and probably all nonverbal behavior are restricted to the comment part or the psychological predicate of the message, which is according to Vygotski the essence of inner speech. We may for this reason assume that gesture is more directly related to the processes of thought underlying sentence production than speech is. Insofar as the first question is concerned, we may conclude that nonverbal aspects precede in one way or another the verbal aspects in sentence production. Furthermore, it can be said with respect to the candy example that before sentence production it is decided that the new part of the sentence will not be uttered verbally, because in this case the first word of the sentence *may* has to receive primary sentence stress. Moreover the intonational pattern changes considerably. This suggests also that the visual channel precedes the auditive one, at least at the level of utterance planning.

From the discussion of ellipsis it is clear that the constraint on ellipsis as formulated above—that the elliptical parts are given—holds for all subdivisions of the term given. It should be added, however, that elliptical sentences accompanied by gesture cannot be analyzed in terms of new and given. It may be doubted whether the latter case is a type of ellipsis in the proper communicative sense, because there is nothing elliptical in it: there is an interrelation between two communicative systems, which means that some functions of the auditory system are taken over by the visual system, or probably more accurately, the other way around.

Communicative Functions

How does the speaker ultimately arrive at the production of communicative acts that are appropriate to his own intentions? For the answer of this central question, different communication functions must be distinguished, because it is clear that an actual utterance gives different kinds of information: 1) it refers to a state of affairs that is spoken about: the referential or propositional structure; 2) it is in one way or another related to the context and the situation: the textual function; 3) it gives information on the speaker's intentions: the intentional function or pragmatic function; 4) it informs us about the speaker's interpretation of the state of affairs he refers to: the attitudinal function; 5) the speaker has to judge the knowledge the hearer can be presupposed to have: the participant function; 6) communication serves to establish and maintain social relations, the speaker has to take into account therefore the participant's intentions with respect to the conversation (interpersonal function); 7) communication serves for getting things done by means of the interaction between the speaker and the hearer: the perlocutive function.

For each function the speaker has sets of options at his disposal at the different levels of the description. The intention operation, for example, consists of a finite set of options (assertion, question, request, etc.). The speaker has to decide on one of these possibilities when speaking. Because thoughts and intentions and judgments pass very fast through the head during communication, it can be assumed tentatively that the communicative content-representation is a rather instantaneous act. This implies a mismatch in time between the message and the linguistic realization, which takes time because of the linguistic planning and monitoring and the principle of linearity in speech. This mismatch is probably responsible for many errors in speech, for many developmental phenomena, and also for the fact that although children are able to realize some communicative features in oral speech, this ability is not acquired until many years later in written language because the mismatch is enormously larger here.

That the mismatch between the content representation and the linguistic realization is intrinsic to verbal communication can be demonstrated with specific features of the communicative system of the deaf, which is to a large extent visual. It allows simultaneous expression of different aspects of the proposition through different channels, for example, gesture, facial expression, and forming words with the lips. The face may express the intention (e.g., question). The language of the society, however, must rely on the linearity principle exclusively for written communications, almost exclusively in non-face-to-face situations, and more than the deaf in normal face-to-face situations. The more the speaker has to rely on the auditory channel exclusively, the more his realization rules will differ from the case of the sign language of the deaf or the case of the visual channel also being available. Children have to develop realization rules that make them more and more independent on the nonverbal channel, although they continue to exploit this channel further, after the introduction of the verbal variant.

DESCRIPTION OF REPRESENTATION AND REALIZATION

This section introduces briefly the headlines of the description of content representation and its realization insofar as we need it to describe the beginnings of language development if we pay due attention to the nonverbal phenomena involved.

In the stage in which Hester, the child in this investigation (see also van der Geest, 1974, 1975), already used three- and four-word utterances, the following sequence of utterances occurred:

(25) A. Hester DEZE. (Hester this + nonverbally indicated "pillow.")
      B. Hester MAKEN deze. [Hester (wants to) MAKE this (pillow).]
      C. Hester maken ditte KUSSEN. [Hester (wants to) make this PILLOW).]
      D. Kussen maken OMA. [Hester (wants to) make (this pillow for) (GRANNY).]

It can be assumed (van der Geest, 1975) that A + B = C and that A + B + C + D together are just one communicational unit with roughly the same meaning as in D. In A, the verb is omitted and the object indicated nonverbally. In B and C, Hester is arriving step by step at a realization without these verbal omissions. In D, the indirect object is added and some given information is deleted. In all four subunits, the attentional desiderative "want to" is realized nonverbally (tone of voice + bodily behavior). It can be assumed furthermore that the "errors" and the trial to arrive at an adult linguistic realization are due to some developmental phenomenon such as limitation of memory span or of planning and monitoring capacities.

I restrict myself here to C and D and demonstrate that addition, deletion, stress, and nonverbal substitutes can be accounted for in the description. As mentioned already, nonverbal visual behavior is related to the comment, nongiven part of the message, which means that it substitutes or accompanies verbal material according to some general rules already mentioned. We therefore abstract from the nonverbally realized desiderative as it concerns only these rules on channel preference.

The logicocognitive rules that can be proposed with respect to C and D are shown in Figure 1. As in adult-child speech, the preferable word order is: (SOV): subject, object, verb (see also Klein, 1974). Therefore $321 \Rightarrow 231$. Some additional notes with respect to the tree diagram of Figure 1 are:

1. SUB(ordinate) INTO, ASS(ert), DES(iderative), and EMPH(asize) are operators that can be considered higher predicates that are also accompanied by one or more arguments. Furthermore: SA = state of

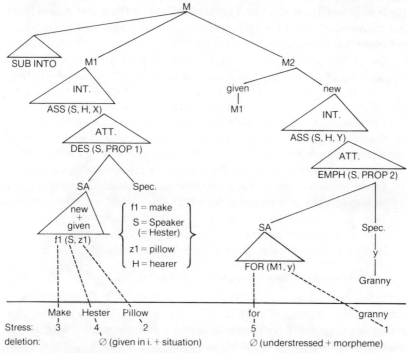

Figure 1.   Logicocognitive rules for examples 25C and 25D.

affairs; M = message; INT = intention; ATT = attention/attitude; Spec = specification, in which also indefiniteness and definiteness (identification) by means of the etha- and iota- operator can be dealt with.

2. The propositional structure has deep VSO order and a "generative semantics"-like description. This acceptance can be motivated from the field of sentential stress assignment (see point 3) and from the field of language acquisition. I hypothesized from my data (van der Geest, 1975) that children acquire cognitive semantic structures in an order that can be deduced from the principle of prelexical predicate raising as worked out by McCawley (1968). Consider, for example, the verb "to kill" = CAUSE [x, BECOME (NOT ALIVE (y)] According to this principle "not alive" (= dead; attribution) is acquired before BECOME dead (= to die; process), and this concept before "CAUSE die" (= kill; action verb). Furthermore, I found in connection with this theory that certain subdivisions of "attribution" that correspond to different logical descriptions parallel the cognitive semantic development of the child: reference or naming ("that is a ball"); essential = definitory identity ("it is round"); accidental but partial identity ("and red"); subjective identity ("and nice"), and noncontrolled state ("and it falls"). See van der Geest (1978a) for further discussion of this topic. Posada

(1980) proved that these hypothetical sequences actually described adequately the facts in early language development of 19 children between 1;0 and 2;0.

3. Stress can be described according to a right-to-left principle, which operates prelexically on the predicate argument structure but after the systematic separation of the given and new elements (van der Geest, 1975). This implies that "Hester" as such is understressed.

4. Deletion is, as argued above, related to stress assignment in the sense that what is most understressed is deleted most easily. Therefore, "Hester" is deleted. Furthermore, it is clear that prepositions, morphemes, and so on tend to disappear in the language production of a language-learning child because these aspects are unstressed in normal nonemphatic speech. It is even probably true that children do not perceive these unstressed elements and therefore are fully unaware of their existence. This may explain why morphemes are acquired so late by the child, and at least why *voor* 'for' is left out by Hester.

Intonation in Early Child Language

In the literature (Lieberman, 1967; Menyuk, 1969, 1971; D. Ingram, 1971; Bloom, 1973; Greenfield and Smith, 1976) the role of intonation is discussed in some detail. It is not sufficient to demonstrate for language acquisition that there is variation in intonation in the data; it also must be determined whether different intonational patterns function systematically differently, and how this interrelation between intonation and intentional function may be expressed. There are two possible ways to investigate this question. One can investigate what functions belong to what contours, and one can investigate the distribution of the contours over the vocabulary, the nonverbal aspects, and over the syntactic structures, if any, present in the data. With respect to the former possibility, Ingram mentioned many observations from the past in the literature in which this type of investigation is described, all detecting the interrelation between intentional function and intonational patterning.

A few investigators, however, (e.g., Bloom, 1973; Posada, 1980) could not find such an interrelation. Most of the time child language studies only mention that children used intonation systematically and functionally, without telling how these conclusions were arrived at.

What kinds of indication one can arrive at? First of all, we may observe how the adults (parents, observers) and older children react to children's intonations. This alone, however, is insufficient because it may prove only that adults interpret the children's intonations as if used by an adult. If the child now accepts the adult's reaction to the child's intonational pattern (therefore the adult's interpretation) of the child's communicative act, we will have more certainty about this matter. It is still insufficient, however. In addition, we could try to interpret the child's intonational pattern counterintuitively, that is, falsely, to observe the child's reaction. For example:

Hester: Naan? (Banana?; friendly, pointing at a banana beyond her range)
Invest.: Yes it is a banana.
Hester: Naan! (Banana! unfriendly behaving)

From this dialogue it may be clear that Hester meant not an information question but a friendly desiderative question/request—but at any rate a question. Apparently also the tone of voice is relevant here. It seems that Hester knew at that time the difference between rising and emphatic into-nation, and what kinds of function can be expressed by them. By applying all techniques discussed in the preceding, I found certain regularities in Hester's speech at the stage of the one word utterance (Table 1). There is additional evidence for the functional use of intonation on the basis of distributional contours over the vocabulary of the one-word stage. In the data, two developmental word classes could be deduced from their occur-rence with intonational patterns (Table 2).

From Tables 1 and 2 it can be deduced that Hester had at least three different intonations at her disposition. There is, furthermore, evidence that both the rising intonation and the emphatic intonation are related to two different functions (see Table 1), as may also appear from the above-mentioned dialogue. Furthermore, the child's bodily behavior may support the intentions of the child: examples include posture, repeatedly bending the knees and/or shaking the body, reaching the arms, and so on, to under-line a desiderative to have or get something, a reaching hand (desiderative) or pointing finger.

Some studies mentioned have no results with respect to intonation. First of all it is unclear whether they investigated in the indicated systematic way. For such an analysis we need audiovisual data or very careful descrip-tions of the observer during sampling of the data. The latter possibility has an additional problem insofar as one is not aware most of the time during observation what kinds of cue should be coded to control the description of intonational contours in connection with their intentional functions. More-over, all the intonational contours do not necessarily develop at the same

Table 1.   Relation between intonation and function in the one-word stage

Intonational pattern	Function
Falling	I assert to you that. . . .
Rising	$\begin{cases} \text{I ask you whether } . . . . \text{ (information)} \\ \text{I ask you that I } . . . . \text{ (desiderative)} \end{cases}$
Emphatic	$\begin{cases} \text{I require from you that you } . . . . \text{ (directive)} \\ \text{I require from you that I } . . . . \text{ (desiderative)} \end{cases}$

Table 2.   Relation between word class and intonation

Word class		Intonation
Child	Adult	
Nounlike word	substantives adjectives pronouns	falling/rising imperative
Verblike word	verbs particles (up/down/in/etc.)	rising/imperative

time and probably not always in the same order, although Liebermann (1967) assumed on reasonable grounds that the normal developmental order is falling, rising, and emphatic. In that case, however, their corresponding functions are not necessarily meant (see Dale, 1980). As illustrations thereof, one may mention that children may use questionlike intonations, although an imperative is meant (Leopold, 1947; van der Geest, 1975). My son Mark many times produced utterances like *Mee?* [(Are you going) with (me)?], although from his accompanying behavior it was evident that an imperative was meant (e.g., dragging off the addressee).

Furthermore, it can be stated that the adult sentence more or less covering the same situation most of the time also has a question intonation. Also in the following examples the incorrect intonation patterns were used:

    (26)   (Een) steenbok? (Een) marmot? (Een) gems? (Een) vlinder?
           (An ibex? A guinea pig? A chamois? A butterfly?)
           (Age: 1;7)

These sentences were used by Mark when he was looking in a book that showed a picture of an animal every two pages. Because the words were too difficult initially for him to produce, we decided to ask him whether a particular name belonged to the picture he was looking at. It is likely for this very reason that the pictures of this particular book were always referred to by Mark with the question intonation.

A last type of sentence in which the child's use of intonation was different from the adult's system has already been mentioned in van der Geest (1977). Some examples are:

    (27)   Aardbei? (Strawberry?) (Age: 21)
    (28)   Kaas hebben? (*litt.*: Cheese have?) (Age: 25)

with the permission meaning *Can I have an X?* which is blocked in the adult's system. If the adult does not explicate the qualifier at a verbal level, he has to rely on the imperative intonation. For example: *Your passport, please!*; *Operator, 3007, please!*; and *Benson and Hedges, please!* mean something like *Give me your passport, please*, and so on. As adult utterances examples 27 and 28 can be understood only as *Do you want to have an X?*

In the present examples the child is not aware that in the adult utterances (example 27) the speaker (the adult) is expected to be the actor of the transfer and the addressee (the child) the recipient. The only thing that counts is that by example 27 the intended state of affairs, "the child is having a strawberry" is effected. Actually the noun + question intonation will not be taken as an offer by the child but just as a kind of yes/no information question that can be used both by the child and by the adult to cover the situation that the child will have the strawberry or the cheese. Thus the meaning of example 27, whether spoken by the child or by the adult, will be according to the child something like:

(27)   Is it true that Mark will have a strawberry?

From these illustrations it may become clear that the analysis of intonation and its corresponding function can be rather difficult. This is why a systematic analysis with positive results is more informative than one with negative results.

Gesture and Its Developmental Function

There were also regularities in the accompanying bodily behavior of the child. The following gestures apparently had communicative function.

Pointing behavior: The child points to a certain object or shows that object and predicates it. This deictic behavior will be referred to as DX_1. Actually, the notion Dx_1 stands for referent-introducing behavior and is, therefore, semantic. *Pointing behavior* is one of its realizations, as are the words *this*, *that*, and so on. As a variation, the pointing behavior can be taken over by the adult. In that case it is sufficient for the child to name the object, although the child may exhibit "redundant" pointing behavior in such cases.

Grasping behavior: The child grasps with his hand in the direction of a certain object while saying such words as *pakken 'take'* or *hebben 'have'*, or saying the object's name. We refer to as Dx_2. Originally Dx_2 was a natural gesture and developed into an arbitrary sign, especially used when the object wanted was beyond Hester's range. I found it also but not always in the behavior of the other children. Other gestures and nonverbal behaviors such as, gaze direction, could assume its function.

The occurrence of these gestures in relation to intonation and word classes is recorded in Table 3. The nonoccurrence of Dx_1 + *imperative* + *noun*, Dx_1 + *verb*, and Dx_2 + *falling* is critical for positing that these are

Table 3.   Relation of gesture to intonation and word class

Gesture	Intonation	Word class
Dx_1	falling / rising	nounlike words
Dx_2	rising / imperative	noun- and verblike words

regularities with respect to gesture, intonation, and word classes. The following paraphrases can be proposed:

> Dx_1 + falling + noun: The thing I am pointing to is an X.
> Dx_1 + rising + noun: The thing I am pointing to, is it an X?
> Dx_2 + rising + noun: The X I am grasping at, can I have it?
> Dx_2 + rising + verb: The thing I am grasping at, can I *verb* it?
> Dx_2 + emphatic + noun: I want to have the X I am grasping at!
> Dx_2 + emphatic + verb: I want to *verb* the object I am grasping at!

By means of the intonational patterns, by considering gestures, and by taking the topic-comment distinction into account, the types of sentences recorded in Table 4 can be accounted for. It should be mentioned that gesture did not necessarily occur in the child's communication—for example, when the object spoken about had been identified already.

With the exception of a few automatisms as *dada* 'bye', *ja* 'yes', and *nee* 'no', the types recorded in *Table 4* were the only ones occurring in Hester's data. It is furthermore remarkable that the stressed (comment) words in the paraphrase were the uttered part by the child (see also Brown and Bellugi, 1964). The intonational pattern seemed initially rather ambiguous, but only for a very short time, at least insofar as the rising and the imperative intonation was concerned (see, e.g., the *Mee?* example mentioned above).

Table 4.   Types of one-word sentence

Word + intonation	Gesture	Paraphrases + stress
Bal (ball)	Dx_1	This is a BALL.
Ditte (this)	Dx_1	THIS is a ball.
Bal? (ball?)	Dx_1	Is this a BALL?
Ditte? (this?)	Dx_1	Is THIS a ball?
Mooi (nice)	Dx_1	This is NICE.
Mooi? (nice?)	Dx_1	Is this NICE?
Appel? (apple?)	Dx_2	Can I have a/the APPLE?
Happen? (eat?)	Dx_2	Can I EAT a/the indicated object?
Ditte? (this?)	Dx_2	Can I have THIS?
Appel! (apple!)	Dx_2	I want to have a/the APPLE!
Happen! (eat!)	Dx_2	I want to EAT the indicated object!
Ditte! (this!)	Dx_2	I want to have THIS object!
Happen! (eat!)	$-/Dx_1$	You ought to EAT!
Ditte! (this!)	Dx_1	You ought to *Verb* THIS!
Bal! (ball!)	$-/Dx_1$	You ought to *Verb* a/the BALL!
Mama! (mommy!)		You (MOMmy) ought to V.

Description of the One-Word Sentence

D. Ingram, describing similar kinds of observation, based his description (1971) of the one-word sentence on the general idea represented in Figure 2. Intonation can be falling, rising and neutral. Gesture can be subdivided into reach (+ wish) (= deixis 2) and point gesture (− wish) (= deixis 1). I argue, however, contrary to the present proposal, that the intention operator, and therefore intonation as the surface expression of intention, ought to be separated strictly from the information part consisting of attention and state of affairs. (+ Wish) is to be considered as belonging to the attentional aspect, which means that intonation and gesture cannot be accounted for under the domain of one modality node. That the young child restricts the usage of the desiderative to the combination with the indirect directive (imperative) function is to be considered a developmental phenomenon, which can be accounted for only by a strict separation of intention and attention in the description. The usefulness of the attention aspect can be motivated independently with such observations (see van der Geest, 1975, 1977) in which it becomes clear that the formal expression of these aspects may cause some major problems for language-learning children and the learning of a second language. For example (Mark, 2;5):

(29) A. Doe ik dat even? (Am I just doing this?)
(30) A. Ik ga even kijken he? (I'm just having a look, aren't I?)
(31) A. Ik moet zitten (I have to sit down.)
(32) A. Ik krijg niets meer (I don't get anything else.)

with (on the basis of context and accompanying bodily behavior) the following meanings:

(29) B. Mag ik dat even doen? (Can I just do this?)
(30) B. Mag ik even gaan kijken? (May I just have a look?)
(31) B. Ik wil zitten (I want to sit down.)
(32) B. Ik wil niks meer hebben (I don't want to have anything more.)

In these observations the following attitudinal functions are violated:

(29) C. Information question versus *permission* question
(30) C. Tag question versus *permission* question
(31) C. *Necessity* versus *desiderative*
(32) C. Assertion versus *desiderative*

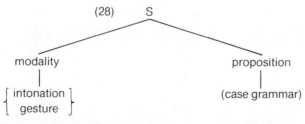

Figure 2.   Schematic representation of the one-word sentence (Ingram, 1971).

There is, furthermore, semantic evidence that Ingram's bipartition into modality and proposition does not hold. Dx_1 means only "the thing I am pointing to," and is therefore considered to be referent-introducing behavior dealt with in the SA description. Dx_2 means "I want to have the object I am reaching at." Therefore, it has a triple function:

1. It is referent introducing.
2. It makes explicit the attitude: desiderative.
3. It expresses the possessive relation between speaker and object (= HAVE).

Because of its first function, Dx_2 is related to the propositional structure and the specification. The same holds for the third function. Because of its second function it must be accounted for in the attitudinal part of the analysis. From the meaning of both deictic gesture types it appears that they ought to be separated from the intention operator, and that their functioning can be accounted for in the proposition as worked out above. The tree diagrams shown in Figure 3 are proposed to account for the child's one-word sentences.

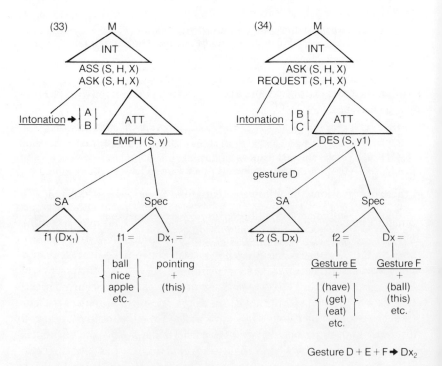

Figure 3.   Formation rules of a child's one-word sentence.

Finally, an output constraint is to be formulated, which says that:

A. At the time that only one word at a time can be produced by the child, it is the rightmost element of the specification (the normally most stressed one) that is realized.

This constraint works the same way as the principle of stress assignment as worked out above. Because it is the primary stressed element that is uttered by the child, the one-word utterance can be regarded to be a special type of elliptical sentence.

Stage of the Two-Word Sentence

At the age of 1;11 Hester used successive one-word sentences that were semantically related to each other, as, for example,

(35)   Kaas // Happen [(I want to) Cheese//bite.]

A reexamination (van der Geest, 1975) of Bloom's (1973) data on successive one-word sentences suggested, contrary to her opinion, that such utterances can be regarded as two-word sentences in that syntactically word order is already very regular, although deviant from adult word order. In my data it appeared furthermore that both words commented on the same topic and that both words had identical intonations and accompanying gestures. What failed was only the child's planning and monitoring capacity to put both words under the domain of one intonation and one procedure of sentential stress assignment. *This transitional stage between the one- and two-word sentence proves that real syntactic development (e.g., a two-word utterance with some syntactic features) may occur only if some developments within the nonverbal aspects of communication already have taken place. It suggests once again that syntactic development can be investigated only in an integrative linguistic communicative approach.*

The two one-word sentences that functioned identically in the one-word stage and occurred successively in the transitional stage are combined to just one sentence in the present stage. For example, a verb like *happen* 'eat' accompanied with emphatic and (or) desiderative gesturing and a noun like *pap* 'pablum' with the same nonverbal features are combined to the sentence *pap happen* 'pablum eat', with identical nonverbal features in this stage. The types of two-word sentence that occurred in Hester's data are given in Table 5. Of course the one-word sentences still continued to occur at that time. They were, at least initially, not systematically different from those occurring in the earlier stages. Only the vocabulary increased remarkably. Afterward also adverbs occurred, such as *ook* 'also', *meer* 'more', *keer* 'again', *zo* 'this way'. The first and the last adverbs occurred with all intonations, the other two with rising and emphatic intona-

Table 5. Types of two-word sentence

Verbal level	Intonation	Gesture	Stress on word 1 or 2 or both
Mama maken (mommy make)	./!/?	Dx_1/Dx_2	1
Koek eten (cake eat)	./!/?	Dx_1/Dx_2	1
Eten koek (eat cake)	./!/?	Dx_1/Dx_2	2
Ditte open (this open)	./!/?	Dx_1/Dx_2	1, 2
Deur open (door open)	./!/?	Dx_1/Dx_2	1, 2
Open deur (open door)	./!	(Dx_1)	1
Meer kaas (more cheese)	!		1
Appel daar (apple there)	.	Dx_1	2
Daar appel (there apple)	.	Dx_1	1, 2
Poes lief (pussy smart)	./!		2
Lief poessie (smart pussy)	.		1

tion. Because the verblike words also occurred in this stage with a falling intonation (this development already had started in the transitional stage), it is not necessary to take these adverbs as belonging to different generic word classes. A very common sentence type already occurring in the very beginning of the present stage was the one-word sentence to which a vocative was added; for example, *Daar, mamma* 'there, mommy' and *mama, cola* 'mommy, cola'. The vocative can be described as a realization of the person spoken to as presented in the intention analysis (second argument). Because the two words in this sentence type are often separated by a pause, and in addition because they have different intonational patterns, this sentence type can be regarded somewhere between the one- and two-word sentence.

Stress Placement and Omission

If we examine the distribution of sentence stress in the two-word sentence in its relation to word classes, we find that in verb-noun constructions nouns generally tend to have primary stress and verbs secondary stress (Table 5, lines 1–3). Furthermore, it can be observed that in predicate-nominal constructions the predicate tends to have primary stress (Table 5, lines 4–6, 10, and 11). The locative adverb *daar* 'there' seldom had primary stress, but *meer* 'more' always had. We are able therefore, to subdivide the words Hester used into subcategories on the basis of stress preference. Furthermore, we can conclude that these observed stress regularities point in the direction of the stress theory as worked out earlier.

1. Because it is stated that the verb is stressed only after the subject and the object, there is a better chance that the stress will be on a noun than on a verb. It explains furthermore that the verb occurs later and less

often anyhow in child speech, because of the corresponding tendency to omit the "understressed part," as worked out earlier.

2. For the explanation of stress dominance in predicate-nominal constructions we need to distinguish between new and given because the nominal is the rightmost element here and can be expected to have primary stress. In one argument structure only one argument needs to be given to arrive at a stressed predicate. Furthermore, one generally qualifies or predicates only something that has already been introduced in the discourse (whether verbally or nonverbally). In our data this something was new only on very special occasions; for example, *deur open* if added with imperative-like intonation. Still, the other possibility (viz., stress on *open*) remains possible and did occur.

With respect to stress in many productions of the child (viz., imitations, and utterances that were expanded by the adults) Brown and Bellugi (1964) found that the main stressed words of the adults' utterances were also the main stressed ones in the child's comparable utterances. They found the same with respect to the words given secondary stress. This investigation by Brown and Bellugi was restricted to rather specific child utterances (imitations and the child utterances that were expanded by the parents); however. Thus to determine whether the outcomes were a consequence of that limitation, I investigated the data of the five children, as reported elsewhere (van der Geest (1974). On the basis of context and situation, paraphrases were made (methodologically, a paraphrase is a specific kind of parent expansion of the child utterance). These paraphrases were as simple as possible; furthermore, they had approximately the same characteristics as the speech used by the parents if talking with their children, so far as this could be deduced from the records. The results of this investigation indicated that Brown and Bellugi's (1964) results could be generalized to all utterances (a thousand) of the five children. The results were:

1. Only the stressed words of the paraphrases were uttered by the children.
2. The distribution of stress was similar in utterances and paraphrases.
3. Utterance and paraphrase had the same word order.
4. The uttered words were content words most of the time.

(The paraphrases were made by trained linguists who did not know the hypotheses of the investigation.) Given now that our semantically based stress rule is also correct in child language, and that the omissions in child utterances correspond with lower stress in the adult's utterances, the child utterances can be accounted for. We can do so by formulating output constraint B, working such that the understressed parts of the information unit must be omitted:

B. If the speaker at a certain time of his development is limited in his speech production to sentences having a maximum of two words, he will produce a one-word sentence by realizing the rightmost element of the specification and a two-word sentence by realizing the two rightmost elements of the specification in such a way that the rightmost of these elements is the primarily stressed one. All elements lower than the secondarily stressed one are not realized, the secondarily stressed one may not be realized.

Finally, I would like to demonstrate how the stress strategy for language production and language development, for example, as worked out in constraint B, may lead to child utterances that are blocked in adult speech. Consider the following child utterances and their paraphrases:

(35) Banaan (Banana?/!) [*May I*(?)/*I want*(!) a banana.]
(36) Koeke happen (Cookie bite) ?/! [May I(?)/I want to(!) bite a cookie.]

in comparison with the following elliptical sentence of the adult's system:

(37) Whiskey? (Do you want to have/drink a whiskey?)

The child sentence can only be interpreted as a desiderative question, the adult one on the contrary as an offer.

Figure 4 shows tree diagrams of examples 38 and 39, to account for these differences. The descriptions differ because the first arguments of the SA are different. However, both arguments are given in the intentional description and can therefore be omitted. It should be noticed finally that although the communication systems of the adult and the child differ systematically with respect to these sentence types, this difference does not

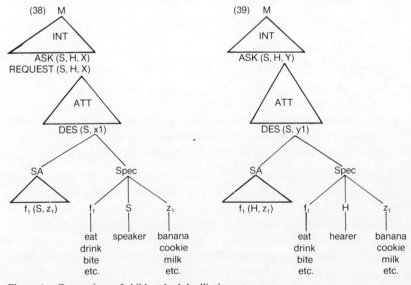

Figure 4.   Comparison of child and adult elliptic sentences.

lead to misunderstandings. That is, the adult and the child differ with respect to what they accept and interpret as hearer and what they produce as speaker in communication with each other. This can be understood only by assuming that both kinds of realization belong to different registers of the same code. In a certain sense, the difference we are dealing with can be related to the pragmatic part of the analysis, while the intended state of affairs in the child-adult communication is the same:

Pragmatic analysis	Intended SA
ASK (child, adult)	f_1 (child, z_1)
ASK (adult, child)	f_1 (child, z_1)

Piaget's characterization of initial egocentrism of the child and its recognition by the adult may explain this remarkable phenomenon. Furthermore, the nonverbal cues of both utterances will remove the ambiguity from the communication, permitting it to act either as a desiderative or as an offer.

DEVELOPMENT OF THE MEANING OF POINTING

This section sketches the development of the central nonverbal phenomenon discussed earlier, namely, the phenomenon of deixis.

One of the essential components in the development of the present nonverbal sign is the child's discovery of the gesture's sign value. This discovery occurs as follows. Initially the adult restricts the use of the deictic gesture almost exclusively to pointing at things that coincide with the end of the forefinger. That is, the gesture is restricted to cases in which attention marker and attention point coincide (e.g., pointing at pictures in a book or things in the child's and parent's direct environment). The present sign has just one interesting feature: marking the child's attention point. This restrictive application of the pointing gesture can be used effectively from the onset in parent-child-topic communication: the child will fix his attention on the top of the adult's forefinger.

An additional and complicating semantics feature of pointing could be the direction of pointing as a necessary prerequisite for the correct interpretation of the sign: the top of the forefinger is not the attention point, but rather, a place somewhere in the near or far distance, in the continuation of the direction line as indicated by the pointing arm, hand, and forefinger. This complex aspect of pointing can be subdivided into two types, with different levels of complexity:

The *first* one occurs when the observing eyes of the sender and the hearer, respectively (the attention marker and the topic to be discussed) are more or less on one imaginary line; this is the single gaze direction type: the speaker's gaze direction and that of the hearer coincide; see Figure 5a.

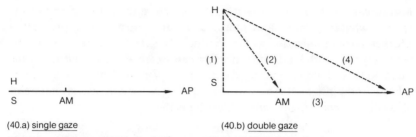

(40.a) single gaze   (40.b) double gaze

(H = hearer; S = sender; AM = attention marker; AP = attention point/topic)

Figure 5.   Complexity levels of pointing: (*a*) single gaze and (*b*) double gaze. In these diagrams H = hearer, S = sender, AM = attention marker, AP = attention point, or topic.

The *second* type of directional pointing occurs when the former condition is not met, so that the message receiver has to construct an imaginary line going through and from the eye of the sender to his attention marker (top of forefinger) and beyond, to the topic to be discussed.

The topic identification may be caused by peculiar attention-attracting features of the topic in the environment or by similarities in the utterance meaning and the topic: the double gaze direction type: speaker gaze and hearer gaze do not coincide; see Figure 5*b*.

In the double gaze type the message receiver H (Figure 5*b*) needs information about 1, 2, and 3, to arrive at the correct interpretation, 4. The single gaze type is and can be used very early in the parent-child-topic communication by the parent. Observations with young children between 0;2 and 0;6 indicate that this type is already effectively used in the baby's first half-year of life. Parents using this type of communication also show themselves to be good teachers, because this pointing gesture is initially used only when the attention point has some additional attention-attracting features (e.g., motion in a motionless environment or noise in a noiseless situation). Airplanes, cars, and birds are good examples of such topics. We may ask whether pointing in this sense, where it is effective, has sign value for the child, because it needs only to accommodate his eye from the relatively unattractive attention marker (pointing hand) to the very attractive attention point, without changing his gaze direction. Formulating the child's activity this way, we can fit it in the young child's sensorimotor intelligence.

Both the "AP = AM" pointing gesture and the "single gaze" type can be considered to be necessary precursors of the real pointing gesture, the "double gaze" type. It appears from numerous observations that this pointing type has a very long developmental route. Initially (until the end of the sensorimotor stage) the present type of gesture is generally interpreted falsely because it is taken in this stage as an "AP = AM" gesture. I noticed that many children before age 1;6 look at the pointing hand instead of the object pointed at, which means that the mediating sign is interpreted as the attentional end of the communicational act. However in the second year of life children develop little by little an adequate understanding of the double gaze pointing behavior if the distance between AP and AM is not too big.

In this light we should also discuss the data of Lempers (1979). He investigated children 9–14 months old to pinpoint their understanding of pointing to a nearby object (50 cm) and a distant object (250 cm), with and without movement, and gaze direction (eyes-face convergent or divergent). He generally found that all children were able to interpret correctly the nearby pointing of the experimenter. The author calls this pointing presymbolic or prereferential, and it can be regarded, therefore, as more or less equivalent to the "AP = AM" type. The "distant object" type is understood only by the children 12–14 months old. The lack of a relation between "AP = AM" and this type suggests to Lempers that different skills are involved, which are necessary for managing symbolic or referential pointing.

It is, however, worthwhile to mention here that the number of objects (3) and the face-to-face position of experimenter and child could have facilitated the child's task to a large extent. If we add that only half the older children accomplished the present task, it will be clear that children of that age are not yet able to perform symbolic thinking with respect to the pointing task. Only the initial step toward full mastery has been taken by these children.

As evidence for the statement that the full development of the pointing gesture takes a rather long route, consider the following observation made, when my son Joost was 7 years old:

(40)   Joost aimed to direct my attention to a rather unusual car standing in a parking place about 100 meters away. After pointing in the adult way (i.e., correctly) to this car, Joost corrected his nonverbal behavior by pointing much higher and saying to me: "No! I will point some higher because you are much bigger than me."

The implication of this self-correction appears in Figure 6a, which shows that initially Joost used the adult pointing system in which the message receiver (F) has the task to construct the J–AM–AP line to arrive at the valid interpretation. Afterward he falsely corrected his message by constructing an F–AM–AP line for the receiver (Figure 6b).

It will be clear from this observation that a child must arrive at a stable concrete operational capacity before he can deal correctly with the nonverbal system of pointing. First he must possess the observational capacity of grouping in the sense that he has to make more than one judgment the same time (the J–AP line, as well as the receiver's capacity to construct the J–AP line). Second to be able to judge the receiver's standpoint as different from his own, he must have left the essential features of preoperational egocentrism. Joost demonstrated that he was able to operate according to the

152   van der Geest

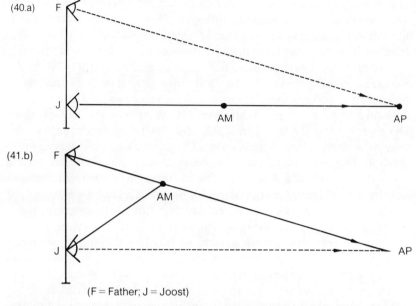

(40.a)

(41.b)

(F = Father; J = Joost)

Figure 6.   (a) Correct and (b) falsely corrected pointing by child; F = father, J = Joost.

operating principles of the concrete operational stage, but he also demonstrated the type of "error" that generally occurs in the beginning of a new
phase, namely, the use of the new operating principles in an exaggerated
way: he gave too much consideration to the distinct position of the receiver.

ACKNOWLEDGMENT

This chapter is dedicated to Walburga von Raffler-Engel, who introduced me to the
problems I dealt with here.

Section IV
METHODOLOGIES

The different goals of the studies of kinesics have dictated different methods of research. The clinical goal of Scheflen is far from the language goal of von Raffler-Engel. Each field brings its one or more accepted research methods to bear on the acquisition of kinesics, including its different premises, methods of data collection, and rules of valid argumentation and hypothesis construction. As has been stated throughout this volume, the convergence of a variety of methodologies on a paradigm, a pattern of development, is the strongest of arguments for validity. This section includes research from other areas and provides a broadening of the scope of research on developmental kinesics.

The vast numbers of child language acquisition studies over the decades provide one control that the study of kinesics does not yet have. When Jakobson (1968/1941) synthesized the observations of child language phonological acquisition from many language families and cultures, he provided us a pattern based on a reliable data base. Similarly Lenneberg (1967) synthesized the results of many studies from a variety of fields such as are included in this volume: linguistics, psychology, psychiatry, medicine, and so on. The results of both investigators are based on a large enough number of children to ensure that the statistical picture of acquisition is well established. The several articles and studies done each year that attempt to alter the pattern by reference to a few children—or, in some cases, one child—ignore the statistical nature of their claims. The patterns of one or a few children may be treated as aberrations, even as may be a different pattern for a single group or language: the pattern for the 98% is not invalidated by the aberrant behavior of 2%.

In developmental kinesics, the control provided by a large number of observational studies done on many children from different cultures does not yet exist. The hypothesized patterns of development may indeed be altered on the basis of small studies; it is just this aspect that adds an exciting element to the research. The paradigm is emerging, and insights may come from any direction at any time; interdisciplinary cooperation is a necessary and enriching practice, especially now.

The chapters in this section provide interesting examples of the multidisciplinary approach. Rosenfeld and Remmers, from a computer-oriented perspective, report on their analysis of mother-infant interaction. The return to a naturalistic, observational method of interactional behavior study, reinforced by the increasing use of videotaping equipment, has not yet been matched by progress in developing more refined analytic procedures for data reduction. Rosenfeld has been using a common data base, a set of mother-infant videotapes, to test the various methods of analyzing the functional relationships in the mother-infant behaviors. He and Remmers report on two recent approaches, the first a deterministic sequential machine, the second a bivariate lag analysis. The discussion of their results highlights the complexity of the problems involved in developmental kinesics.

Yoder's chapter extends her previous work on the processes of differentiation and integration when examining the verbal and nonverbal communicative resources the child uses. In her study of the child's vocalization patterns, she adds to the observation of word output two important kinds of data: discourse structure coding, and systematic coding of gesture and gaze direction accompanying the vocalizations. The resulting research offers a much fuller picture of communication development in the mother-infant interaction.

In the next chapter, Marcos comments on the possible misdiagnosis by practitioners in his field of psychiatry of schizophrenic bilinguals whose Spanish language and kinesics are dominant. The resulting kinesic pattern in English may be misread by a clinician. The misreading is intensified as the English language ability approaches native fluency while the kinesic system retained from Spanish causes interference. As an example Marcos discusses certain types of hand movement activity, which had earlier been related to psychopathology in some patients but are now seen to be related to the more demanding tasks of verbalization in a subordinate second language. The development of full and partial bikenesic systems is a fruitful area for research.

Hutcheson treats the implications of epidemiological research methods for developmental kinesic study. One major difference in method is the special use of rates for comparing events rather than plain occurrences of events. One application is in the diagnosis and intervention of language learning disabilities. Although not caused by disease, the disabilities exhibited by a population can be studied with these methods and effective intervention strategies planned. The multiplicity of influences on kinesic behavior leads easily to the idea of using statistical methods of analysis. The computer can more rapidly handle factors enumerated for age, sex, culture, class, intended receiver of message, muscular coordination, personality traits, talkativeness, mothering behavior, emotional disturbances, and so on. Sophistication in statistical methods is fundamental to a social science, although, as this book makes clear, methodologies that use statistics are diverse.

Chapter 9
SEARCHING FOR TEMPORAL RELATIONSHIPS IN MOTHER-INFANT INTERACTIONS

Howard M. Rosenfeld and Willard W. Remmers

In recent years there has been a remarkable increase in efforts by re-searchers to analyze the process of interaction between infants and their mothers as well as other social figures. Much of this new trend is attribut-able to the popularization of the ethological concept of "attachment" (Bowlby, 1969). Also there has been a renewed interest in studying the early development of communicative ability in relationship to the adult speech environment (Snow and Ferguson, 1977) and to the prior nonverbal com-munication skills of the infant (Schaffer, 1977). This book treats the early development of nonverbal aspects of communication as a topic of inquiry in its own right.

A popular methodology of contemporary researchers for the analysis of early communicative skills has been the observational study of naturalis-tic social interactions. This method was characteristic of research by devel-opmental psychologists in the 1930's, but was substantially abandoned in subsequent years in favor of less complex and less confounded experimen-tal procedures. The recent renewal of interest in naturalistic observational studies probably is attributable to several sources. One is the reemergence of biosocial theories, and particularly the associated belief that ethological methods for studying animals in their natural habitats are productively applicable to the study of humans (Blurton-Jones, 1972; McGrew, 1972).

Developmental linguists also have had a relatively long tradition of descriptive study, although it was used primarily for the assessment of the normative emergence of linguistic forms in the child. More recent natural-istic studies have attempted to assess the structure of the adult communicative environment, both verbal and nonverbal, that surrounds the child. But thus far little progress has been made in the descriptive analysis of how the interaction of the behaviors of infant and other persons contributes to the development of communicative skills.

The return to the method of naturalistic observation requires renewed faith in the ability of the researcher to detect meaningful, coherent structure within the complexity of human social interactions. For many researchers this faith has been fostered by recent evidence that infant nonverbal behavior is quite precisely synchronized to maternal speech rhythms at several microscopic levels of activity (Condon and Sander, 1974b). The evidence is controversial on several grounds (Rosenfeld, 1980). For example, the findings have not been successfully replicated by independent researchers. Also, there is considerable evidence that only limited aspects of adult interpersonal behavior are synchronized and that even these are synchronous only to a probabilistic degree.

The recent surge in interest in naturalistic observational methods also had been reinforced by the increasing availability of videotaping equipment and computers. Unfortunately, however, there has not been corresponding progress in the development of analytic procedures for meaningful data reduction. Consequently, many researchers have found themselves in the frustrating position of having a large and expensive collection of videotapes but not knowing how to code them or how to analyze the coded data in ways that are likely to facilitate their substantive objectives.

The authors are among a growing number of researchers who have been concerned with developing better analytic methods for descriptive studies of social interaction. During the past decade the senior author has used a common data base for the purpose of testing and comparing the usefulness of a variety of analytic approaches. The original data consisted of naturalistic interactions within two mother-infant dyads during the infant's ages of 2 to 6 months, purportedly a major phase in the development of social attachments (Schaffer, 1964). Each dyad was videotaped for 14–16 sessions, averaging 45 minutes per session. The data were coded at a level that was intended to be sufficiently comprehensive and differentiated to permit analysis of a wide variety of behaviors of substantive interest. Preliminary progress was described in a set of technical reports (Rosenfeld, 1971) and a symposium presentation (Rosenfeld, 1973). Since the time of the earlier reports the authors have collaborated in the development and testing of several additional analytic programs.

The major purpose of this chapter is to review and evaluate two of our most recent approaches to the analysis of functional relationships between the behaviors of mother and infant, and to illustrate their application to data relevant to the study of developmental kinesics. One of the approaches, a deterministic sequential machine, provides a holistic, comprehensive model of the interaction process. This method is not common in behavioral research. Its application to our data was urged by colleagues in electrical engineering, who, like Condon, were confident that a simple structure would be found to underlie the apparent complexity in the initial data set. The second approach, bivariate lag analysis, focuses on probabilistic relationships between pairs of time-lagged variables. This is a common approach in behavioral research. However, the ordinary analysis is likely to confound a variety of underlying processes, thereby producing results that are spurious at worst or ambiguous at best. Thus our major interest in the bivariate lag approach was to develop efficient "filtering" techniques for separating various possible forms of temporal relationships and for removing spurious relationships attributable to univariate distributional properties rather than to actual interactions between behavioral classes.

The authors feel that sufficient progress has been made in the development and assessment of the methods above to warrant a review of their implications. It should be emphasized that the goals of the research thus far have been primarily methodological. Although the limited data structures that have been analyzed may be of interest to developmental kinesiologists, their purpose has been to illustrate and evaluate rather than to provide normative substantive information.

BASIC METHODOLOGICAL CONSIDERATIONS

In selecting the descriptive study of natural social interactions, rather than the experimental control of the laboratory, the investigator forgoes potential simplicity and clarity of analysis in favor of the opportunity for discovery. By means of the comprehensive inspection of the complexities of social interaction, researchers hope to identify important functional classes of variables and to gain some insight into the nature of the relationships among the variables. Countering this opportunity is the likelihood that there will be an indeterminately large number of functional variables, some not yet well defined, some not known at all, and many that interact in very complex ways. The success of the research enterprise in finding useful information in the simplest form possible depends on two major decisions—the selection of the elemental variables or primitives and the choice of procedures for determining relationships among the primitives. Of course, the number of analytic models that can be applied to any finite set of data is also infinitely large. Thus the best the investigator can hope to accomplish is to have selected methods that result in meaningful data reduction.

Selection of Primitive Variables

There are a variety of bases for the selection of primitive variables. These include the investigator's own natural perceptual discriminations and hunches about which of these are likely to be important, previous distinctions made by other investigators, and the implications of psychological theories. It is tempting to include all variables imaginable, since the greater their number, the greater the number of possible relationships to be discovered; but it must be remembered that the complexity of the data analysis rises at least in proportion to the square of the number of variables and perhaps as the factorial of their number.

Higher Order Classification Within a Time Unit

Formation of new classes of events from the initial set of elementary classes may be accomplished by the use of the simple logical operations "and," "or," and "not"($\sim$). All possible derivative classification schemes within an elementary time unit may be formed from the initial classifications and their negations by means of concatenations in which behavioral classes alternate with the logical operations. The inclusion of the logical operator "not" is important since the nonoccurrence of a behavioral event class (denoted by $\sim$ E) can be considered an event in itself. For example, if the event classes E_1, E_2, E_3, . . ., E_j are thought to be functionally equivalent, a new event may be formed from them using the logical "or" as follows: $E_k = E_1$ or E_2 or E_3 or . . . E_j. This means that the occurrence of any of the initial events E_1 through E_j will be reclassified as an occurrence of the new event E_k. Two such examples appear in Figure 1. In the case of "superordination," the event classes were combinations of a common general feature (i.e., all directions of visual orientations). In the case of "functional" equivalence, classes are combined on the basis of similar circumstances of usage even if the forms are dissimilar [e.g., leaning or reaching toward an object (12.A) "ored" with visual orientation toward an object (11.B)]. If some of these events are not mutually exclusive and if the researcher feels or has evidence that the co-occurrence of two behavioral classes is functionally different from the "ored" single occurrences, he may use exclusive "ors" to separate out these single occurrences.

It should be noted, however, that although combinatorial methods can simplify primitive classification systems by reducing redundancy, they also run the risk of combining incompatible elements or adding noise (error) to a class. For example, in a study of elements of nonverbal reactions of teachers to student performance, one significant empirically derived cluster of teacher behaviors permitted the inclusion of either head nods or head shakes or both when they occurred within a larger set of elements in common (Rosenfeld et al., 1979). But it was also found that the teacher head nods were almost perfectly associated with successful student performance, whereas the head shakes were strongly associated with unsuccessful performance. In this case the individual elements were better predictors

Figure 1 — Simultaneous combinations of primitive variables for four code categories.

Elementary time units	0	1	2	3	4	5	6	7	8	9	10	11	12	13	14	15	16	17	18	19	20	21	22	23	24	25	26	27	28	29	30	31	32
Occurrence:																																	
I1.E	1	1	0	1	0	0	1	1	1	1	0	0	0	1	1	1	1	1	1	0	0	0	0	1	0	1	1	1	0	1	1	0	0
I1.B	0	0	1	0	1	1	1	1	1	1	1	0	1	0	0	0	0	0	0	0	0	1	1	1	1	0	0	1	1	0	0	0	0
I4.A	0	0	0	1	1	0	0	0	0	1	0	1	0	0	0	0	0	0	0	0	0	0	0	1	1	1	0	0	0	1	0	0	0
I2.A	0	0	1	1	1	0	0	1	1	0	0	0	0	0	0	0	0	0	0	0	0	0	1	1	0	0	0	1	1	0	0	0	0
N-Tuple categories	a	a	b	c	d	e	f	g	g	h	e	i	e	a	a	a	a	a	j	j	j	b	k	i	a	f	f	b	c	a	j	j	
extended	a		b	c	d	e	f	g		h		e		a					j			b	k	i	a	f		b	c	a	j		
Superordinate I1.	1	1	1	1	1	1	1	1	1	1	1	1	1	1	1	1	1	1	1	0	0	1	1	1	1	1	1	1	1	1	1	0	0
extended																																	
Functional, I1.B or I2.A	0	0	1	1	1	1	1	1	1	1	1	1	1	0	0	0	0	0	0	0	0	0	1	1	0	1	1	1	1	0	0	0	0
extended																																	

Note Translation of code categories: I1.E = infant looks at mother; I1.B = Infant looks at mobile; I4.A = Infant coos; I2.A = Infant leans or reaches forward.

Figure 1. Simultaneous combinations of primitive variables for four code categories: I1.E = infant looks at mother, I1.B = infant looks at mobile, I4.A = infant coos, I2.A = infant leans or reaches forward.

than the cluster. On the other hand, a cluster containing the occurrence of a headshake and a smile was perfectly associated with unsuccessful performance, even though the smile occurring alone was more often associated with success.

The empirical identification of functional classes commonly is done by means of discriminative analysis whereby primitives are clustered on the basis of their common association to criterion variables. An example of an empirically derived functional classification is the identification of a diverse class of potential instigators of aggression on the basis of significant transitional probabilities. Each element in the derived set consisted of behaviors that significantly increased the probability that the recipient of the behavior would hit the instigator (Patterson and Cobb, 1971).

The data used in the present investigation have also been used for the identification of a set of elementary behaviors of mothers that were predictive of episodes of crying. Using an elementary time unit of 25 seconds, single and combinatorial classes of mother behavior were weighted for their contributions to the predictability of subsequent periods of infant crying versus contentment (Young, Browne, 1972).

One interesting case is the concatenation of all behavioral classes or their negations with "ands." This procedure might be thought of as consisting of all possible combinations of co-occurrence of behavioral classes in a single time unit. If there were three initial primitive behavioral classes A, B, and C, each having a possible value of 0 or 1 representing occurrence or nonoccurrence in an interval, we could represent the new classification generated as a set of triplets. The first place in each triplet would refer to A, the second to B, and the third to C. The new classification would then be (0,0,0), (0,0,1), (0,1,0), (0,1,1), (1,0,0), (1,0,1), (1,1,0), (1,1,1). Note that there are 2^3 or 8 new behavioral classes. In general this procedure produces a new classification whose size is 2^N, where N is the size of the initial classification scheme. If N is greater than 3, each member of the classification is usually referred to as an N-tuple for ease of pronunciation (i.e., triplet becomes 3-tuple). If N is large, the number of possible new behavioral classes is extremely large. If all these combinations actually occurred in the data string, the analysis would be very unwieldy. However, in our experience with behavioral data, relatively few combinations actually occur. This we assume indicates underlying structure in human behavior.

In the data used in our systems analysis of mother-infant interaction, the initial classification of mother behaviors consisted of 23 mother behaviors that could have resulted in the occurrence, in our data, of a large subset of the 2^{23} possible derived behavioral classes. The number of possible classes found is of course limited by the length of the data string, which in our case was approximately 4000. If all the 23-tuples were equally likely, then given the number of possible 23-tuples, the probability of multiple occurrences of any behavior in a data string of length 4000 is very small (about 0.0005); hence in this case one might expect 3998 different 23-tuples. In our data 61 mother patterns actually occurred with a frequency of greater than 10. This seems to be a result of restrictions on the number of behaviors the mother can do at once, as well as the functional structure of various combinations of behaviors.

Figure 2 gives an example of occurrence/nonoccurrence data with various coding manipulations. The top row lists the elementary time units, and below the time units the behavior to be coded is graphically represented, showing the times during which the behavior is occurring and (in the troughs) its periods of nonoccurrence. The points of change (i.e., the starting points of the behavior and the stopping points) are represented by right angles in the "behavior" line. The third line represents the observer's initial coding within each elementary time unit of starts (+) and stops (—). This is a simplified version of our actual coding scheme in which the behavior was represented by an alphanumeric symbol (e.g., Ml) followed by a "+" or "—" and a number indicating the time interval. Momentary behaviors represented by "×" are those in which both a "+" and a "—" occur in the same time interval and were actually coded by merely noting the behavioral class and interval of occurrence. Note that all features of the original behavior can be reconstructed from this code, with a resolution of one elementary time unit. It is not necessary to enter codes for intervals between starts and stops; these can be derived if needed.

The fourth, fifth, and sixth lines of Figure 2 show the starts, stops, and momentaries as separate behaviors. The seventh line illustrates a binary coding of occurrence and nonoccurrence in each time interval, and the next three rows define and represent starts, stops, and momentaries, respectively, in terms of sequences of three binary entries. Note that these two coding systems are not informationally equivalent. Although the first system may be used to generate the second, the reverse is not true because the stop at 14, the start at 15, and the stop at 26 can not be recreated from the binary data. If a researcher believes that starts and stops are salient features of behavior regardless of the brevity of the intermission in ongoing behavior, the first method would be better. However, the binary method of representation has in its favor a simplicity not shared by the first system, and it loses information only because of the momentary ons or offs of the behavior.

We used the first method for our time lag analysis, which emphasized starts and stops, and we used a derivative of the binary N-tuple method described above for the sequential machine analysis because its holistic character was in keeping with that method.

Returning to Figure 1, we see that each of the infant behavioral classes has its occurrences in each time unit listed in a row to its right. Each column headed by a time interval and going across all the infant behaviors repre-

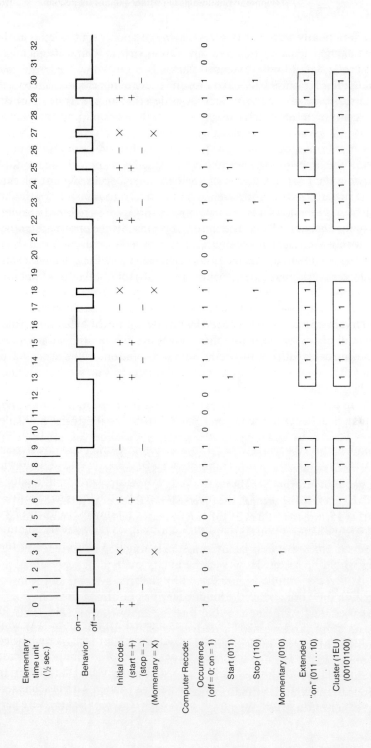

Figure 2. Temporal features of a coded variable; entries are simulations of analyzed data.

sents a 4-tuple of infant behavior, which is renamed with the letter at the bottom of each column. Adjacent intervals having the same events might then be collapsed into one extended unit.

If the researcher believes that only the order of occurrence is relevant, not the real time of occurrence, a time-ordered sequence made up of extended units of behavior may be formed as in the example and analyzed as was done in our sequential matching analysis.

Smoothing Spurious Discontinuities

Most behavioral data contain variance that is due to processes not relevant to the major underlying structure. In occurrence/nonoccurrence data this "noise" may appear as short interruptions in the flow of ongoing behavior. For example, breath taking during the performance of a spoken utterance may not be perceived as a meaningful discontinuity by the listener. If this is true, then leaving these discontinuities intact will make the detection of any underlying interactional relationship more difficult. These discontinuities may be smoothed as illustrated in the last row of Figure 2, which gives an example of combining three separate interludes of extended behaviors into one interlude by clustering when interludes are separated by less than some criterion distance (in this case, one elementary time unit). The reformed data may then be analyzed with a reduced set of starts and stops.

THE DATA BASE

Almost a decade ago the senior author instigated a small project for the purpose of exploring the ability of different analytic methods to detect apparent causal relationships in the interaction of mother and infant. Several mothers of recently born infants were asked if they would be willing to come to a nursery setting in a university behavioral science building for a weekly hour-long period throughout several months so that the investigators could collect some naturalistic videotapes of infant development. Two of the mothers were able to attend with reasonable regularity throughout the period. One of the dyads (dyad A) provided the data used in this chapter.

Collection of Data

The dyads were videotaped, 45 minutes per session, in a $12' \times 14'$ room by means of a camera with a wide angle lens located behind a one-way window. Nine to ten sessions per dyad, including the first four, were labeled "baseline" sessions to reflect two conditions: no modifications were made in the environment, and no special instructions were given to the mother. In five to six additional sessions per dyad, which alternated with baseline sessions after the fourth session, one or both of two manipulations were performed. Toys were removed from the setting, the mother was instructed not to interact with the child unless she felt it was necessary, or both actions were implemented. The latter sets of "experimental" sessions were included to check on the validity of certain inferences about the capacities of the infant or the mother that might be drawn on the basis of naturalistic data alone.

Coding of Primitives and Data Reliability

Initially, the principal investigator and several students and assistants casually observed large samples of the videotapes to get a sense of what elementary units might be worth coding. The basic mind-set recommended by the investigator is that minimal acts be defined on the grounds of being intuitively or theoretically meaningful and having some reasonable likelihood of being discriminated as such by the other member of the subject dyad. After extensive observations and consultations, one particular code was selected for general analytic purposes.

The code consisted of a hierarchical system of behaviors of each actor (mother or infant), organized within major modalities of action (visual, vocal, locomotion, object manipulation, and person contact). Each binary event was coded in terms of its start time and stop time to the nearest half-second, using a digital clock superimposed on the videotape. Events that lasted no more than a half-second (momentary) also were recorded. Many events could occur simultaneously in an interval. For example, the infant might simultaneously look at an object or a person, vocalize, change position, and manipulate an object.

A variety of computer programs, labeled UTILITY programs, were developed to detect logical errors, provide simple distributional summaries, and perform other mundane manipulations of the data. Another diverse set of programs, labeled RELATIONAL programs, were concerned with detecting temporal relationships within the data.

Reliability coefficients were collected on a substantial subset of the data. Coefficients of agreement between the principal investigator and an assistant, whose data were used in the computer analysis, ranged from 0.70 to 0.95 per category. The written coding system was used as the basis for additional reliability coding by a graduate student unfamiliar with the data. Her agreement with the prior assistant ranged from 0.32 to 0.97. After observation of discrepancies, the code was revised to include implicit assumptions shared by the investigator and the first coder. The second coder observed additional data sets, with reliability coefficients ranging from 0.70 to 0.97.

These coefficients were computed on the basis of occurrence of events during a time interval. A more restrictive feature of the coded events was their start and stop times. Allowing a half-second leeway between the start times perceived by coders, agreement ranged from 61% to 84% over categories. Allowing a full second (two-interval) leeway, the coefficients ranged from 70% to 84%. Several potential variables were reluctantly discarded because of low reliability; for example, pointing by the infant in the direction of an object was not reliably discriminable from motor excitement.

METHODS OF DATA ANALYSIS

Systems Versus Bivariate Analysis of Interpersonal Relationships

Among the indefinitely large number of analytic procedures that can be used in the search for interpersonal structure in complex distributions of classes of behavior, two basic approaches stand out. One is the holistic or systems approach, in which the entire set of data is analyzed simultaneously for structural properties. This approach is intuitively more compatible with the reasoning that underlies the naturalistic descriptive method, and particularly with the field theoretical assumption that the parts of complex systems tend to interact. The associated drawback of the procedures is that unless human social relationships are composed of relatively simple structures of action patterns, such as those that have been observed in other species, or of the precise synchronies observed by Condon, the resulting structure may still be too complex to be comprehended by the investigator.

An alternative is to analyze the data in a more piecemeal fashion, such that any relationships that emerge will be more easily interpretable. In its simplest form, this method applies the bivariate relational strategy of experimental studies to parts of the descriptive data. A major problem with this approach is that it is likely to miss the opportunity to detect multivariate interactions among variables (e.g., when neither event A nor B affects C, but the combination of A and B does affect C, either in a sequential manner or as a co-occurring pair). Also it may be difficult to integrate and interpret the pattern of relationships between large numbers of significantly interrelated pairs of variables, particularly if the temporal direction and the time lag of each related pair are taken into account.

As in any other scientific search for structure, we say we have "found" a temporal pattern of events when that pattern is repeated often enough to make its accidental happening unlikely. Otherwise we have only noted a temporal sequence or series whose structure may not have any useful implications. Both methods presented in this chapter rely essentially on redundancy to find relationships. One can imagine an indefinitely large number of temporal patterns that might connect behavioral events. When a data structure and an analytic model are chosen as tools for conducting investigations into the structure of interaction, these tools can be thought of as filters that select out certain temporal structures, but let other possible ones slip through.

There seems to be no certain way to choose the "best filter." We think therefore that the application of a variety of methods and data structures to mother-infant interaction might yield a greater depth of knowledge about the interaction and provide information about which techniques filter out the most useful structures. Hence we chose to search for temporal patterns in our data at both ends of the spectrum of methods. To search out candidates for simple classical causal relationships, we used bivariate lag analyses that yielded the frequencies or, equivalently, the sample probabilities of one event class following another at various time lags. In contrast, for a holistic systems method we chose a completely deterministic sequential machine model fitted to our data, to be able to completely and exactly recreate the original data string given the appropriate inputs.

Sequential Machine Model   The term "sequential machine" has ordinary language connotations of a mindless mechanism, and thus might have offensive implications for psychologists with a humanistic orientation. However, it is merely a formal technical term that describes a decision-making device, consisting of a network of states that respond to an input (while in a given state), with both an output and a transition to another state. In applying this concept to the human being, states of the device may be thought of in terms of colloquially apprehended "states of mind" or of body. Similarly, inputs and outputs may be thought of as stimuli and responses.

Description and Example of a Sequential Machine and Its Minimization   To investigate the behavior of a system relative to the external events bearing on that system, without knowledge of the internal structure of the system, one may construct a mathematical model of the system that relates the inputs to the system to the outputs from the system. If this relationship is not single valued (i.e., if the same input produces different outputs at different times), a set of relationships between the inputs and outputs must be constructed so that each relationship is single valued but occurs at a different time in the sequence of events composed of inputs and outputs to and from the model. These different single-valued relationships are called "states" of the model of the system.

Automata theory is a part of systems theory that deals with discrete inputs, outputs, and states. As such it is adaptable to the study of human interactions in which behavior is characterized in discrete categories. A deterministic, finite, automaton that produces an output for each input is called a sequential machine model and can be defined as follows:

Let: (1) $I = (i_1, i_2, \ldots)$ be the set of inputs.
        (2) $O = (o_1, o_2, \ldots)$ be the set of outputs.

(3) $S = (s_1, s_2, \ldots)$ be the set of states.
(4) f be a function of the current input and state ($I \times S$), which yields the next state. This function is known as the "next state function."
(5) g be a function of the current input and state, which yields the output. This function is called the "output function."

When the number of inputs and states are finite, f and g may simply be represented by two-dimensional tables associated with each state, giving the relationship between the input and the next state, and between the input and the output, respectively.

Suppose we have a set of data representing the sequential interaction of a mother with her infant, and we wish to construct a model of this interaction. Ideally our model would have two properties:

1. Given a representation of the original mother input string of behaviors, we would like the model to produce an exact representation of the original output string of behaviors produced by the infant.
2. The sequential machine model should have the minimum number of states necessary to satisfy item 1, to give the most parsimonious model fitting the data.

The first of these requirements is easily met by simply having one state for each input-output pair in the sequence. The machine thus produced is called a chain sequential machine Booth (1967) has a general description.

The second requirement depends on the recognition of patterns in the data whose descriptions are more succinct than the original data strings.

As an example, suppose we have the following categories of behavior:

I. Mother behaviors
    1. Mother looks at infant (ML)
    2. Mother asks question of infant (MQ)
    3. Mother lightly stimulates infant (MLS)
    4. Mother stimulates infant in a rough or arousing manner (MAS)
    5. Mother exhibits no behavior impinging on the infant (MN = mother nonactive)

II. Infant behaviors
    1. Infant looks at mother (IL)
    2. Infant coos (IC)
    3. Infant grunts (IG)
    4. Infant cries (ICR)
    5. Infant exhibits no exogenous behavior (IN)

Suppose the following sequential events are recorded: MN, IG, MQ, IG, MN, IG, MLS, ICR, MN, ICR, MLS, IG, MLS, ICR, MAS, IC, MLS, IC, MN, IG, MQ, IG, MLS, ICR, MAS, IC, MQ, ICR, MN, ICR.

A transition diagram of the chain sequential machine for these data is given in Figure 3. The states are represented by numbered circles, the state

170   Rosenfeld and Remmers

Figure 3.   Transition diagram of the chain sequential machine.

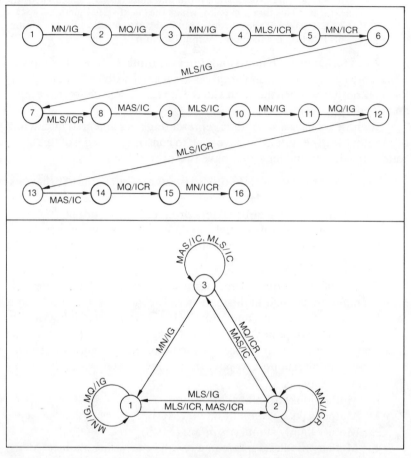

Figure 4.   Input-output sequence for the chain sequential machine of Figure 3, modeled with fewer states.

transitions by the arrows, and the inputs or outputs by the labels on the arrows.

This same input-output sequence is modeled with a much smaller number of states in Figure 4. Each state in Figure 4 can be thought of as consisting of a set of states from the chain machine of Figure 3. State 1 of Figure 4 consists of the set of states (1, 2, 3, 4, 7, 11, 12) in Figure 3, state 2 of Figure 4 consists of the set of states (5, 6, 8, 13, 15, 16), and state 3 of Figure 4 consists of the set of states (9, 10, 14). Note that this is an incompletely specified machine because f and g are not given for all possible inputs.

The machine constructed above might be called an "infant machine" because it models the coded infant behavior (output), given the string of coded mother behavior (input). By using the series of infant behaviors as inputs and the series of mother behaviors as outputs, we could create a "mother machine." We could also consider the mother-infant pair as an entity using their joint behavior, successively, as output and then as input for the construction of a "mother-infant machine." We have so far concentrated on the infant machine; however it might be interesting to attempt to compare the size and structures of the "mother machine" and the "infant machine" with the joint mother-infant machine.

Several computer programs were written to effect the transition from a chain sequential machine to a minimized sequential machine as illustrated by the transition from the machine in Figure 3 to the minimization in Figure 4.

Several knotty problems became evident as the algorithms were written and tested. The most interesting and serious was that beginning with a large, incompletely specified chain sequential machine, it is usually possible to find several different irreducible machines (i.e., machines that are minimal in that no further reduction is possible by combining states). This happens because during the reduction of the original machine there were always choices to make of which state collapses first. To choose one state reduction, in many instances, excluded the possibility of some other collapse. Thus the order of collapse of potentially redundant states interacted with the final form and size of the irreducible machine obtained. We were not able to find any reasonably inexpensive method for determining when we had obtained an irreducible machine that was minimum among all possible irreducible machines equivalent to the original chain sequential machine. (A very expensive method is to generate all irreducible machines and choose one of the minimal ones.) This problem does not appear for completely specified machines, whose more restricted nature forces single minima for which algorithms are known.

We proceeded by programming several different heuristic algorithms, running each with the data, and choosing the minimum machine produced. The various programs were also run on many sets of randomized data. In each case the same program produced the smallest machine. For example, one heuristic was to reduce the machine by first collapsing the two longest compatible strings of states and repeating this procedure on each new machine generated until no further collapses were possible. Another heuristic was to first collapse the largest number of compatible strings of states, each of which was at least of length two.

The second procedure worked the best, and using it we were able to reduce a machine of 1197 infant states (modeling infant behavior given mother input behavior) to 215 infant states or 18% of the original number of states. This is a seemingly large reduction, but we had no clear idea of how much of this reduction was due to chance and no known statistical methods to guide us.

We therefore resorted to using experimental techniques on our model. By reversing the time order of either the mother or the infant behavior series, or by dividing each in half and reversing the time order of each half and concatenating the parts, we formed four sets of test data in which the mother-infant relational sequence was destroyed but most of the distributional structure of each individual was maintained. Running these data sets through the program gave us a benchmark of "nonsocial structure" to which we might compare the machines derived from the fully structured data. We ran these benchmark data sets, obtaining reductions from 1197 to 570, 588, and 629 states, which is about a 50% reduction. Comparison of these results to the 215 states obtained from the unmodified data set indicates that there is a substantial amount of structure in the relationship of mother behavior to infant behavior.

Although this reduction in complexity was substantial, it still left a model that was beyond our perceptual and cognitive abilities to understand and codify for general consumption and application. This lack of intuitive comprehension and easily codified laws does not, however, preclude the usefulness of the model for predictive purposes. "Experiments" (simulations) may be run on the model to indicate the optimal choice between various schemes of intervention an experimenter or a therapist may wish to employ. This is an advantage to the experimenter, who without confounding future experiments may run pilot studies on the machine, formed from naturalistic data taken on the subjects' interactions. Simulation techniques have been used successfully by industry and government agencies to solve a great variety of problems occurring in systems that are too complex for comprehension by ordinary means.

Bivariate Lag Analysis

In the sequential machine analysis of our data we sacrificed comprehensibility for comprehensiveness. This led us to reconsider the complementary value of less holistic approaches, which are likely to provide a clearer understanding of subparts of the larger data structure. The simplest level of structure in the social interaction process is the bivariate temporal relationship. The detection of structure at the bivariate level is fundamental to a variety of theories of social development and performance. For example, social learning theory emphasizes the systematic association of behavior with short-term consequences (reinforcers) and antecedents (discriminative stimuli, models) in the development of classes of behavior (Gewirtz, 1969). Similarly, ethologists seek the immediate social "causes" of a class of behavior and its "functional" consequences (Blurton-Jones, 1972).

One could seek analogous evidence in naturalistic data. For example, a social behavior might be designated as a reasonable candidate for the label "social reinforcer" if evidence of its increasing rate of occurrence following a particular category of subject behavior were followed by evidence of an increase in rate of the subject's behavior class. Similarly, if the addition of a regularly occurring social antecedent to the sequence above also resulted in an increase in probability of performance of the subject's behavior class, the antecedent could be labeled a likely "discriminative stimulus." In either case, the subject's class of behavior could reasonably be considered to be an "operant." Thus we considered bivariate temporal analysis to be a basic first step toward the extraction from naturalistic data of evidence for the structure and development of interpersonal relationships.

Our development of bivariate analytic methods generally followed a progression of successive approximations. Initially we used conventional statistical methods to scan large numbers of paired variables for evidence of gross temporal relationship. For example, early in the project a computer search was performed in which the data string was segmented into 4-second blocks by collapsing across sequences of eight half-second elementary time units.

Gross temporal relationships at the 4-second level in each of the nine baseline sessions of dyad A were assessed by means of the chi square statistic. A "positive" association was attributed to the pairs of behaviors that mutually occurred in the same 4-second intervals significantly beyond the level expected on the basis of their individual frequency distributions. For example, the pairs M1 (mother looks at infant) and I1.E (infant looks at mother) were significantly positively related in seven of the nine sessions. When this analysis was rerun with the data segmented at 1-second intervals, significant positive associations were found in all nine sessions.

However, such evidence of temporal association is compatible with a variety of interpretations about the specific nature of the connection between the classes of behavior. Was the mother's behavior contingent on the occurrence of the infant's? Vice versa? Both? At what time lags? Or did the two classes of events tend to co-occur, perhaps as the result of some unassessed additional behavioral variables or a tendency to synchronize rhythms? How much of the strength of the association was attributable to spurious inflation of numbers of events, such as the counting of continuations of a single long look as separate events because these events overlapped adjacent intervals? Even if the events in each distribution were separate, to what degree was the infant's response due to the immediately preceding mother act rather than to some number of replications of the act?

To pursue such questions, a set of computer programs were written (by author Remmers) for assessing directional relationships at different time lags.

A lag analysis determines the frequency with which events of one class follow events of another class at various time lags. The strength and statistical significance of a lagged relationship is a function of the amount by which the frequency of the lagged event differs from the level expected by chance. A useful measure of the relationship between events is the relative frequency of occurrence of a lagged pair of events, that is, the frequency of occurrence of the lagged pair divided by the number of opportunities for its occurrence. If the lag is k time units, this relative frequency is usually called the sample transitional probability of order k. Other researchers have used bivariate programs for assessing relationships at successive time lags between occurrences of two classes of events (e.g., Bakeman and Dabbs, 1976; Kaye, 1977; Sackett, 1978). The present programs differ from the others primarily by providing a set of procedures for "filtering" out the effects of occurrences of events from one or both event classes when these intervene between single pairs of events.

To illustrate the need for such filters, consider the three data sequences:

A. _ _ _ _ _ _ M M M _ I I I _ _ _ _ _
B. M _ M _ I _ _ M M _ _ I _ M _ _ M I
C. M _ _ _ I _ M _ _ _ I _ _ M _ _ _ I.

If these small data sets were each representative of much longer sequences of mother-infant data, they would indicate very different temporal relationships. However, totaling up all the M → I pairs at lags between 0 and 18, all three reach the maximum possible frequency of 3 at lag 4.

This is the most straightforward method of lag analysis. It picks up all three examples of a lag 4 relationship but it does not discriminate among them.

An intuitive classification of these examples might consider sequence A to be the infant's rhythmic imitation of the pattern of mother behavior after a wait of four time units. One can imagine the sequence going on with different patterns of mother behavior followed by replications in the infant's behavior (e.g., M _ M _ I _ I _ _ M _ _ M I _ _ I, etc.)

In the second data set the infant is evidently responding to particular instances of mother behavior after a lag of 4 and ignores mother behaviors that fall between the initial mother behavior and its response. The reaction time of the infant seems to be set and intervening mother behaviors do not change it.

The third data set seems to be a very pure example of mother behaves—lag—infant behaves. Notice that the I-to-M intervals do not indicate a reversed lagged relationship, thus one might speculate either that the infant is reinforcing (extinguishing) the mother's behavior or that the mother is providing discriminative stimuli that elicit the infant's behavior.

Three computer programs were written to discriminate among these possibilities. Four types of simple bivariate lag analysis can be distinguished on the basis of permissible intervening events.

Different versions of our basic lag program were written to discriminate among the examples given above. The most general, which we call type I, considers all lagged pairs from each antecedent event A to each subsequent event B, regardless of other occurrences of A and B that fall between. This is the type of time lag analysis discussed by Sackett (1978). The remaining programs filter out the bivariate distributional properties corresponding to data sets B and C. Significant results in the more filtered analysis permit more specific interpretations than in the less filtered analyses. Also, if the more general analyses produce significant results, but not the more filtered analyses, the results can be attributed to the residual distributional properties remaining at the more general level.

The types of analysis discussed here are not the same as those discussed by Sackett. His typology refers to combinations of events classified as starts and stops, whereas ours refers to the differing importance of intervening occurrences of events. In the present examples, all events are starts (e.g., infant starts looking after mother starts talking) and correspond to Sackett's typology. (Our programs also will produce stop to start, start to stop, and stop to stop histograms, each of which may indicate quite different relationships in the data.) Initial applications of the filtering procedures to the mother-infant data base have proved to be very informative. Thus a relatively detailed explanation of the filtering methods is presented. To exemplify the method, actual results are presented in Figures 5 through 9 from the relationship infant looks at mother (I1.E) following mother vocalizes (M4).

The I1.E variable was selected because of its widely recognized importance as a measure of attention and interest, and because of the special importance attributed to the mother as a recipient of infant attention. The M4 category includes a wide variety of verbal and vocal subcategories. They were collapsed in the present illustration to increase the number of cases, thereby ensuring statistical reliability.

Type I Analysis   Given the null hypothesis of no relationship between A and B, the expected frequency distribution for the type I histogram (Figure 5) is the uniform distribution whose height can be best estimated by the formula:

$$\frac{N_A N_B}{N_{TU}} = N_A \, p(B)$$

where N_A is the number of A's, N_B is the number of B's, N_{TU} is the total number of time units in the data sample, and $p(B)$ is the relative frequency of B or the sample probability of B occurring in a time unit. The standard error (SE), can be estimated by:

$$SE = \sqrt{N_A \, p(B) \, (1 - p(B))}$$

The last formula must be qualified because the data string is finite, hence an A closer to the end of the data string than the lag being considered will have no opportunity to be paired with a B at that lag. Therefore N_A

should be reduced, to account for the data truncation, by an amount equal to that which is indicated by the formula:

$$k \; \frac{N_A}{N_{TU}}$$

where k is the lag. So

$$N_A - k \; \frac{N_A}{N_{TU}}$$

should be substituted for N_A. In our potential application we simply removed from consideration all A's whose distance from the end of the data string was within the maximum lag considered. This meant that we could use the same statistics for all lags in the type I histograms. We could do this with little relative loss of data because we had several thousand time units in our data string. For short data strings one should recalculate for each lag.

If there are insufficient data on the occurrences of either A's or B's, the use of the formula for SE given above may prove to be inaccurate. Our heuristic criterion, derived from the analysis of our data, is that whenever the height of the frequency histogram is greater than 20/(expected height), the formulas will prove accurate enough. [A stricter criterion given by Hays (1963:230) requires $N_A \, p(B)$ and $N_A \, (1-p(B))$ both ≥ 10.] However, frequencies F below that level must have their significance judged by the exact computation of the binomial probabilities given by:

$$P(F \geq FO \text{ (observed frequency))} = 1 - \sum_{i=0}^{FO} \binom{N_A}{i} (1-p(B))^{FO-i} \, p(B)^i$$

In interactional analyses there is always the danger that the univariate distributional properties of the variables will confound the analysis of the bivariate lagged distributions. The tendency for some mother and infant behaviors to occur in bursts (momentary in nearly every time interval) would cause problems in the interpretation of histograms produced by type I analysis. If in the distributions of the mother and infant behaviors there is a large burst of behavior in each case, there will be an elevation in the type I histogram corresponding to the lag between each mother and each infant burst. This elevation will occur even if there is no "real" relationship between the two categories of bursts.[1]

---

[1] If there are a great number of bursts in the data, these bursts may be reclassified by the programs as behaviors in themselves. These new events might then be analyzed for their interactional significance. The study of univariate bursting behavior, an interesting area in itself, is discussed by Fagen and Young (1978) and by Kaye (1977).

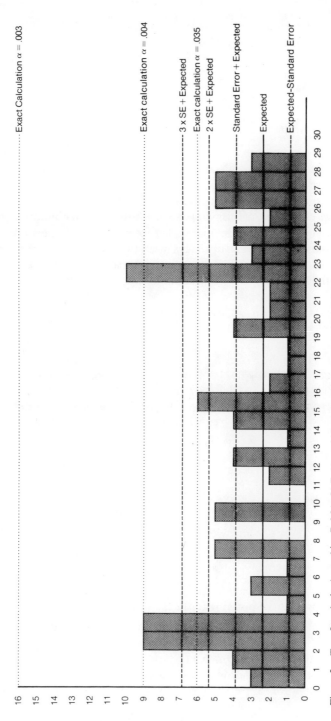

Figure 5.   Type I analysis, A anything B, M4→II.E, N_{M4} = 237, $N_{II.E}$ = 45, expected = 2.35, SE = 1.49, N_{TU} = 4546.

One discovery was that some significant "bumps" (elevations) in our type I histograms were indeed the result of a burst of A behaviors followed at some lag by a burst of B behaviors, rather than by a repeated pattern of A lag B . . . A lag B . . . . After that experience we always ran the auto-histograms from A to A and B to B to check for bursting in the data.

At the same time we had looked more carefully at some possible relationships that fell just below the level of significance using type I analysis and discovered that those relationships were quite significant when removed from the din of background noise inherent in the very general type I analysis. We then decided that programs should be written to detect much more specific types of relationship.

Type II Analysis   Type II analysis acts as a finer filter than type I and allows only those A → B pairs to contribute to the histograms in which B is the first occurrence following an A. Figure 6 is an example of type II analysis on the same data analyzed by type I in Figure 5. Note that the frequencies at lags 2, 3, 15, and 22 are not as significant under type I analysis as they are under type II.

The null hypothesis for type II analysis can be considered to be the result of a Poisson process; hence the expected frequency (F_k) at lag k can be estimated from the continuous Poisson model by:

$$E(F_k) = N_A \left(e^{-r(k+1/2)} - e^{-r(k+3/2)}\right)$$

where r is the sample rate of occurrence of B per time unit. Of course, r is equal to $p(B)$ if rate is defined relative to the observational time units rather than some external time base. The formula above is easily derivable from the reverse cumulative frequency distribution for intervals between events in a Poisson process (note that intervals between events are one time unit shorter than lags). The probability that the lag is greater than or equal to k is given by $e^{-r(k+1)}$, hence the cumulative frequency of lags of size k or greater is given by $N_A e^{-r(k+1)}$ (see Breiman, 1969; Cox and Lewis, 1966). These formulas represent continuous processes and only approximate the discrete processes dealt with in this chapter. If $p(B)$ is large, the approximation may not be satisfactory and it may be necessary to calculate exact probabilities. These calculations, which are not too difficult if a computer is used, are given for the null hypothesis by:

$$E(F_k) = N_A (1-p(B))^{k-1} p(B)$$

where $(1-p(B))^{k-1}p(B)$ is the expected transitional probability of B at lag k, given A. For example, if $p(B) = 0.05$, the continuous approximation gives 0.04757 and the exact calculation gives 0.04750. These values are virtually identical, but with $p(B) = 0.5$ the continuous approximation gives 0.3064 and the exact calculation gives 0.2500 N_A. Thus in the second example the approximation overestimates the expected value, making it more likely

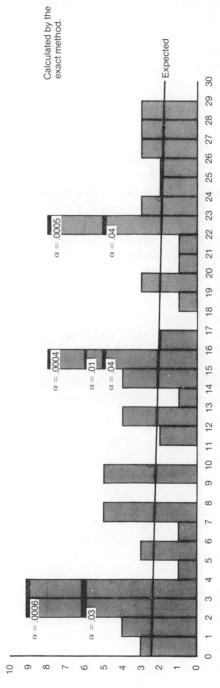

Figure 6. Type II analysis, A next B, M4→ II.E, $N_{M4} = 237$, $N_{II.E} = 45$; calculated by the exact method.

that a truly significant "bump" would be falsely rejected and a nonsignificant suppression would be falsely accepted. The statistical significance may be tested by means of the same formulas used for type I, but with the substitution of the transitional probability expected at each lag k under the null hypothesis for the quantity $p(B)$. For example, the formula for the calculation from the binomial would become:

$$P(F \geq FO) = \sum_{\substack{iMO \\ i=o}}^{FO} \binom{N_A}{i} \; [1 - (1 - p(B))^{k-1} p(B)] \quad {}^{NA-i} \; [(1-p(B))^{k-1} p(B)]^{i}$$

Type III Analysis   Lag analysis type III only allows B's but not A's to fall between any AB pair included in the histogram. The statistical properties of the histogram generated by this analysis are more complicated in that they depend directly on the temporal autorelationships of the A's as well as on the transitional probabilities relating the A's to the B's. There is a hierarchical relationship between type I and either type II or type III in that a type I histogram includes all the pairs in the II and III histograms, but the type II and III histograms are not hierarchically related to each other. Type IV pairs are included in both type II and type III histograms. We decided to utilize the hierarchical chain of analyses I, II, and IV, excluding for the present type III.

Type IV Analysis   The finest filter, type IV, allows only AB pairs that are devoid of intervening occurrences of either A's or B's. The statistical properties of type IV histograms, like those of type III, also involve the distribution of A's; however, the importance of type IV as a filter for only the clearest A lag B relationships repays the more difficult computations. The expected for a type IV histogram at lag k is given by:

$$N_A \; [(1 - p(B)) \; (1 - p(A))]^{k-1} p(B)$$

The substitution of this value divided by N_A (the expected probability of B lag k, given A) for $p(B)$ in the type I formulas gives the appropriate significance values.

Illustrative Results

Figure 5 presents the results of a type I analysis of the relationship "I1.E follows M4" for infant A at age 29 weeks. The abscissa lists 30 time intervals, an arbitrary number set at the beginning of a computer run. These range from the zero interval, in which infant behavior occurs in the same interval as mother behavior, to lags of 1 through 29 intervals. The ordinate in Figure 5 shows the number of times the infant behaviors occurred at each time lag from the mothers' behaviors.

The interval size selected was the elementary coding unit (a half-second). Larger sized units can be (and were) used for heuristic purposes. But they cannot be used legitimately because a larger interval could include

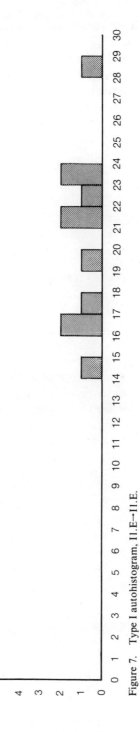

Figure 7. Type I autohistogram, II.E.—II.E.

several occurrences of mother or infant behavior. Each of the occurrences of mother behavior in one interval would then be paired to each infant behavior in a later time interval. This would result in an artificially inflated histogram interval, falsely indicating a lagged relationship. If the elementary half-second unit were used, however, no infant or mother act could be paired more than once at a given lag.

The entire session from which the data were drawn consisted of 4540 elementary units (about 43 minutes). During the session the infant initiated gazes toward the mother 45 times, and the mother initiated vocalizations 237 times. The maximum possible height of the lag histogram is 45, which would have occurred if each of the 45 infant acts had followed a separate mother act at exactly the same time lag. In actuality, the highest interval frequency obtained was 10.

Visual inspection of Figure 5 suggests that there may be relationships between mother and infant behaviors at lags 2 and 3 and again at lag 23. Statistical tests were performed to determine the frequency needed to assume a significant relationship. Using the formula expressed earlier, the mean expected frequency per lag is found to be 2.35. Using the normal curve approximation, the standard error is calculated as 1.49. For a particular lag frequency to reach the 0.05 level of significance it must be 1.96 standard errors above the mean, or 5.27, or in integer terms, 6. Four of the 30 lag frequencies are 6 or greater, an outcome that is unlikely to occur by chance ($\alpha = 0.045$). But inasmuch as the data in the histogram did not reach our minimal criterion for the applicability of the normal curve approximation, the obtained frequencies were tested for their exact probabilities of occurrence using the binomial test. The probability, given the null hypothesis, of obtaining a frequency of 6 or greater is 0.035. The probability of obtaining 9 or greater at lags 2 and 3 is 0.004, and the probability of a 10 or greater at lag 22 is 0.0035.

Thus Figure 5 indicates that there were significant relationships at four lags: 2, 3, 15, and 22. That is, the infant initiated gazes at the mother 1, 1.5, 7.5, and 11 seconds after the mother initiated a vocalization. We know that the looks at lag 2 and at lag 3 were in reaction to different occurrences of mother vocalization because the autohistogram of infant looks (Figure 7) indicated a minimal lag of 14 units before this behavior occurred again. But were the gazes at 8 and 11.5 seconds also independent? Or might the infant have given several looks to a single vocalization? Or might the mother have given several vocalizations in a sequence, each of which was related to the same infant gaze? These possibilities all were confounded in the type I analysis.

Thus type II and type IV analyses also were performed to remove the ambiguity from the results.

The type II analysis (Figure 6) eliminated or filtered out all intervals in which a mother vocalization was followed by more than one infant gaze. The results of the type I analysis were upheld using the exact calculation. All four previously significant lag frequencies remained significant (with respective α levels of 0.0006, 0.0006, 0.01, and 0.0005). Thus the different lagged relationships contained different infant looking responses.

In the type IV analysis shown in Figure 8, however, the first two lags (frequencies of 8 and 6) remained significant: 0.0013 and 0.019). The previously significant frequency at lag 15 was reduced to zero. The frequency at lag 22 was reduced to 2 from 8, with the loss of a convincing significance level and frequency, indicating that the relationship is type II but not type IV. This is not surprising, given the distribution of the autohistogram of M4 (Figure 9), which makes type IV relationships at this lag unlikely. Thus the significant relationships at lags 2 and 3 were the results of independent occurrences of both mother and infant events and were not confounded by intervening repetitions of either, whereas the initial relationships at lags 15 and 22 may have been attributable to repetitive occurrences of the mother's vocalization, or at least were not destroyed by the intervening other vocalizations.

A whimsical possibility is that the behaviors at lags 2 and 3 follow the last of these intervening mother vocalizations in either the lag 15 or 22 relationships and the infant is waiting until the mother stops talking before looking at her (possibly reinforcing the cessation of vocalization). To further elucidate these possibilities, the set of programs should be run from stops in the mother vocalizations (M4) to starts of infant looks at mother (I1.E).

The major point is that significant relationships were found at specific lags. These results enable the researcher to know where to look in the "naturalistic" data to discover the intricate details of interaction, and they may indicate the forms to be taken by the controlled experiment necessary for validation of the results.

CONCLUSIONS

The holistic sequential machine and the bivariate filtered lag approaches that were developed and tested were successful in two respects. Workable computer programs were written for each method. And both methods produced some meaningful results in the initial applications to mother-infant interaction data.

The amount of data reduction obtained in the application of the sequential machine model was encouraging. However, the complexity and uninterpretability of the reduced model was disappointing, at least in rela-

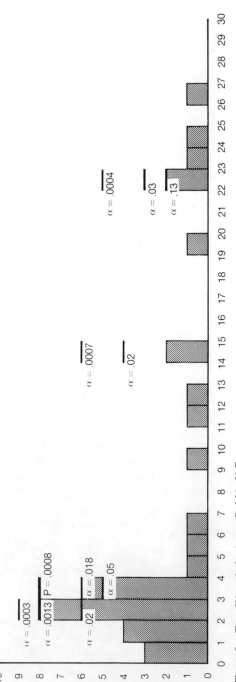

Figure 8. Type IV analysis, A zero B, M4→II.E.

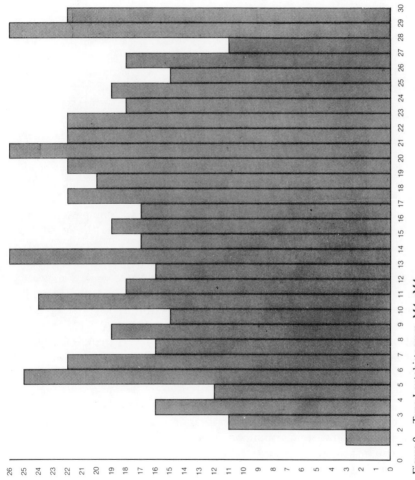

Figure 9. Type I autohistogram, M4→M4.

tion to what the beliefs of other researchers suggested one should have obtained. Still, there is an indefinitely large number of ways in which complex descriptive data can be modeled; thus it is possible that some variations in the design and usage of the sequential machine idea may result in simpler and more interpretable outcomes.

Several possibilities have occurred to the authors. One is to select, as the mother and infant input strings, sets of behavior classes all of which are a priori meaningful to the investigators. In the present case, meaningful elementary variables were combined into N-tuples, many of which were not themselves meaningful. This practice might have led to the splitting of coherent event classes on the basis of presence versus absence of trivial covariates. Another possibility would be to select fewer variables than the 61 mother and 27 infant classes presently included (although one must accept the risk of discarding some potentially important distinctions). Also, one might consider constructing a probabilistic sequential machine (see Paz, 1971) in which the relationships between inputs and outputs, and the relationships between inputs and states, are probabilistically, not precisely, described as in the present deterministic model. Finally, one might consider defining the input-output relationships in terms of real time lags rather than the sequences of extended units used in the present analysis. Although the addition of the real time feature may add to the complexity of the model, time lag did prove to be an important characteristic of mother-infant relationships in the bivariate lag approach.

Alternatively, or additionally, one might seriously ponder the possibility that natural mother-infant interaction truly is very complex, and that a comprehensive model of the data will necessarily be correspondingly difficult to interpret. This does not imply that behavior in social settings is not determined; but in humans it is likely that many of the explanatory variables are located in the heads of the participants rather than in their overt behavior. Even if this is true, an accurate though incomprehensible model may prove to have predictive value for human relationships just as it has had for complicated business organizations.

The illustrations of the application of the bivariate lag programs were encouraging; our new filtering methods for the lag analysis were helpful in sorting out different distributional properties of the behavior classes that contributed to the lag relationships. Thus, we recommend the addition of the filtering methods to the currently available array of methods for bivariate lag analysis.

The bivariate lag analyses did point to the serious problem of running out of data. After years in the laboratory, evoking behaviors at high rates in sessions lasting only minutes, it is sobering to have obtained sparse distributions of many interesting variables in sessions lasting three-quarters of an hour, or sometimes even across sets of sessions totaling several hours.

One might alleviate this deficiency to some degree by arranging settings that will evoke higher rates of behavior or by selectively coding episodes in which high rates occur. But many important classes of behavior are likely to be manifest as rare events (e.g., the infant's earliest words and gestures, the parent's use of strong sanctions), and these are problematic for purposes of inferential statistical analysis.

In particular, we demonstrated how the use of continuous distributional estimates of sampling distribution parameters, when the data consist of small samples of discrete events, can lead to erroneous conclusions about statistical significance. Thus we recommend the calculation of exact probabilities when the number of events is too small to meet conventional criteria. The exact tests for testing statistical significance in the various filtered lag approaches should be helpful in protecting against biased evaluations. However, it would be even better for students of early social development to develop the patience to collect much larger data samples on single cases than has hitherto been customary.

ACKNOWLEDGMENTS

The research reported here was supported by grant HD002528 from the National Institute for Child Health and Human Development (NICHHD), administered through the Kansas Center for Mental Retardation and Human Development and by an NICHHD predoctoral traineeship (T32HD007173) to the junior author. Many individuals contributed to the project. Gail Young Browne was centrally involved in the recruiting and videotaping of subjects and Virginia Stark in the coding of data. Others who contributed to coding and data preparations were Margaret Hancks, Richard Levin, Paul Greenbaum, Joe Holman, and Carol Lollman. The computer programs written by Remmers were intended to improve on initial bivariate lag programs written by Jeff Bangert, Bill Maxwell, and Jim Waldby at the University of Kansas Computer Center, and initial efforts toward the development of a sequential machine program by Nimitra Kattiyakulwanich under the direction of Robert Haralick of the Department of Electrical Engineering.

Chapter 10
DEVELOPMENTAL PROCESSES IN PRELINGUISTIC DISCOURSE

Cecelia K. Yoder

One of the most fundamental and generally agreed upon principles of human development is that of integration. Wapner and Werner (1957) have discussed hierarchical integration from the perspective of organismic psychology. It is, however, almost impossible to discuss integration without considering the complementary process of differentiation. Bruner (1969), for example, has detailed the process of integration with respect to the development of eye-hand coordination in the infant. However, integration must be preceded by some important preliminary developments in the areas of visual attention as well as prehension. One of the critical components of visual attention that must be established before eye-hand coordination involves not only "the regulation of attention *placing* but also the withdrawing and shifting of attention" (Bruner, 1969:227). In short, a certain amount of differentiation is required before the process of integration can begin.

Integration is not an all-or-none phenomenon, it is a process. Again drawing from Bruner's study, the early stages of eye-hand coordination are marked by invariance and inflexibility. The sequence "Reach — Grasp — Retrieve — Mouth" (Bruner, 1969:230) is at first "mainly successive with little anticipatory priming" (p. 229). The sequence always terminates at the mouth, and at 7 months interruption of visual contact with the object interrupts the action.

During development, the sequential acts of reaching and grasping seem to require cessation of all other enterprises. Like so much of the child's complex behavior, it involves a total commitment. What is interesting, once visually guided reaching achieves some rough competence, is that attention enters a new phase in its deployment. (pp. 229–230)

189

It is entirely appropriate in the early phases of research into some aspect of development to follow a particular behavior as if it were a unitary phenomenon. For example, since our primary interest here is language, most studies of language development focus on syntax, semantics, or phonology, or more recently, with the shift toward an interaction perspective, communicative skills including kinesics. As a result, we have at least a limited account of development during critical growth periods in some of these areas, but we have very little idea of the overall process of integration of the various communicative resources that make up the repertoire of the normal human adult. Subsequently, we are periodically bewildered by the apparent appearance then disappearance or disintegration of a particular bit of language skill when, for example, a child seems to have mastered the past tense of irregular verb forms such as *came* and *went* only to begin using incorrect forms such as *camed* and *goed* (Ervin, 1964; McNeill, 1970). Similarly some researchers have observed the early occurrence of intonation contours that do not, however, seem to be contrastive (Weir, 1966).

One very reasonable hypothesis for explaining some of the apparent discontinuities in language development is that developments in one area may seem to regress or come to a standstill while development in another area is accelerating. It is well known that development in physical and motor areas interacts with language development. Clark and Bertha Hull (1919) plotted learning curves for vocabulary growth and voluntary bladder control in one infant and found that the bladder curve contained a plateau that coincided with the rise of language development. Likewise as infants begin to walk, language development may hit a plateau; once walking is well under way, language development, particularly vocabulary growth, may spurt. These developmental patterns suggest the fruitfulness of investigating simultaneous developments in areas that show varying degrees of sophistication in an attempt to get at the developmental processes of integration and differentiation of communicative skills.

In 1976 von Raffler-Engel proposed that the task of the decade was "to return to empirical research and to refocus language acquisition within the context of the child's process of socialization" (1976d:287). Not only did she propose placing language development research within the context of socialization, but she also suggested that language development be regarded as one part of the total developing communication system.

> I do not believe that we can fully understand how language is acquired unless we observe it with its context of socialization and unless we look at it as a means of communication together with the other modalities that accompany the process of verbalization. The act of communication seems to involve a pluri-modal behavior. (1976d:288)

The present study takes seriously both proposals and has been strongly influenced and stimulated by much of von Raffler-Engel's pioneering work, particularly in the area of intonation (von Raffler-Engel, 1964, 1972).

BACKGROUND

The period selected for this exploratory study is the portion of the prelinguistic phase during which the child is beginning to make the transition to single-word speech. This phase was chosen because it maximizes the chances of observing varied vocal phenomena, and thus should maximize the possibility of observing the processes of integration and differentiation. In addition, beginning when the system or systems are relatively simple with respect to structure and meaning facilitates an attempt to do a relatively comprehensive in-depth analysis.

The data for this study[1] are transcribed audio- and videotaped verbal and nonverbal behavior from a portion of a 40-minute observation session of a mother and her young son Andy. They played together in a small windowless room equipped with a cabinet, several chairs, and a box of toys. The child was 16 months, 3 weeks of age at the time of the observation. Further details concerning the subjects and the data-gathering procedures and circumstance will be published separately (Tamir, to appear; Yoder, to appear). Only the first half of the observation session, approximately 19 minutes, was used in this analysis. The corresponding corpus is referred to as AI(A).

Elsewhere (Yoder, to appear) the entire AI corpus is analyzed, and it is argued that Andy's vocalizations represented two vocal systems operating in synchrony. One system, referred to as the type X system, was made up of vocalizations that were phonologically approximations of adult English *Huh?*, *huh uh*, and *uh uh* with the additional form, *?V*. However, the intonation on *uh uh* was virtually always a rise rather than the expected fall, indicating disagreement or *no*. The type X system comprised 52% of the 256 vocalizations recorded: 96% of the one-syllable forms had rising intonation, and the remaining 4% had level contours. The two-syllable forms showed greater intonation variation: 32% rises, 16% falls, 4% level, and 48% complex. The high percentage of complex contours on two-syllable vocalizations is to some extent predictable because of the increased options for stress placement, which is a key factor in the identification of intonation contours. Complex contours were defined as any contour type other than a single primary contour with a single primary stress. Most complex contours were either two successive primary contours or a primary with a precontour: syllables preceding a stressed syllable that are "pronounced in the

---

[1] Data for this study were gathered as part of a larger child language development research project codirected with Lynne Bernstein and assisted by Lois Tamir. These data were collected from February to July 1974, using the facilities of the Institute for the Study of Mental Retardation and Related Disabilities, Ann Arbor, Michigan.

same burst of speed with that primary contour but which themselves are unstressed" (Pike, 1945:29).

The type X system appeared to be multifunctional in the sense that no single apparent function or meaning, either referential or pragmatic, could be attached to these forms. Most frequently they seemed to perform a discourse function that permitted Andy to be an adequate though limited conversational partner. A small percentage of these vocalizations (7%) were used for a very interesting interaction in which Andy "showed" or handed his mother an object. On these occasions vocalizing and gesture were simultaneous and, unlike the vast majority of type X turns, these were initiations rather than responses.

The second system of vocalizations was designated type W forms. These forms were either Clear Words (CW), phonetic approximations of a known English form with evidence of meaningful use, or Ambiguous Words (AW), wordlike forms that although possibly phonetically similar to an English form, could not be related to either the verbal or the nonverbal context. An analysis of the five most frequently occurring Clear Words for evidence of productive use of intonation yielded the conclusion that rising intonation was associated with behaviors indicating *engagement*, and falling contours were associated with an attitude of *detachment*. These very general and admittedly tentative meaning characterizations were seen to be consistent with Pike's (1945, 1966) description of the basic contrast in the adult system as incompleteness (rise) versus relaxation or finality (fall).

In addition to formal and functional differences clearly distinguishing the two vocal systems, there was further evidence for considering the two vocalization types as systems from an analysis of mother's discourse acts and moves in relation to Andy's vocalization types. This analysis was based on the system developed by Sinclair and Coulthard (1975) for analyzing discourse structure. The results of this analysis showed differential consequences at the discourse level of Andy's use of type X versus type W vocalizations. Type X vocalizations were most frequently followed by a Directive or a Prompt, acts that structure an Opening (i.e., initiating) move, whereas type W vocalizations were most frequently followed by an Accept or a Reply, acts that structure Answering or Followup moves. These findings were interpreted as indicating that Andy's mother tended to treat and ultimately reward type W vocalizations as appropriate discourse acts in that she was more willing to take a response role. Type X vocalizations were less likely to be treated as appropriate discourse and so mother continued to take the role of initiator.

Although this analysis was fairly comprehensive, it left a number of questions unanswered concerning the function of the type X vocalizations and the function of the AW vocalizations. The analysis did suggest the fruitfulness of analyzing and categorizing prelinguistic forms on purely formal grounds as a step toward discovering functional differences and ultimately developmental processes.

The present work is an extension of this earlier study. It investigates the processes of differentiation and integration by examining verbal and nonverbal communicative resources and using discourse act and vocalization as the main structures for organizing the data. Obviously there are many features, linguistic and nonlinguistic, verbal and nonverbal, that can be classified as communicative resources. The features that are of major interest are intonation (i.e., pitch contour shape and stress); type of pitch movement, glide or step on one-syllable vocalizations; syllable length; voice quality (i.e., loudness, length, interval width, crescendo or decrescendo and key); gesture, particularly arm/hand gestures such as pointing, handing, reaching; gaze direction; and function or meaning. These features were chosen empirically as the most salient and productive or potentially productive in the data under study.

Intonation contours were transcribed using Pike's notation and model of American English intonation (Pike, 1945, 1966). Although this system is based on a phonemic approach, it was utilized in this analysis as a phonetic system comprised of four pitch levels: 1) extra high, 2) high, 3) mid, and 4) low. Pitch contours were characterized in terms of initial pitch, final pitch, and mid-located direction change point, if there was one. Contours begin on stressed syllables and may be preceded by a precontour that is secondary to, although part of, the primary contour. Stress marking then is an important part of the intonation analysis. Type of contour movement was noted for one-syllable vocalizations because both steps and glides were used and gave the impression of contrast.

Voice quality features that were most salient were loudness, key or general pitch level, and length. Three degrees of loudness (soft, normal, and loud) seemed to adequately characterize the observed variations in loudness. Similarly, three degrees of interval width as well as general pitch level seemed to adequately describe these features: narrow, normal, wide, and low, normal, and high. Length was included as a voice quality feature because the phonological features of interest here were nonsegmental rather than segmental. Furthermore, the interesting uses of length were deviations from the norm that occurred in the nonstandard type X vocalizations and seemed to be more appropriately classified with voice quality features. Syllable length was noted as a potentially important feature, along with intonation. Finally crescendo and decrescendo, variants of normal stress described by Pike (1945), were noted.

Gestures that were utilized by the child in accompaniment to his vocalizations were incorporated in the transcriptions. No attempt was made to do a fine-grained analysis of body movement or posture, and frequently the child's face was not visible. In fact, determining exact gaze direction (e.g., at mother's face or at the object she was holding up) was not always possible. However the investigator noted the gestures that seemed to give the most information about the function of the vocalization. Hence arm/hand/finger gestures were of crucial importance, as were general changes in body orientation or positioning (e.g., climbing down from sitting on a chair). Gaze direction with respect to the object of gaze was noted, as was general body positioning with respect to mother.

The final and most difficult aspect of the analysis was that of determining the function of Andy's vocalizations. One very clear aspect of the type X vocalizations that had emerged during the earlier analysis was the observation that at the very least, these utterances served a turn-taking function. They provided material for Andy to take a response role in the dialogue. In the general analysis only mother's utterances had been coded for discourse function, using the system of discourse analysis presented by Sinclair and Coulthard in their book "Towards an Analysis of Discourse" (1975). Although several researchers have developed systems for analyzing the meaning of prelinguistic vocalizations in terms of function, namely, Halliday (1975), Dore et al. (1976), and Carter (1978), none of these systems are embedded within a discourse structure framework. Furthermore several features of the Sinclair and Coulthard system made it appear promising for analyzing mother-child interaction. The system had been developed using classroom behavior (teacher-student interaction) as data. Thus there were role similarities to mother-infant interaction as well as contextual similarities, since the playroom, like the classroom, limits physical movement as well as the unpredictable intrusion of other people or events from the outside world.

The aspects of the Sinclair and Coulthard system that are relevant to this analysis are the bottom two ranks of the analytical hierarchy: act and move. The act is the smallest and most basic unit of the hierarchy. It can be compared most closely to the clause at the grammatical level; however, "when we describe an item as an act we are doing something very different from when we describe it as a clause. Grammar is concerned with the *formal* properties of an item, discourse with the *functional* properties, with what the speaker is using the item for" (Sinclair and Coulthard, 1975:27–28). The act seems to be closely tied to the speaker's intent. However, Sinclair and Coulthard also suggested that "the *discourse* value of an item depends on what linguistic items have preceded it, what are expected to follow and what do follow" (1975:34).

The next level up is the move, which is composed of acts and is the smallest free unit in the discourse. The move is at least in part the posture or attitude of the speaker with respect to the listener. Neither the move nor the act necessarily corresponds to the concept of turn, which has been used quite extensively in much of the literature on early interaction (e.g., Kaye,

1977). A single turn, if defined as all the utterances of a single speaker before another individual begins to speak, may consist of more than one move. Even in a simple greeting we can observe a change in move within a single turn.

Example 1:
A. Hi.
　　How are you?
B. I'm fine.
　　How are you?

Speaker B responds to A's greeting with a move called Answering and then poses the same question himself, with an accompanying change in move to an Opening. These two moves correspond to the most basic positions in any system of interaction: initiation and response.

Table 1 presents the functions and coding criteria for the discourse acts and moves that were of primary importance in this analysis. It is im-

Table 1. Functions and coding criteria for vocal/verbal discourse moves and acts observed in corpus AI(A)

Rank:	Class	Function[a]	Coding criterion
Move:	Opening	To get others to participate in an interaction	"Sets the stage"[b] for an interaction; elicits a reply
	Answering	To provide a response to an initiation	"Sounds like a response;" linked to previous speaker's utterance primarily through timing
Act:	Directive	To elicit a non-verbal response	Listener's acknowledgment of speaker's intent
	Loop	To take the interaction back to where it was before the speaker spoke	Followed by repetition (or paraphrase) of preceding utterance
	Reply	To provide an appropriate vocal response to an Elicitation[c]	See Answering

[a] These definitions are adapted from Sinclair and Coulthard (1975).

[b] Based on coding criteria for mother-infant interaction developed by Patricia Self (personal communication).

[c] An Elicitation is an act that functions to elicit a verbal (vocal) response.

portant to remember that the material to which this coding system is being applied is prelinguistic in form and function. Therefore timing, in relation to the previous speaker's utterance, as well as general "sound" plus the listener's response, were the primary criteria available for distinguishing between the different elements in the system.

THE AI(A) DATA

Discourse Analysis

The AI corpus is composed of 80 separate vocalizations. Of these 80 vocalizations, 64% (51) could be coded for discourse act. The remainder of the vocalizations either could not be coded at all—no code, 24% (19)—or were coded as tentative—12% (10). Three discourse acts accounted for 86% of all codable vocalizations: Reply, 35%; Loop, 27%; Directive, 23%. Five additional discourse acts occurred but at frequencies of 2 or less. These acts were: Elicitation, Nomination, Accept, Acknowledge, and Prompt.

The first analysis involved examining the relationships between two of the major variables, discourse act and vocalization type. This analysis was of particular interest because it would expose one level of the extent of flexibility or rigidity in the overall system and ultimately would indicate where the processes of differentiation and integration were most active. Table 2 shows the frequency and percentage of vocalization type for the three primary discourse acts.

Two of the discourse acts show a perfect relationship between form (i.e., vocalization type) and discourse function. Loops and Directives were only realized via type X vocalizations. Reply, although predominantly realized by type X (67%), was also realized by type W (33%). There were a total of 9 Clear Words in this corpus. In addition to the CW item coded Reply, three additional CW's were the sole examples of three of the five low frequency discourse acts. Of the remaining five CW's, four could not be coded for discourse act and one was tentatively coded a Reply. The four items not coded were all part of the same sequence and followed similar forms coded

Table 2.   Distribution of vocalization types for three discourse acts for corpus AI(A) ($N = 44$)

Vocalization Type[a]	Reply		Loop		Directive	
	N	%	N	%	N	%
X ($N = 38$)	12	67	14	100	12	100
AW ($N = 5$)	5	28	0	—	0	—
CW ($N = 1$)	1	5	0	—	0	—

[a] This analysis accounts for 86% of the vocalizations that could be coded for discourse act.

as Reply. In other words, had the coding criteria been less conversative, all the CW's not coded in this analysis would have been considered Replies. On the other hand, the present analysis reflects that at this stage in development there is still a fair amount of functional ambiguity even for CW forms.

These data were also coded for moves, the next rank in the Sinclair and Coulthard analytical hierarchy. Since moves are structured by acts, a single move may coincide with a single act or may be made up of several acts. Of the 80 vocalizations, 87% (70) could be coded for move; two vocalizations received tentative codings, and eight were coded as no code. Two types of moves, Opening and Answering, accounted for 99% of the coded moves. There was one instance of a Followup. Openings were more frequent than Answerings: 61% (43) versus 38% (27), respectively. Openings were as difficult as Answerings to code for discourse act. Of the 43 Openings, 72% (31), were discourse act coded, with 12% (5) coded as tentative and 14% (6) as no code. In comparison, 74% (20) of the Answerings were coded for discourse act, with 12% (3) tentative and 12% (3) no code.

The discourse analysis suggests that although the discourse act is the most basic unit in the analytical model, the next rank up, move, is more basic developmentally because a higher percentage of vocalizations were coded for move (87%) than could be coded for discourse act (64%). The two main moves that Andy used, Opening and Answering, correspond to the two fundamental postures or roles in communication, initiation and response. Yet although the literature on early mother-infant interaction clearly supports the interpretation above (e.g., Travarthen, 1977; Fogel, 1977), it also clearly indicates the extent to which mother structures such interactions. The designation of discourse act, even though it is defined in functional terms, hence depends heavily for its interpretation on mother's response, clearly requires greater differentiation of communication ability than that of move.

It is interesting that the child used not only the two fundamental and complementary moves, Opening and Answering, but two of the discourse acts, Directive and Reply, respectively, that structure these moves. Thus the child has the minimal discourse act resources for realizing the basic moves. The area of greatest formal variation at this level is the Reply, which can be realized by all three main vocalization types. In addition, Reply was the most frequently occurring of the discourse acts. The second most frequently occurring act, Loop, is classed as an Opening, but it is almost a mechanical function corresponding to *What did you say?* or as Andy in fact says, *Huh?*[2] The third act, the Directive, like the Loop, is realized only by type X vocalizations. However, such classification implies a certain degree of dif-

---

[2] It is interesting that in the interview following the 4-month period during which Andy was videotaped, when mother was asked about the type X vocalizations, she said that they were attempts to say something, not indications that the child had not heard the speaker.

ferentiation, presumably being utilized at the nonsegmental and/or non-verbal level.

The Directive is one of three major discourse acts that according to Sinclair and Coulthard (1975), probably occur in all forms of spoken discourse. The other two acts are Elicitation and Informative. It appears that developmentally the most important of these is the Directive. At this phase children have less need either to elicit talk (via Elicitations) or to provide information (via Informatives) than to learn to get others to respond to them. Just how they are able to do this will be further explored as we move to the next level of analysis, intonation.

Intonation and Voice Quality Analysis

As was mentioned earlier, analysis of the intonation of the entire AI corpus showed that the most complex and varied contours occurred in type W vocalizations and two-syllable type X. All the one-syllable type X vocalizations were found to have rising contours only. To continue the search for evidence of differentiation and integration between various levels of communication resources, however, these results must be examined in greater detail and in relation to the discourse analysis. The major question concerns the extent to which intonation and voice quality are employed in relation to discourse act and move.

Vocalizations in the three major discourse act categories were analyzed and compared for contour shape, type of pitch movement, syllable length, and the voice quality features of loudness, key, interval width, crescendo or decrescendo, and length. The results of this analysis are summarized in Tables 3a, 3b, and 3c.

The patterns that emerged from this analysis are complicated and difficult to interpret because the frequencies are small, once the vocalizations have been classified by several variables. Nevertheless there are some very suggestive differences.

Table 3a.   Intonation and voice quality features for loops $(N = 14)$[a]

N	Number of syllables		Pitch movement[b]		Contour[c]				Voice quality[d]				
	1	2	Gl	St	R	F	L	C	Ld	K	IW	Ln	D/C
10	x		x		x								
1	x			x	x				x	x			
3		x	—	—	x								
14	2	3	10	1	14	0	0	0	1	1	0	0	0

[a] All vocalizations are type X.
[b] Gl = glide, St = step.
[c] R = rising, F = falling, L = level, C = complex.
[d] Ld = loudness, K = key, IW = interval width, Ln = length, D/C = decrescendo or crescendo.

Table 3b. Intonation and voice quality features for directives X (N = 12)[a,b]

	Number of syllables		Pitch movement		Contour[c]				Voice quality				
N	1	2	Gl	St	R	F	L	C	Ld	K	IW	Ln	D/C
1	x		x		x								
1	x		x		x				x			x	x
3	x			x	x								
3		x	—	—	x								
2		x	—	—				x[c]				x	
(R)[d] 1	x		x		x								
(R) 1	x		x		x				x			x	
12	7	5	4	3	10	0	0	2	2	0	0	3	1

[a] All vocalizations are type X.

[b] Abbreviations as in Table 3a.

[c] One overall fall and one overall rise.

[d] R = Residue: forms that deviate from the basic X form but are clearly phonetically derived from it.

Table 3c. Intonation and voice quality features for replies (N = 18)[a]

Vocalization type	N	Number of syllables		Pitch movement		Contour				Voice quality				
		1	2	Gl	St	R	F	L	C	Ld	K	IW	Ln	D/C
X (N = 12)														
	1	x		x		x								
	2	x		x		x							x	
	(R)[b] 1	x		—	—			x				x		
	1	x		—	—			x				x		x
	3		x	—	—		x							
	1		x	—	—			x				x	x	
	1		x	—	—			x				x		
	2		x	—	—				x[c]					
AW (N = 5)														
	3		x	—	—		x							
	1		x	—	—		x							
	1		x	—	—				x[c]					
CW (N = 1)														
	1		x	—	—	x								
	18	5	13	2	0	4	7	4	3	0	4	0	3	0

[a] Abbreviations as in Table 3a.

[b] R = residue: forms that deviate from the basic X form but are clearly derived phonetically from it.

[c] Overall fall.

In general the greatest amount of variation was found in the act Reply, particularly with respect to intonation contours. More than half the contours are falling, even though two-thirds of the vocalizations are type X, which predominantly carry rising contours. However, more than half the type X Replys are two-syllable vocalizations, and it is mainly here that we find falling contours. In fact overall, nearly three-fourths (72%) of the Replys were two-syllable vocalizations.

Voice quality features utilized were key and length, and these were observed only on type X vocalizations. Length was always short and key was always low. In summary, the Reply vocalizations were very likely to have two syllables and more than twice as likely to have a falling contour as a rising or a level contour. Despite a fair degree of variation with respect to the various features utilized in this category, the major portion of the variation was found in the type X forms. In fact the type W forms by contrast are highly predictable: all are two-syllable vocalizations and two-thirds have falling contours.

The next two acts, Loop and Directive, show interesting contrasts with Reply as well as with each other. Both realize opening moves, whereas Replys realize Answering moves. Both were composed only of type X vocalizations, and both carry rising contours nearly 100% of the time. However Directives show greater variability in syllable structure and pitch movement. Nearly 80% of Loops are one-syllable vocalizations, with pitch movement a glide in almost all cases. By contrast, Directives are almost as likely to be two-syllable as one-syllable vocalizations, and of the latter, pitch movement is about as likely to be a step as a glide. Only one-fourth of the Directives carried special voice quality features, which tended to be extra length or loudness or both.

In summary, both Loops and Directives structure Opening moves and utilize only type X vocalizations with primarily rising contours, but the typical Loop, a one-syllable rising glide with no special voice quality characteristics, is the least typical Directive.

There is one other important point concerning similarities and differences among the intonation and voice quality features of the three acts. Although the Loop is considered to be an Opening move, it is such by definition and was so coded only after it had been established as a Loop. In terms of timing and "sound," Loops could have been coded as Replys. To qualify as an Opening, a vocalization could not occur too quickly after mother's previous utterance. Therefore, and because Loops most frequently sounded like Replys, it is all the more remarkable that Loops are so similar to Directives in certain features, while Directives show somewhat more overall variation, thus are in turn more similar to Replys.

Gesture and Gaze Analysis

The final set of variables to be examined in relationship to those previously discussed consists of gesture and gaze.

Gaze was analyzed simply in terms of apparent direction of gaze. Table 4 shows the percentage of vocalizations accompanied by gaze at mother. The main difference observed in frequency of gaze at mother was between Directives and Loops as compared with Replys. More than half the Directives and Loops were accompanied by gaze at mother, as compared with one-fourth of the Replys. However the results for Loops were influenced by the impossibility of coding gaze for four of the 14 vocalizations. In all four cases Andy had moved quickly out of camera range and may have been oriented away from mother. The category Other was included to permit comparison of gaze patterning on discourse items with all other vocalizations. Slightly less than half these vocalizations, which were the vocalizations classified as Directives and no code in the original discourse analysis, were accompanied by gaze at mother.

The similarity between gaze at mother in Directives and Loops is somewhat perplexing because the function of these acts is so different. However when gestures are considered in relation to gaze and discourse act, clear differences emerge. All the Directives accompanied by gaze at mother also involved specific gestures that can best be glossed as "showing" or "handing" mother an object. In four of the seven cases the object is a toy and the context appears to be what Bruner (1975) has described as the game of give and take. In the other three cases, Andy extended a paper cup to his mother, "asking" for more juice. It should be recalled that all Directives were type X vocalizations.

When we look at gestures for Loop accompanied by gaze at mother, we find a great deal of diversity. In only one instance is there vocalizing accompanied by a hand/arm gesture. The vocalization occurs in response to mother asking about the object Andy had just picked up: *What color is*

Table 4. Percentage of vocalizations for three discourse acts involving gaze at mother ($N = 72$)

Discourse act	N	Percentage	Could not see
Loop ($N = 14$)	10	60	4
Directive ($N = 12$)	12	60	0
Reply ($N = 18$)	17	24	1
Other [a] ($N = 29$)	28	43	1

[a] Includes vocalizations that could not be coded or were tentatively coded for discourse act.

it? He responds and holds the object, a red block, out to her. Mother repeats her question, thus qualifying Andy's vocalization as a Loop, not a Reply. Two more of the vocalizations with gaze occurred during a "talk" routine in which mother asked questions and Andy replied.

> Example 1
> Mother: Did you play with Kenna today?
> Andy: $°3\overset{X}{\frown}2$
> Mother: Kenna? Did you play with Scotty?
> Andy: $°3\overset{X}{\frown}2$
> Mother: Scotty?

Three of the remaining four items involved gaze movement during vocalization, a phenomenon that did not occur at all with Directives. In two cases Andy moved his gaze from a paper cup he was holding to mother's face. He clearly wanted juice. In both cases mother ultimately responded, but the timing of the vocalizations led to their classification as Loops rather than Directives. The final item occurred when Andy's mother asked him to sing for her. He vocalized but removed his gaze from her face, bending over to pick up a plate from the floor.

The function of Andy's gaze at mother in Directives and in the majority of the Loops seemed to be that of getting her attention. Gaze most frequently occurred as part of his intonation. Only in the routine in Example 1 is there an instance of mother holding Andy's gaze during talk. It is therefore interesting that when we look at Replys, we find gaze occurring with only about 30% of the vocalizations, less than half as frequently as during Loops and Directives. In all five instances, the topic or activity was food: drinking juice or eating cookies. In two cases Andy was extending his hand, holding a paper cup toward mother for juice. As in Directives, these Replys involved Andy wanting something, but the behavior came as a response to an initiation by mother.

At this stage in development, the child's use of gaze at mother simultaneously with vocalizing is closely tied to the use of specific hand/arm gestures. Gesture and vocalization are in turn tied to the goal of getting and directing mother's attention to play a game or give him something he wants, particularly food. Given the apparent validity of the foregoing statement, it is interesting to examine Directives that do not involve gaze at mother. These Directives as well as several of the tentatively coded Directives all occurred in the interactions with the shapes "box." Those items were coded as Directives that were so recognized by mother. The recognition came through her giving instructions, directions, or encouragement. All the vocalizations were one-syllable steps or two-syllable type X vocalizations with rising intonation. There was no specific gesture except Andy's attempts to manipulate the plastic shapes so they would drop into the box.

Coding of these items was difficult because it was not clear whether Andy wanted mother to do something, wanted a change in the situation, or was simply venting his frustration.[3] Since function was the main coding criterion, only the items that mother "recognized" were coded as Directives.

The difference in frequency between gaze at mother during Directives as contrasted with Replys is striking. A shift in gaze to mother was clearly not a necessary part of an adequate vocal response to mother's initiation. It is important to recall that coding a Reply depended in part on mother treating the vocalization as such. There were also situational factors conditioning gaze direction during a Reply. For five out of the 12 Replys during which gaze was not at mother, Andy and his mother were looking at a book together. It is interesting that all five utterances were type W vocalizations. The remaining seven Replys with gaze elsewhere than at mother were quite diverse.

The most interesting Replys, however, were the two instances of Andy both looking at mother and vocalizing. In the first example, Andy and mother have competing agendas. Mother is trying to get Andy to sing[4] a song. He is playing with his empty juice cup and apparently ignoring her.

> Example 3
> Andy: X — extending cup, which he's crushed, to mother
>   °3–2 while gazing at her.
> Mother: Can you sing for mommy?
> Andy: X — looking down at cup in hands.
>   °2–1
> Mother: Wanna play ring around the rosey?
> Andy: XX — looking at cup which he then extends.
>   °2–3
> Mother: Okay — takes cup from Andy.

The XX vocalization carries the Reply intonation, but it was accompanied by gaze and gesture, which signal that Andy wanted something. In adult English a falling contour on the equivalent utterance *huh uh* would signal *no*. A second example (Example 4) occurred when again Andy used a Directive XX while extending the juice cup to mother. Mother pressed for a "better" vocalization.

> Example 4:
> Mother: Tell mommy what you want.
> Andy: (jargon) — turning cup in hands.
> Mother: Juice?

---

[3] So Foster (1979) describes an analogous problem in her discussion of difficulties in positively identifying attention-getting versus attention-directing devices in prelinguistic discourse.

[4] Singing a song or "reciting" a poem was one of the activities that mother was requested to initiate during the observation session.

Andy: XX — gazing at mother and holding out cup.
        °2–3
        (Mother takes cup from Andy)
Mother: Okay.

Once again Andy has marked his vocalization as a Reply with falling into-nation, but has signaled his wanting the juice through the combined and now familiar gaze at mother, plus hand/arm gesture.

These two examples show the beginnings of the separation of gesture and gaze from vocalization. This separation clearly introduces a new flexi-bility into the system. It permits the child, to use Halliday's (1975) phrase, to do more than one thing at a time, an operation and degree of integration that is fundamental to the adult system. The separation of intonation from gesture and gaze may well be the precursor of the distinction that is funda-mental to the adult system between content and expression: what is said and how it is meant. However with his limited structure, Andy could not yet realize this distinction.

DISCUSSION

The goal of this analysis was to examine in depth a small corpus of prelin-guistic data for evidence of the operation of the developmental processes of integration and differentiation. Although the data base came from one time period, the author has suggested previously that there was evidence for two developmentally different vocalization systems operating syn-chronically. What was fascinating about the two systems was that they were distinguishable both formally and functionally. The type X system was clearly prelinguistic and highly predictable phonetically, although dif-ficult to categorize functionally except at the discourse level of filling a conversational slot. The type W system was less homogeneous. It was com-posed of Clear Words, which were forms clearly linked to the adult English system both segmentally and nonsegmentally; evidence was presented for contrastive use of intonation contours, rise versus fall. The other type W forms, Ambiguous Words, were clearly wordlike and seemed to be closer to the adult system than the type W, but their functional status was not clear. Finally the two systems showed differential impact on the discourse level. Mother tended to follow type X vocalizations with discourse acts that structured Openings. She was more likely to follow a type W vocalization with discourse acts that structure Followup moves, thus treating the vocal-ization as an appropriate Reply.

To fill in the blank spots in the picture sketched above and to get a firmer grasp on developmental processes within a single observation, two important kinds of data were added to the analysis: discourse structure coding of the child's vocalizations, and systematic coding of gesture and gaze direction accompanying the vocalizations.

The picture that emerges from the descriptive analysis of discourse, intonation, voice quality, gesture, and gaze, combined with the formal vocalization type categories, is highly complex. The examples are frequently few in number. However there are several rather clear patterns that taken together, provide several substantive and coherent findings.

The data show perhaps most clearly that the area of greatest differentiation lies at the level of discourse move: Opening is marked in a number of ways that distinguish it from Answering. This statement holds even if we consider Loops together with Directives. As stated earlier, Loops, although categorized functionally as Openings, are not truly initiated items in the same sense as Directives. Therefore in this discussion, the term Opening refers to Directives only.

The clearest distinction between Opening and Answering is found in intonation. All the Openings used a rising intonation contour, but Answerings used a rising contour in only four out of 18 cases (22%). Conversely seven out of 18 Answerings had a simple primary contour fall and an additional three had an overall fall using a complex counter: $°2-2$ $°3-3$, $°3-3$ $°2-4$, $°2-1-3$. Although these figures are small, the significance of the high proportion of falls becomes apparent when we consider the frequency of rises and falls in the entire AI corpus. Seventy-five percent of all type X vocalizations had rising contours. All the falling contours on Type X vocalizations occurred on two-syllable forms. These two-syllable forms were the one major resource for Andy's Answering moves.

The other major formal resource for Replys was type W forms, notably Ambiguous Words. The entire AI corpus reveals that the distribution of contours on the type W forms is quite different from that on the type X. More than one-third (37%) of the contours are rises, with approximately the same number of falls (38%). Twenty-five percent (22) are complex, and half of these are falling in overall movement. This means that approximately half the type W forms have falling contours.

The data strongly suggest that there is some relationship, not a perfect one, between discourse move and intonation. An analysis of the Clear Words in these data suggested contrastive use of intonation, with a rise indicating *engagement* and a fall indicating *detachment*. There seems to be an additional contrastive use of intonation to mark a response (Answering) versus an initiation (Opening). This interpretation is further supported when we consider the Loops. These forms often "sounded like" Replys, yet the intonation was always a rising contour. A finding similar to that described above is presented in Halliday's (1975) discussion of his son Nigel's early language development. At 19–19½ months Nigel used a rising versus a falling tone to distinguish pragmatic (requiring a response) utterances from mathetic (not requiring a response) ones. This distinction according to Halliday is fundamental to the transition to the adult system.

The next set of resources Andy utilized for marking the distinction between Opening and Answering consisted of gaze and gesture. In initiating, Andy combined gaze at mother, the major object of attention, and a hand/arm gesture, when he wanted to play give and take or when he wanted juice or cookies. However when his focus of attention and therefore his gaze or activity was on an object, such as playing with the shapes box, he could not yet differentiate visual attention and activity. He seemed to want mother's attention, yet his gaze, his most unambiguous attention-wanting signal, remained on the shapes box. Presumably if mother had allowed Andy's frustration to increase, both gaze and vocalization would have changed.

The lack of differentiation at the level of vocalization form, which is necessary for unambiguous reference, further adds to the difficulty in interpreting these interactions. Mother "reads" the child's need through his activity (e.g., not getting the shape in the hole) and probably through the sound of the vocalization. Presumably, she knows too that two-syllable type X forms with rising intonation mean that the child wants her attention. There was an interesting example of Andy using a two-syllable type X as an Opening. Having given mother his cup for more juice, he looked at her, looked away, then looked back at her and vocalized XX with a rising contour; mother answered *What*? This remarkable vocalization unambiguously functioned as though Andy had called *Mama*.[5]

Interpreting the less frequent use of gaze with Answering moves in terms of Andy *not* needing mother's attention is far too simple. Although he does not obviously monitor where mother's gaze is directed with glances, he is undoubtedly well aware that most of the time it is on him. There were several instances of Andy orienting toward mother as she changed her position from sitting on the floor or chair to getting something from the cabinet or toy box. In addition, although Andy could not easily shift his gaze from the initial object of attention to mother, keeping gaze on the object while vocalizing a response, as in looking at a book,[6] may have been highly appropriate. As Murphy (1978) emphasized in her study of pointing, it is vitally important to consider situational factors when assessing the frequency of gestures such as pointing.

The resources of intonation and gesture are the most differentiated at this point in development, at least in relation to discourse move. This differentiation is no doubt facilitated by its initial occurrence in conjunction with a system of highly predictable segmental forms, the type X vocalizations. However comparing the resources within the two basic moves, we

[5] There are three examples in AI(B) of Andy calling *mama* (with a rising contour), to which mother replies *What*? In two cases he is looking at mother while vocalizing. In the third case he is out of camera range.

[6] Murphy (1978) found only one instance of pointing at a book while looking at mother in a sample of eight infants from 9 to 24 months of age.

find that there are a small number of relatively fixed patterns within Directives, whereas Replys show greater variation in resources being utilized. There is some hint that it is in the area of Replys that the transition into the adult system is most advanced. The few type W forms in AI(A) occurred only in Replys and in several low frequency acts. In addition, there was some evidence of the beginning separation of intonation from gesture and gaze, as was shown in Examples 3 and 4, which may herald the distinction in the adult system between content and expression. In Andy's system the separation perhaps marked the beginning differentiation between discourse move and act.

It is possible that the increase in use of different resources within Replys (Answering) will lead to greater differentiation as a precursor to further expansion of discourse acts, particularly the important acts, Elicitation and Informative, which structure Openings.

Since neither discourse act nor intonation has a strict tie to structure in the adult system, the full operation of all communicative resources requires that each achieve a certain degree of functional autonomy. The overall degree of autonomy in the system at this point in development is small compared to what will ultimately be achieved.

The finding that discourse move, initiation versus response, is the most differentiated resource in the communication system is congruent with the literature on early caregiver-infant interaction. The additional finding that intonation is used to mark contrast between discourse moves, Opening versus Answering, is also consistent with observations of young infants' sensitivity to intonation (Lieberman, 1967) as well as reports of early occurrence of identifiable intonation contours (von Raffler-Engel, 1964).

The process of differentiation and the precursors of differentiation (i.e., variation) are much easier to delineate at this phase than integration partly because of where the system is in relationship to its ultimate goal and partly because a limited amount of data has been observed from a single point in time. This analysis demonstrates the fruitfulness of utilizing a modified version of Sinclair and Coulthard's system of discourse analysis for studying infant speech at the prelinguistic or transitional phase of language development. Using discourse structure as a basic framework has illuminated the early development of the many resources involved in the communication system. The application of this approach to longitudinal data should lead to a more complete description of the processes of differentiation and integration in early language development.

ACKNOWLEDGMENTS

The author wishes to thank Ralph Cooley for constructive critiquing during the preparation of the manuscript. Thanks are also due to Patricia Self for pointing out the importance of child-initiated behavior.

Chapter 11
BODY MOVEMENT
AND VERBALIZATION
The Bilingual Model

Luis R. Marcos

In the field of human communication, body movement was first conceived as a "discharge" and "expressive" behavior (Darwin, 1929). Within this model, Freud (1906) proposed that motor activity expressed conflicting unconscious impulses and memories, Reich (1928) postulated that an individual's defenses were frequently displayed in his motor behavior, Allport and Vernon (1933) observed that motor activity conveyed personality traits, and Deutsch (1952) integrated these views in his work. The contributions of Efron (1941) illustrate the extent to which culture may pattern human gestures.

During the 1950's there occurred a shift in emphasis from the view of movement as a discharge and expressive activity to its communicative and interactional values. The pioneer in this transition was Birdwhistell (1952), who coined the term "kinesics" for such a field of research. This school of thought argued that body movement consists of culturally learned communicative units that are patterned in ways analogous to language and serve in the maintenance of face-to-face interaction. Thus a movement is considered to be "a communicative structural event" (Scheflen, 1963). This model has, therefore, placed the emphasis on the interpersonal rather than the expressional function of movement. Supporting the assumption that movement constitutes a language of interpersonal relations, Watzlawick et al. (1967) have regarded motor behavior as a form of communication that in analogous ways defines the implicit relationship of two participants in a given social context.

In the experimental field, researchers have found a diversity of interrelationships between nonverbal and verbal content aspects of speech, affective reaction, interpersonal relations, and psychodynamics (Ekman, 1965;

Dittman, 1966; Mahl, 1968). However, there is still controversy about the nature of the emotions that can be inferred from a person's facial expression and body movement (Marcos, 1974).

Nonverbal behavior has also been viewed as an overt manifestation of centrally organized sensory motor schemata (Piaget, 1952; Werner and Kaplan, 1963; Bruner, 1966). Recently, some indirect evidence has accumulated that points to the possibility that movement may be associated with the transformation of thoughts into words (Freedman, 1972). For instance, it has been shown that movement during speech persists even when there is no visible object of communication (Mahl, 1968), at times of verbalization failures (Krout, 1954), and during pauses that seem to be related to syntactic planning (Dittman, 1972).

Based on the conceptual framework that considers nonverbal behavior as a participant component of information processing mechanisms is the movement-coding system developed by Freedman and collaborators (1972). This system, which has been the instrument in our work, studies hand movement activity. But before describing this coding method and reviewing the evidence attesting to the central role of hand movement behavior in the process of information, it is desirable to conceptualize the mechanisms of verbalization and present the bilingual model.

The process of verbalization is linked to the concept of codification. This term was first used by communication engineers to refer to the substitution of one type of communicative event for another, such that the event substituted stood in some sense for the other. Along these lines, it was conceived that in the communication process the source produces messages that must be transformed by the transmitter into signals that are carried by a channel. These signals must then be transformed by the receiver back into messages, which can be accepted at the destination. The activity of the transmitter is usually referred to as encoding and that of the receiver as decoding. Human beings, however, can function simultaneously as source and destination, and as transmitter and receiver of messages. Indeed, the individual is a decoder of the messages he himself encodes through various feedback mechanisms. This information-processing paradigm has been applied with great generality to different psychological and social systems (Osgood and Jenkins, 1954; Ruesch and Bateson, 1968).

The concept of verbalization, as it is used here, refers to the process commonly called "the expression of ideas." It may be defined as the mechanism whereby a speaker's ideas, feelings, and imagery become coded into the verbalizations that produce intelligible sounds in a given language. Operationally, the verbalization process may be considered as having two major components:

1. *Imagery*: A preverbalization stage that refers to the nature of the idea

to be verbalized, specifically its abstractness-concreteness dimension (Paivio, 1971).

2. *Verbalization*:   This component includes the lexical, syntactic, and phonetic steps. Respectively, these verbalization steps depend on the number of words available to the individual, the capacity for grammatical ordering, and the individual's ability to articulate the words (Marcos, 1976a).

THE BILINGUAL MODEL

A person who can speak two languages is of particular interest and offers unique possibilities for the study of cognitive processing mechanisms. Bilinguals have been classified in different ways according to dimensions such as the level of language dominance, degree of independence of the language, language acquisition contexts, semantic characteristics of the languages, and other sociological and psycholinguistic variables (Marcos, 1976b). According to the degree of linguistic competence bilinguals have in their two languages, they may be classified as subordinate when there is a differential linguistic performance in the two languages, or proficient, for some "true" bilinguals, when they display a native speaker's command of both languages. The fundamental characteristic of subordinate bilinguals is the language barrier or degree of linguistic deficit and difficulty involved in the verbalization in the nondominant language.

To study the relations between verbalization mechanisms and movement behavior, subordinate bilinguals constitute ideal subjects because the same person offers two verbalization conditions, dominant and nondominant languages. Evidently in comparison with their dominant language verbalization, subordinate bilinguals have to perform more elaborate and difficult verbalization work in their nondominant language. Verbalizing in a nondominant language implies greater cognitive work because the number of words available, the capacity for grammatical ordering, and the articulation facility are significantly poorer. A subordinate bilingual, therefore, may serve as self-controlled subject when comparing different levels of verbalization work and any dependent variable such as movement activity.

HAND MOVEMENT BEHAVIOR

It is apparent that hand movements are the most frequent, quantifiable, and psychologically revealing bits of overt nonverbal behavior available for objective study. Hand activity has been considered to be the fundamental vehicle for the study of the structure of thought (Wolff, 1952), it is one of the most important foundations of human capabilities (Stone, 1961), and it has been found to have critical developmental roots (Piaget, 1952).

In this chapter, hand movement activity is assessed according to the coding system developed by Freedman (1972). This system, which has been extensively utilized in clinical as well as in experimental studies, has the advantage of having been developed within the conceptual framework that considers nonverbal communication to be a component of central information-processing mechanisms.

When conceptualizing hand movement activity, Freedman distinguished two broad classes of hand movements: object-focused and body-focused movements. Object-focused movements (OFM) are speech-related movements and are intimately linked to rhythmic and/or content aspects of the verbal utterance. The OFM relations to speech appear to range from instances of the movement being subordinate to the verbal statement to instances of the movement substituting for the verbal message. Body-focused movements (BFM) comprise a range of stimulation of the body by the hands. These are movements that seem to be unrelated to speech and have been regarded as a form of tension regulation and focusing. Examples of BFM range from repetitive and unpatterned to circumscribed and patterned motions.

Hand movements are organized according to different sub-categories of movement behavior. For this study the following categories of movements were considered:

1. *Speech-primacy movements* (SPM):   This activity consists of short, rhythmic movements that convey a beat quality without carrying content of their own. These small hand movements tend to occur in bursts, and they are intimately coordinated with the rhythmic aspects of the speech. The hand either traverses an essentially straight vertical path or performs a simple turning of the wrist. Empirical studies assessing this hand movement behavior have given indirect support to their relation to the process of verbal encoding. Thus the amount of SPM did not change when the participants in a dialogue were facing away from each other (they were seated back to back) (Hoffman, 1968). This finding suggests that this movement may not have a solely communicative or message value.

2. *Representational movements* (RM):   This motor activity expresses some content message, an image, a feeling, or a thought. The judgment of the relative enactment of a message is always made by reference to the verbal content. The RM hand activity is frequently a literal outline of an image, is sometimes a condensation of it, and often provides more information than is carried by speech alone. RM activity decreases significantly when the subjects involved in a dialogue are seated back to back (Hoffman, 1968). This finding suggests that RM may not

have a function in the process of verbalization per se, but rather, play a role in face-to-face communication context. RM have also been related to the imagery component of the process of verbalization—namely, the identification and delimitation of the images to be verbalized (Freedman, 1972). In effect, RM tend to precede the onset of verbalization (Barroso et al., 1976), and are more frequently deployed when there is an image in focus that cannot be readily verbalized. For instance, more RM are produced when subjects are presented with and asked to describe Rorschach cards as opposed to TAT figures (Hoffman, 1968).

3. *Pointing movements* (PM):   This movement is used by the speaker to indicate a person or an object in the immediate or distant environment. PM identify and emphasize objects in the space. By pointing, the individual appears to reaffirm the self, others, or things in the space. PM function seems to be similar to that of RM in the sense that they participate in the confirmation and buttressing of an object image or a self-image.

4. *Groping movements* (GM):   These are hand activities that lack a verbal referent and thus seem to have a substitutive function. GM have also been referred to as speech-failure movement. This activity is not used to represent but rather to indicate the individual's struggle to find words. Descriptively, these are short, rhythmic movements that occur in outbursts during hesitations in speech. These hesitation pauses have been thought to represent the speaker's difficulty either in making a lexical choice or in casting it into the right syntactic form (Lounsbury, 1954).

5. *Continuous finger-to-hand movements* (CFHM):   These body-focused movements include one or more fingers of one hand rubbing against the other hand. These stereotyped, repetitive movements are continuous in time (i.e., longer than 3 seconds). These movements seem to be unrelated to speech and have been regarded as a form of tension regulation. CFHM have been linked to different states of psychopathology (Grand, et al., 1975), to situations of stress (Mahl, 1968), and to cognitive interference as studied by the Stroop color word test (Grand, et al., 1973). These hand movements have also been related to affective states such as depression and anxiety (Steingart and Freedman, 1976).

All hand movement behavior is scored by viewing the videotapes on a monitor and by playing back any segment of the tape as many times as the rater may need for a satisfactory identification of the movement. SPM, RM, PM, and GM are scored in relation to speech and are computed in terms of rates that take into account the subject's total word output (i.e., frequency of the movement $\times$ 100/total words). Body-focused movements, such as CFHM are expressed as time scores and are referred to as the number of seconds spent in that particular activity. The distribution of scores is then normalized by using the formula: $\sqrt{X + 0.5}$, where X = number of seconds of movement. In our studies using the bilingual model, 5 minutes of parallel portions of the English and Spanish verbal tasks is coded for analysis.

The scoring is carried out by a trained bilingual rater. The level of reliability is determined by having an independent bilingual rater score the hand movement activity of half of the sample randomly chosen, and by computing a category placement coefficient. This coefficient refers to the concordance between the two judges in identifying the same movement as belonging to any of the categories studied, divided by the total number of movements scored by the two raters in the same category. The average coefficient for all the movements scored in the studies using the bilingual model has been 0.75. The coefficients have ranged from 0.71 for GM to 0.86 for CFHM. These coefficients are comparable with those achieved in previous studies with monolingual subjects (Freedman, 1972).

EXPERIMENTAL STUDIES

The background for the use of the bilingual model to study relationships between movement behavior and the process of verbalization was the finding that Spanish-speaking schizophrenic patients, with a deficit in the English language, were rated by clinicians as significantly tenser motorically and more manneristic when interviewed in English than when the interview was conducted in Spanish (Marcos, et al., 1973a). In this study, tension was rated solely on the basis of physical signs and motor behavior, not on the basis of the subjective experiences reported by the patient. Mannerisms referred to unusual motor behavior. The sample consisted of 10 schizophrenic patients, all recent admissions to the Adult Services at Bellevue Psychiatric Hospital in New York City; Spanish was their dominant language, but they were fluent enough in English to participate in psychiatric interviews in that language. The differential competence in the two languages, apart from being obvious to the clinicians, was reflected in the WAIS Vocabulary subscale scores in English and Spanish.

The analysis of the content and vocal components of these videotaped psychiatric interviews disclosed that in the English-language evaluations the patients produced a series of speech changes that have been related to verbalization difficulties (Marcos, et al., 1973b). For instance, the patients' verbal productions were shorter, had simpler grammatical structure, and showed more frequent speech disturbances and longer silent pauses. These changes appeared to be associated with a speaker's uncertainty about cognitive decision making in the process of verbalization (Marcos, 1976a).

The patients participating in this experiment were part of an ongoing project initiated to explore the effects of interview language on the evaluation of psychopathology in Spanish-American schizophrenic patients (Marcos, et al., 1973a). Closed-circuit television recordings were made of standard psychiatric interviews in English and Spanish. Two psychiatrists rated independently the interviews utilizing the Brief Psychiatric Rating Scale (Overall and Gorham, 1962). This scale permits the clinical evaluation of 18 symptom areas. Pathology scores for each of the 18 symptom dimensions were obtained separately for the English and Spanish interviews. A comparative study of the hand movement activity of these patients during the English- and Spanish-language interviews suggested that the increased motor activity observed by the clinicians during the English interviews was related to the more demanding verbalization tasks in that language, not to psychopathology (Grand et al., 1977). This study addressed the effect of psychopathology and verbalization stress on hand movement behavior. The effect of such stress was most clearly indexed during the interview in the nondominant language by a cluster of significant positive correlations between nonrepresentational movements that carried no message content and lacked verbal referents, and motor-discharge symptoms such as tension, withdrawal, excitement, and mannerisms.

Nonrepresentational movements such as groping movements occur mainly when word finding falters and the speaker is searching for adequate means of expressing ideas. The increase in such movements with the upsurge of tension, excitement, mannerisms, and emotional withdrawal during the English interviews means that they are not simply overt motoric manifestations of such symptoms. If this were the case, similar positive correlation would have occurred in the Spanish-language interview. Indeed, it is this discriminating upsurge of nonrepresentational activity in the nondominant language that supports its link to verbalization stress.

This study, however, was limited by several methodological problems. For instance, the possibility that the difference in hand movements in our patients during their English and Spanish interviews was attributable to the intrinsic characteristics of the languages cannot be ruled out. Furthermore, the patients participating in these interviews were schizophrenics under chemotherapy, and there is evidence indicating that nonverbal behavior is affected by psychopathology as well as phenothiazines. Another experiment was then designed to disentangle these confounding factors by utilizing a sample of opposite bilinguals, that is, English-primary and Spanish-primary subjects, and by studying normal individuals.

For the next study, normal adult bilinguals with a significant language deficit in their nondominant language were selected (Marcos, 1979a, 1979b). The sample was divided in two groups, each with eight linguistically opposite bilinguals. One group consisted of eight bilinguals whose dominant language was English and their nondominant language, Spanish; and the second group was formed by eight bilinguals with Spanish as the dominant language and English as the nondominant one. Linguistically opposite bilinguals were selected to control for changes in kinetic behavior that might result either from the cultural pattern of the subject or from the intrinsic characteristics of the languages rather than from differences in the subjects' verbalization work.

To select a linguistically comparable group, a language-dominance battery was administered to each subject on an individual basis. This battery included the *Subjective Estimation Scale*, a *Word-Naming Test*, and the *WAIS Vocabulary Subtest*. Bilinguals' own estimation of their nondominant language fluency has been found to be a valid measure of their proficiency, and the word-naming and vocabulary measurements have been extensively used to estimate the degree of bilingualism (Marcos, 1978). These language proficiency scores in the dominant and nondominant languages were compared for the total sample, and the results indicated that the subordinate bilingual subjects constituted a linguistically homogeneous sample. Each subject was seen individually, and all the experimental tasks were videotaped. The subject was requested to verbalize in each language, for 10 minutes , 5 minutes on a high imagery topic, and 5 minutes on a low imagery topic. The task of verbalizing high and low imagery material was intended to help distinguish movements with a function in the imagery component of the verbalization process from those associated with the lexical, syntactic, or phonetic components.

To analyze these data, a multifactorial analysis with repeated measures was first computed. Results indicated that more SPM and GM were produced during the nondominant language verbalization. The level of imagery of the subjects' verbalization did affect PM activity; more PM were produced during the low imagery topics than during the high imagery verbalization.

To explore the patterning of hand movements in relation to the level of language fluency, correlations were computed with the language dominance scores and the movements produced during the nondominant language verbal tasks. This analysis generated a 3×5 correlation matrix containing significant negative correlations for GM and all the measures of language fluency, and a positive correlation for CFHM and the scores of the Subjective Estimation Scale.

IMPLICATIONS

The studies described addressed the conceptualization of kinetic activity, specifically hand movements, as bearing a function in central cognitive processes, such as the mechanisms involved in the process of verbalization.

The major assumption was that definite categories of hand movements have a function in the process of transforming ideas into words. Bilinguals, by having two language systems, offer unique opportunities to the investigator of mental processes. Subordinate bilinguals, with a differential competence in two languages, constitute the ideal population to explore the kinetic consequences of different degrees of verbalization work. Furthermore, in the latter experiment with normal bilinguals, high and low imagery topics were introduced as a convenient way of separating movements with the preverbal function of identifying the image to be verbalized (*imagery component*) from movements with a function in the lexical, syntactic, and phonetic work (*verbalization component*).

In general, the results of these studies support the function of kinetic behavior in central processing of information and call into dispute the notion that nonverbal behavior has simply a transmission or communicative value in human communication. Thus, when the verbalization work was made difficult by having the subjects speak in their nondominant language, movements such as SPM and GM significantly increased in frequency. A crucial difference between SPM and GM is that GM occur during hesitation pauses in which the individual appears to struggle to find the proper word or group of words to express an idea. In this regard, indirect evidence may be marshalled in support of a more specific assumption linking GM with the lexical and syntactic planning steps of the verbalization process. The negative correlation of the rate of GM with scores in language dominance tests involving lexical and syntactic factors corroborates this hypothesis.

These studies also attempted to investigate the movements discussed with the function in the imagery component of identifying the images to be verbalized. In effect, more PM activity was produced when low imagery material was being verbalized than when the ideas encoded were of high imagery, regardless of the language of the task.

Body-focused activity such as CFHM was not directly affected by the level of language verbalization work nor by the imagery of the topics verbalized. However, in contrast to the other movements, this body-focused movement showed a positive relation to the measures of language proficiency in the nondominant language. This finding gives support to the notion that body-focused activity may have a role in mechanisms other than verbal encoding, for instance, in attention focusing and endogenous affective states such as depression or anxiety. It may then be that when the individual has a better command of the language and fewer restrictions in verbalization, tension states and attention focusing become more evident in kinetic behavior.

The results of these studies with bilinguals may also be understood in terms of the function of hand movements as verbalization facilitators. Thus SPM and GM may be considered to have a facilitatory function in the verbalization work. In contrast, PM may facilitate the verbalization stage in which the image to be verbalized is identified and delineated. One is reminded of popular sayings such as "Neapolitans can be made mute by tying their hands behind their backs."

When attempting to understand these findings, however, interpretation other than verbalization facilitation should also be considered. For instance, our results could also be explained in terms of a motor overflow attributable to a central effort, either to verbalize in a poorly commanded language or to encode abstract ideas. Similarly, it may be that the increase in movement activity reflects a conscious attempt to reach and establish contact with the object of communication in a nondominant language, or to communicate poorly delineated abstract images. Also, we must bear in mind that these studies were based on a population of bilinguals. Although subordinate bilinguals are known to process information like monolinguals, namely, by utilizing an unitary language code (Marcos, 1976a), they often use translation mechanisms as part of verbalization work. Our results might, then, reflect this additional encoding task.

Several implications should be considered at this point. This line of research contributes to the current integrational tendency to study diversified data within one system, and to eliminate boundaries that obscure the orderly relationships among parts of the real world. Specifically, in these studies we have attempted to integrate "central" cognitive processes with "peripheral" physical nonverbal activity, two phenomena that for a long time have been compartmentalized under separate fields of investigation. An immediate implication of this work is that those invisible mental processes (e.g., imagery, lexical and syntactic planning), by being integrated with visible kinetic activity (i.e., hand movements) may be subjected to study and monitoring through the examination of the latter.

In the area of basic and developmental research, one central problem has been the identification of the hypothetical constructs that constitute the encoding and decoding components of verbalization processing. By identifying specific peripheral activities with the function in the information-processing mechanisms, the investigator may be able to explore sequential steps involved in central cognitive processes that otherwise will not be available for study. In this regard, the identification of kinetic activity that is not just a vestige of the past, but serves specific verbalization functions, offers unique opportunities to the investigator of cognitive and language development. For instance, by reliably relating external motor activity to central cognitive processes, the understanding of the development of information-processing mechanisms, including lexical, syntactic, phonetic, and abstraction capacities, may be significantly facilitated.

This line of investigation has also implications for the area of speech disturbances, particularly for the study of aphasia, the motor and sensory language disturbances caused by brain lesions. The field of language disorders is an extensive one, and it is clearly out of the scope of this chapter to review it. However, it is important to remember that clinicians in this area have often related movement to speech by proposing gesture as a source of speech. Early neurologists suggested that manual gestures became associated with oral gestures. Sounds then became linked with the meaning of the gestures; later, gestures were largely shed, and sounds were left as the main symbols.

Aphasias have been classified according to different parameters. Most of the aphasic disturbances, however, consist of problems with symbolization or perception (e.g., nominal, semantic, sensory aphasias), problems in verbalization planning (e.g., syntactic, verbal aphasias), problems in articulation or expression (e.g., motor, expressive aphasias), and any combination of the three (Brain, 1961). Although aphasic disturbances are often associated with muscular deficits, when possible the examination of hand activity of the patients could offer the clinician clues to the specific information-processing component that has been affected. For instance, in relation to these findings, we may speculate that GM would become more apparent in aphasics with faulty syntactic or lexical decision making, and pointing movement would increase in frequency when the symbolization and imagery components were most affected.

In addition, the results of these studies carry implications to the realm of psychotherapy. Let us repeat that these findings, by supporting the function of nonverbal activity in the encoding process, reject the use of kinetic behavior either as simply discharge or expressive behaviors or as a mere communication channel for the transmission of messages, whether resting on the analogue or the digital principle. Psychotherapists, then, who choose to focus on the latter communicative aspects of motor activity should develop some way of eliminating those verbalization-related movements, to avoid being misled. On the other hand, the study of these external clues to central information-processing may provide unique opportunities for gaining understanding of important aspects of the psychotherapy process. For example, we may speculate that the detection of certain verbalization-facilitatory movements permits the distinction between motivated repression and information retrieval difficulties. Motivated repression would probably not elicit facilitatory movements, whereas verbalization failures would reveal an overproduction of these movements. At the same time, since specific categories of kinetic activity might be linked to specific cognitive mechanisms such as imagery or verbalization, a certain kinetic behavior would indicate to the clinician whether the patient is struggling for images or for words.

A major implication of these studies concerns the area of psychodiagnosis and assessment of psychopathology in bilingual patients. Thus, clinicians evaluating subordinate bilingual patients, with a significant deficit in the language of the interview, should be careful to distinguish the movements that reflect verbalization work from motor behavior having expressive or interpersonal value. Specifically, when interviewing a patient who is not speaking in his dominant language, clinicians should be careful to interpret hand movements such as GM or SPM.

Regarding further research, apart from replication studies, it is important that more refined measures of the imagery, lexical, syntactic, and phonetic components of the verbalization process be developed, so that specific movements can be reliably related to specific encoding steps. An additional analysis might involve the microanalysis of one case in which the verbal and vocal productions during dominant and nondominant language monologues could be brought into relation with the exact occurrence of the motor act. Also, in the bilingual model, there is evidence that following cerebral vascular accidents or during deteriorating organic brain diseases, bilinguals exhibit differential impairment in their two languages (Marcos and Alpert, 1976). A comparative analysis of hand movements produced in the aphasic language and in the intact language may reveal the movements with function in specific verbalization factors.

A more general expansion of this research area could involve the study of other body movements, or the study of other components of information processing such as verbal decoding, since it is well known that people move while listening. Finally, the bilingual model could also offer its unique advantages to the study of the effects of cultural factors on patterning movement and the identification of the effects of the intrinsic characteristics of languages on kinetic activity.

Chapter 12
EPIDEMIOLOGY IN DEVELOPMENTAL KINESICS

Robert H. Hutcheson, Jr.

Principles of epidemiology, like other tools that may be employed in research, have their own ground rules, strengths, and weaknesses. This chapter highlights the implications of epidemiological research for the study of developmental kinesics.

Because principles of epidemiology are not consciously known and practiced in the field of kinesics, background information is necessary to understanding some of the jargon and thought processes that epidemiologists use. Austin and Werner (1974) have written a short, easy-to-read book designed to convey an understanding of epidemiologic concepts more rapidly than is possible with standard textbooks. A few high points can be summarized as follows.

Epidemiology is just a way of looking at things in a slightly different way reflecting an appreciation of what is important. Throughout the years people have used their observations Sherlock Holmes fashion, to understand causes of disease and to stop epidemics. The slightly different approach that epidemiology has contributed to the world is the use of rates for comparing events instead of plain numbers. Epidemiologists have taken the concept of using rates and polished it so that it seems sophisticated; actually it is quite simple: a rate is a number divided by another, just like a fraction. It is special because the denominator is almost always 100, 1000, or 10,000. Rates are used with such denominators to make comparison easier. It is much easier to compare 20/1000 versus 16/1000 than 50/2500 versus 52/3250 even though the comparisons are equivalent. Simply, a rate is events divided by population at risk $\times$ 100 (or 1000 or 10,000).

$$\text{rate} = \text{events} / (\text{population at risk}) \times 10^n$$

All the counts in the numerator are also in the denominator.

HISTORY

To appreciate the significance of epidemiology to the field of public health, a few historical concepts and insights need to be recapitulated. Many epidemiologists believe that the laws attributed to Moses are not just a religious code but also were directed toward prevention of illness. "The swine he is unclean" (Leviticus 10–17) was an extremely useful guideline if the disease trichinosis was to be avoided by a large colony of former slaves spending years in the desert with very primitive cooking facilities. After Moses, Hippocrates has been recognized as teaching correct principles for the prevention of diseases.

Two epidemiological concepts, environmental influences on disease and the notion that some diseases are contagious, can be traced back to the beginning of history. The Hippocratic work *On Airs, Waters and Places* stated: "Whoever wishes to investigate medicine properly, should proceed thus: in the first place consider the seasons of the year, and what effects each of them produce. . . . Then the winds. . . . We must also consider the qualities of the waters . . . and . . . the inhabitants . . . whether they are fond of drinking and eating to excess. . . ."

Isolation of persons with contagious diseases such as leprosy was practiced and written about in Biblical times. "Contagious," however, was given little formal expression until Girolamo Fracastoro published *De Contagione* in 1546. His proposal that infection could be transferred by minute, invisible particles led to long and sometimes acrimonious debate that was not resolved until the end of the nineteenth century.

EPIDEMIOLOGY AS A SCIENCE

During the eighteenth and nineteenth centuries two breakthroughs in medicine occurred *without* conscious use of rates. It was found that scurvy could be prevented among British sailors (limeys) by feeding them citrus fruit, and typhoid was linked to sewage. In the middle of the nineteenth century rates were used by Semmelweis and Snow in the control of childbed fever and cholera. Appreciation of their work in disease control was great, although understanding of their methodology was slow in coming; indeed, it is still not appreciated by the majority of physicians.

Why do epidemiologists compare rates? One answer is that they are searching for *association*. Epidemiologists look for associations to help them find "causes" of diseases. The term "cause" is used in its broad sense. Most diseases have multiple "causes," just as nonverbal expressions have a complex etiology. Automobile accidents may be "caused" by drinking, speeding, bad equipment, poor visibility, heavy traffic, and a whole host of other "causes." Similarly, one does not always know the "causes" of developmental delays in the acquisition of kinesis, and it is in this context that the principles of epidemiology may provide some insight.

The various definitions of epidemiology suggest that these definitions usually incorporate the word "disease"[1] and therefore would not, at first glance, apply to developmental kinesics. Before the turn of the century, Hirsch (1883–1886) defined epidemiology as "a picture of the occurrence, the distribution, and the types of the diseases of mankind, in distinct epochs of time, and at various points on the earth's surface; and render an account of the relations of those diseases to the external conditions." J. N. Morris (1964) presented a much shorter definition: "the study of health and disease of populations." "Populations," it should be noted, is the key word. However, the definition of epidemiology as given by Wade Hampton Frost (1936) is particularly meaningful in relation to this chapter. He said that epidemiology "is something more than the total of its established facts, it includes their orderly arrangement into chains of inference which extend more or less beyond the bounds of direct observation."

Conventional wisdom, supported by research data, holds that delayed language development is an educational handicap for the child having the delay (von Raffler-Engel, 1976a). Such children are believed to be at a real disadvantage both socially and educationally. Thus it does not require too great a leap of faith to accept the notion that delayed language development (including kinesics) is a psycholinguistically negative experience. To cope with this retardation, many have argued for some formal intervention (von Raffler-Engel and Hutcheson, 1975). Similarly, epidemiologists have been successful in the use of intervention strategies. Therefore, why should we not use some of the very tools that have been so advantageous in coping with diseases? We have an interest in finding out the determinants that are either risk factors or preventive factors in respect to the "disease," delayed language acquisition.

It was not until the papers of John Snow (1855) were published that today's brand of epidemiology using rates began to be practiced. His papers, over a century old, provide a nearly perfect modern model for today's epidemiology. Until that time, observations were made by practitioners of the healing arts and, from these observations, theories were formulated, advice given, and laws and codes instituted. This statement is not intended to demean Hippocrates, Moses, and other great minds. Observation is endemic to all sciences. Consequently it is not surprising that physicians, teachers, and many of the helping professions use the techniques of careful observation. They provide a thorough recording of the data, produce theories, and act on or publish their findings without consideration of rates.

---

[1] "Disease" originally was used in the broad sense of the term, that is, any condition that interferes with human functioning.

Snow did not spend all his energies on these well-recognized techniques in recording the cholera epidemic that devastated London in the 1850's. Instead, he went two steps further by: 1) carefully observing the people who did *not* get cholera and 2) calculating attack rates. The physicians of his day believed correctly that the disease cholera was multifactoral in its causes, and many of them observed and believed that the disease afflicted mainly the poor, the crowded, and unclean, the bad water drinkers, and persons exposed to bad air. Snow carefully observed hundreds of cases of cholera and, as he did this, he developed a theory that the *sine qua non* was the consumption of fecal material, usually from bad water and occasionally through the hands of the caregivers. Then, having developed this theory, he sought to prove it with the new tool epidemiologists call attack rates.

In London there were two different episodes of a dramatic cholera epidemic in which hundreds died. The first one occurred in the 1840's and the second one in the 1850's. A certain district of London was supplied by two different water companies, the Southwark and Vauxhall Company (S&V) and the Lambeth Company. In the period between the epidemics, the operators of the Lambeth Company moved their source of supply to a relatively uncontaminated area, but S&V continued to use the polluted part of the river that it and Lambeth had used during the earlier epidemic. It was quite fortunate for Snow that some districts of London were served by both companies, meaning that next-door neighbors and neighbors across the street from each other in some parts of London had water supplied by the two different water companies.

For convenience, Snow used as a case definition of cholera a sudden death associated with colorless, watery diarrhea. He used the simple technique of long division to calculate the attack rates of cholera per 10,000 households in that district of London in both outbreaks. In the outbreak of the 1840's, there was little difference in attack rates between persons served by the two companies. However, in the outbreak in the 1850's the respective attack rates were 71 and 5 per 10,000 households, showing a fourteenfold (!) difference. Snow went on to prove that the attack rates for persons served by the Lambeth Company were significantly lower than those for the rest of London. Those believing in the multifactoral causes of cholera were *not* shown to be wrong. What was shown was that the *most important ingredient* in the spread of cholera was the drinking of polluted water; crowding and poor sanitary conditions certainly contributed, but not nearly as much as drinking polluted water.

John Snow made the Broad Street pump and its handle a symbol for epidemiologists everywhere. It seems that hundreds of persons were dying of cholera in the area surrounding the Broad Street pump, but those working in the brewery next to the pump were not stricken: these individuals had access to a different deep well, but probably drank very little water because free beer was available to them. Snow suggested that the handle of the pump be removed, and the resulting control of the epidemic was truly dramatic. The John Snow Pub stands today at the brewery site in memory of his contribution. Long before the organism causing cholera was discovered, John Snow was able to identify the mode of transmission and the most important risk factor in the disease. It should be emphasized that in the epidemiology of communicable diseases there are some diseases, like cholera, that will not occur in the absence of the organism. However, even in cholera, there is no such thing as *a* cause of a disease. *All* diseases have many factors of host-agent environment in their causation. Some of these are age, sex, religion, ethnicity, culture, physical factors, and in general the personal and geographic factors that vary enormously from person to person.

STRUCTURAL PARALLELS

With this background, and with the overview of the issues presented by von Raffler-Engel (1976a), it becomes immediately obvious that this investigator uses the same sort of intellectual curiosity and careful recording of data that Dr. John Snow employed when he was studying cholera and its risk factors. Among the many factors that may influence development kinesics, von Raffler-Engel noted age, sex, culture, intended receiver of the message, muscular coordination, personality differences, talkativeness, mothering behavior, handicapping conditions, mental retardation, emotional disturbances, motor readiness, and social awareness. The factors that influence development of kinesics can influence the development of diseases.

Nationality and culture according to von Raffler-Engel (1980) influence kinesis: Americans and Greeks have opposite head movements for *yes* and *no*. The hand gesture that signifies the number 2 to an American signifies 3 to a German. The emotional release of profound grief is expected to be contained in Great Britain, but not in many societies in the Middle East.

Nationality and culture influence disease distribution also. Suicide is more common (has a higher rate) in Japan than in Israel. Black persons have a higher rate of sickle cell disease than other groups, yet the same sickle cell risk factor is protective against malaria. Americans are more likely to suffer from high blood pressure than Japanese. Culture influences diet, and diet influences high blood pressure.

Von Raffler-Engel (1980b) shows that much learning including acquisition of kinesics takes place through osmosis (incidental learning) with reinforcement by models, often parents. The structural parallel is the observation that children imitate all sorts of adult and peer behavior, including behaviors that prevent accidents (usually noted from parents) and reckless behavior that causes accidents (often copied from peers).

Age and physical maturity influence the acquisition of kinesics. Thus an American or an Italian infant may imitate the hand motion for leave taking correctly, although the "correct" gesture is different in the two cases. The Japanese girl described by von Raffler-Engel in Chapter 1 had to be able to stand and bow to execute the proper body movements in her pretend telephone conversation.

The structural parallel is that age is the most important determinant in all forms of disease. Children under age 4 die at a higher rate than older persons in auto accidents when the proper denominator (per million passenger miles) is used. High blood pressures, strokes, and heart attacks occur at a higher rate among persons over 45.

Sex differences exist in kinesics. Von Raffler-Engel (1980d) observed that when girls disapproved of the content of a story being told, they became stiffer, whereas boys showed bewilderment in their faces. The structural parallel is that disease rates are influenced by sex. Boys in elementary schools in the United States have a higher accident rate than girls, as all school teachers know. Cancer of the breast is uncommon in males, but it does occur. Females, especially those over 20, have a much higher rate of breast cancer than males. Males have a higher rate of high blood pressure than females, especially among 35–45 year olds.

Von Raffler-Engel (1980e) observed nonverbal behavior in Down's syndrome and normal children. The Down's syndrome children made no use at all of illustrators. The structural parallel is that Down's syndrome children are at higher risk of tooth decay and heart disease than normal children are.

Age, sex, social class, and culture, four factors that have an enormous effect on developmental kinesics, also have an enormous effect on the acquisition or nonacquisition of cholera in Bangladesh. Von Raffler-Engel states that some of the problems in the research of developmental kinesics include the difficulty in producing an inventory of nonverbal language and the extreme fatigue associated with the study of videotaped nonverbal interaction. It seems clear not only that a learning paradigm is the best way to study developmental kinesics, but also that a learning paradigm *requires* an inventory of nonverbal language for different cultures and ages. Both the inventory and the analysis described by von Raffler-Engel will require an enormous amount of work. An epidemiological paradigm gets around some of these problems, as we shall see, but the answers it produces will not necessarily address the questions that the people in the field want answered.

IMPLICATIONS FOR DEVELOPMENTAL KINESICS

The epidemiologists approaching the questions relating to determinants in developmental kinesics may directly benefit from reading the position paper by von Raffler-Engel (1976a). They could, for example, form a hypothesis that because only a few weeks might be available to study the "disease" (i.e. delayed acquisition of kinesics), it would be necessary to do two things:

1. Develop a case definition to distinguish cases from noncases. In developing the case definition, one would probably look for presence or absence of the most used forms of nonverbal language such as leave taking, yes/no, and deictic motion. A "case" could then be a child who uses none of the three during a stated period of observation. Each of the three should be described unequivocally.
2. Form a hypothesis, such as "age is the most important determinant." But other factors such as social class, position in a family in respect to the siblings' ages, and presence of emotional disturbances would be associated with delayed acquisition of kinesics.

At this point, the educators and linguists would probably jump up and down and say "Hey, wait a minute, you can't do that. Instead, you must describe in detail each child's behavior. Acquisition of nonverbal language is *not* an all-or-nothing phenomenon." Then the reply would be "Well, I am not using a learning paradigm. Let me continue before you judge me too harshly." It is important to note that if the epidemiologist were studying measles, the physicians would jump up and down and say "You cannot do this because your case definition for measles will clearly identify some cases as measles who do not really have it and some cases without measles who really do have it." The answer would still be the same. "Wait until I make my case before you judge me too harshly."

The next step would be to collect data on as many children as possible. Obvious sites for data collection include day care centers, nursery schools, and nurseries at the sites of religious programs when parents gather for services. The data on each child would include identifiers, presence or absence of the case definition, and personal characteristics that are fairly easily measured, such as number of caregivers, date of birth, position in the family, occupation of parents, and cultural indicators such as skin color and parents' religious preference. After examining the raw data, the investigator might form a hypothesis that when age is held constant, the number of hours of caregiver time per child can protect the child against "disease" (i.e., developmental delays in nonverbal behavior), and when the number of hours per child is low (e.g., in a family with one adult caregiver and many small children), it would seem logical to collect more data to attempt to verify that hypothesis, which is similar to the hypothesis of Zajonc (1975).

Like John Snow (1855), the epidemiologist will collect "attack rates" for different groups. Although numbers alone may tell the story, optimal analysis of the data *must* be converted to appropriate rates or ratios using accepted mathematical techniques. The resulting figures provide a better measure of occurrence of delays because they take into account the approximate size of the population at risk. If the background rate for developmental kinesics delays in 2 year olds in nursery schools is 3 per 100 (i.e., 3%), and nursery school X has a rate of 15% among 2 year olds, it becomes useful to find out what the risk factors may be. Small differences are difficult to interpret, but a fivefold increase in nursery school X indicates a real problem, that is, an epidemic.

An epidemic is by definition the occurrence of bad events clearly in excess of the number expected. Regardless of what the risk factors may be, the nursery school will need some additional early childhood intervention techniques. Which intervention technique based on which theories shall the investigator employ? The literature on language intervention programs, including its controversies, has been reviewed (von Raffler-Engel and Hutcheson, 1975), and that review offers an overview of what has been tried, based on what theories. Such an overview may: 1) save the investigator library time, 2) point out some of the risk factors in delayed language acquisition, and 3) describe some of the intervention techniques and their problems. If the risk factors are those that can be changed (e.g., "no breakfast"), the intervention may be enhanced by removing the risk factor.

The next step would be to gather more data, attempt publication with enough information to permit the duplication of the observations by others, and perhaps make a strong case for the hypothesis. It is at least within the realm of possibility that such epidemiological studies could influence public policy. John Snow asked that the handle be removed from the Broad Street pump. This was done, and then disease diminished remarkably.

Tactics such as those described in this chapter might identify the Broad Street pump handle for delayed acquisition of kinesics. There may indeed be a critical number of caregivers per child, or a number of caregiver hours per child, required to avoid delayed language development including nonverbal language. Of course, the investigator might quickly disprove that hypothesis and find another one that fits the data set.

When carried out correctly, the principles of epidemiology should allow one to define high risk populations for delayed acquisition of language and kinesics with the hope of initiating specific control measures. Unfortunately, control measures that may be recommended based on the investigation will necessitate the cooperation of a number of individuals who may be unfamiliar with the techniques and even suspicious of them. If those involved then fail to reach the same conclusions as the investigator, it will be difficult to obtain cooperation.

Those interested in the theory and practice of language intervention programs did not have easy access to a summary and bibliography of accomplishments in the field until von Raffler-Engel and Hutcheson (1975) published their monograph. Unfortunately, without a work such as this, a computer-assisted librarian cannot produce a fairly complete, fairly selective bibliography on language intervention in normal children. This is because the key words for indexing and the titles themselves have not been specific enough. The lack of specificity requires the investigator to go to the original work, often to find that the article is of no use.

Which theory and which control measure are appropriate in developmental kinesics? The monograph does not answer that specific question, but it does catalogue theories and intervention procedures for delayed development of *spoken* language. The most optimistic theory—namely, that language behavior can be changed by developing appropriate training procedures—is potentially the most useful, especially if it includes proper attention to the health social needs of the child (von Raffler-Engel and Hutcheson, 1975: 2). The conclusions are analyzed with respect to their similarities and differences. The central issue of language stimulation amounts to where, when, how, and by whom the presentation of language to the child should be accomplished.

Works on language enrichment are concerned primarily with cognitive factors, affective, neurophysiologic, and other factors rarely appear in the literature (von Raffler-Engel and Hutcheson, 1975: 3). This unfortunate circumstance may reflect problems of quantitating affective factors and the lack of agreement in other factors. The author's involvement with Tennessee Child Development Projects has afforded an opportunity to learn how much administrators like things that can be measured in budget justification documents. The sympathy and caring with which the workers approach their jobs and the attempts to see that all the child's health needs are met are less impressive to bureaucrats than a demonstration that children are at or ahead of the expected milestones for their age.

The theories about language and dialect are numerous, and a few are absurd. The epidemiological approach would be to read the suggestions of von Raffler-Engel and Hutcheson (1975: 5) and set about simple observation of children less than 36 months old in various group settings, and select what seems to be appropriate. If observed data do not fit the theory, do not use the theory!

Although there has been much research on how and where language intervention should take place, and the bibliography is large, we do not know whether language is best improved by instructing children individually or in groups, or by alternating the individual with the group setting. We still do not know, and need research to determine, the suitability of the methods above depending on such risk factors as age, ethnic background, family situation, attitude of the family, and attitude of the community toward the program. We believe that attitudes will be related to the program itself, how it is structured, and its principal immediate objective (von Raffler-Engel and Hutcheson, 1975: 24). We do not believe that the research problems will be solved soon, nor do we believe that the many experts who have written on the subject will be speaking with a single voice at any time in the distant future.

Since the experts disagree, what are the new epidemiologists to do? In all probability they will visit programs that seem to work and try to pick a methodology to improve kinesics from a methodology to improved spoken language that not only seems to work but also has the affective, medical, nutritional, and social components that also seem to work. Furthermore, principles of epidemiology will assist in developing the background prevalence of developmental delays and will enable the investigators to locate epidemic foci of the disease, which is the group needing language intervention the most.

SUMMARY

Since the dawn of history, epidemics have been studied and controlled using theories based on observation. Until rates were used to observe epidemics in the nineteenth century, epidemiology was only occasionally a successful science. By the use of rates, epidemiology has been used to find associations and causes of diseases. Associations have been observed in the studies of developmental kinesics. Because many such associations have structural parallels in diseases (age, sex, nationality, culture, etc.) that influence both kinesics and diseases, epidemiology could be used as a tool for determining more associations and for locating groups in need of intervention. Furthermore, the newly discovered associations should provide the opportunity to develop and test theories to explain the differences observed and the remediation needed. A review of the literature has been done, which may assist future investigators when the research begins.

LITERATURE CITED

Abravanel, E., Levin-Goldschmidt, E., and Stevenson, M. B. 1976. Action imitation: The early phase of infancy. *Child Dev.* 47:1032–1044.

Alexandre, P. 1972. *An Introduction to Languages and Language in Africa.* Transl. by F. A. Leary. William Heinemann Ltd., London. (Original title: *Langue et Langage en Afrique Noire,* 1968.)

Allport, G. W., and Vernon, P. 1933. *Studies in Expressive Movement.* Macmillan Publishing Company, Inc., New York.

Antinucci, R., and Parisi, D. 1973. Early language acquisition. In: C. Ferguson and D. Slobin (eds.), *Studies in Child Language Development.* Holt, Rinehart & Winston, New York.

Argyle, M. 1972. *The Psychology of Interpersonal Behavior.* 3 Ed. Penguin Books, Inc., Baltimore.

Austin, D. F., and Werner, S. B. 1974. *Epidemiology for the Health Sciences.* Charles C. Thomas, Springfield, Ill.

Austin, J. L. 1962. *How To Do Things with Words.* Oxford University Press, Cambridge.

Bakeman, R., and Dabbs, J. M. 1976. Social interaction observed: Some approaches to the analysis of behavior streams. *Pers. Soc. Psychol. Bull.* 2:335–345.

Barker, R. G. (ed.). 1963. *The Stream of Behavior.* Appleton-Century-Crofts, New York.

Barroso, F., Freedman, N., Grand, S., and Bucci, W. 1976. The evocation of two types of hand movements in information processing. Paper presented at the 47th Annual Meeting, Eastern Psychological Association, New York.

Bates, E. 1976. The emergence of symbols: Ontogeny and phylogeny. In: W. A. Collins (ed.). *Children's Language and Communication: The Minnesota Symposia on Child Psychology,* Vol. 12. Lawrence Erlbaum Associates, Hillsdale, N. J.

Bates, E., Benigni, L., Bretherton, I., Camaioni, L., and Volterra, V. 1977. From gesture to the first word: On cognitive and social prerequisites. In: M. Lewis and L. Rosenblum (eds.), *Interaction, Conversation and the Development of Language.* John Wiley and Sons, Inc., New York.

Bates, E., Benigni, L., Bretherton, I., Camaioni, L., and Volterra, V. 1979. Cognition and communication from nine to thirteen months: Correlational findings. In: E. Bates, L. Benigni, I. Bretherton, L. Camaioni, and V. Volterra (eds.), *The Emergence of Symbols: Cognition and Communication in Infancy.* Academic Press, New York.

Bates, E., Camaioni, L., and Volterra, V. 1975. The acquisition of performatives prior to speech. *Merrill-Palmer Q. 21*:205–226.

Bates, E., and MacWhinney, B. 1979. The functionalist approach to the acquisition of grammar. In: E. Ochs and B. B. Schieffelin (eds.), *Developmental Pragmatics*. Academic Press, New York.

Bellugi, U. 1971. Simplification in children's language. In: R. Huxley and E. Ingram (eds.), *Language Acquisition: Models and Methods*. Academic Press, London.

Bellugi, U., and Fischer, S. A. 1972. A comparison of sign language and spoken language. *Cognition 1*:173–200.

Bellugi, U., and Klima, E. 1979. Language: Perspectives from another modality. In: *Brain and Mind*, Ciba Foundation Series no. 69 (new series). Elsevier–Excerpta Medica, Amsterdam.

Benedict, H. 1979. Early lexical development: Comprehension and production. *J. Child Lang. 6*:183–199.

Berlyne, D. E. 1965. *Structure and Direction in Thinking*. John Wiley and Sons, Inc., New York.

Birdwhistell, R. L. 1952. *Introduction to Kinesics*. University of Louisville Press, Louisville.

Birdwhistell, R. L. 1966. Some relations between American kinesics and spoken American English. In: A. Smith (ed.), *Communication and Culture*. Cambridge University Press, Cambridge.

Birdwhistell, R. L. 1970. *Kinesics and Context*. University of Pennsylvania Press, Philadelphia.

Bloom, L. 1970. *Language Development: Form and Function in Emerging Grammars*. MIT Press, Cambridge, Mass.

Bloom, L. 1973. *One Word at a Time*. Mouton, the Hague.

Bloom, L., Lightbown, P., and Hood, L. 1975. Structure and variation in child language. *Monographs of the Society for Research in Child Development*. Vol. 40, No. 2, Serial no. 160.

Blumenthal, A. L. 1970. *Language and Psychology: Historical Aspects of Psycholinguistics*. John Wiley and Sons, Inc., New York.

Blurton-Jones, N. (ed.). 1972. *Ethological Studies of Child Behavior*. Cambridge University Press, Cambridge.

Bode, L. 1974. Communication of agent, object, and indirect object in spoken and signed languages. *Percept. Mot. Skills 39*:1151–1158.

Bolinger, D. 1975. *Aspects of Language*. 2 Rev. Ed. Harcourt, Brace, Jovanovich, New York.

Booth, T. L. 1967. *Sequential Machines and Automata Theory*. John Wiley and Sons, Inc., New York.

Bower, T. G. R. 1977. *A Primer of Infant Development*. W. H. Freeman & Company, Inc., San Francisco.

Bowerman, M. F. 1973. *Early Syntactic Development*. Cambridge University Press, Cambridge.

Bowlby, J. 1969. *Attachment and Loss*. Hogarth Press, Ltd., London.

Brain, L. 1961. *Speech Disorders*. Butterworths Scientific Publications, Ltd., London.

Braine, M. D. S. 1963. The ontogeny of English phrase structure: The first phase. *Language 39:*1–13.

Braine, M. D. S. 1971. The acquisition of language in infant and child. In: C. Reed (ed.), *The Learning of Language*. Appleton-Century-Crofts, New York.

Braine, M. D. S. 1973. On learning the grammatical order of words. *Psychol. Rev. 70*:323–348.

Braine, M. D. S. 1976. Children's first word combinations. *Monogr. Soc. Res. Child Dev. 41*(1), Serial no. 164.

Brazelton, T. B., Kolowski, B., and Main, M. 1974. The origin of reciprocity: The early mother-infant interaction. In: M. Lewis and L. A. Rosenblum (eds.), *The Effect of the Infant on Its Caregiver*. John Wiley and Sons, Inc., New York.

Breiman, L. 1969. *Probability and Stochastic Processes*. Houghton-Mifflin Company, Boston.

Bresnan, J. W. 1971. Sentence stress and syntactic transformations. *Language 47*:257–281.

Brown, N. 1959. *Life Against Death*. Wesleyan University Press, Middletown, Conn.

Brown, R. 1973. *A First Language: The Early Stages*. Harvard University Press, Cambridge, Mass.

Brown, R. 1977. Introduction. In C. Snow and C. Ferguson (eds.), *Talking to Children; Language Input and Acquisition*. Cambridge University Press, Cambridge.

Brown, R., and Bellugi, U. 1964. Three processes in the child's acquisition of syntax. *Harvard Educ. Rev. 34*:133–151.

Brown, R., and Fraser, C. 1963. The acquisition of syntax. In: C. N. Cofer and B. S. Musgrave (eds.), *Verbal Behavior and Learning: Problems and Processes*. McGraw-Hill Book Company, Inc., New York.

Brown, R., and Hanlon, C. 1970. Derivational complexity and order of acquisition in child speech. In: J. H. Hayes (ed.), *Cognition and the Development of Language*. John Wiley and Sons, Inc., New York.

Brown, R. H. 1978. *A Poetic for Sociology: Toward a Logic of Discovery for the Human Sciences*. Cambridge University Press, Cambridge.

Bruner, J. S. 1966. On cognitive growth. In: J. S. Bruner et al. (eds.), *Studies in Cognitive Growth*. John Wiley and Sons, Inc., New York.

Bruner, J. S. 1968. *Processes of cognitive growth: Infancy*. Clark University Press, Worcester, Mass.

Bruner, J. S. 1969. Eye, hand, and mind. In: D. Elkind and J. H. Flavell (eds.), *Studies in Cognitive Development*. Oxford University Press, New York.

Bruner, J.S. 1973. Organization of early skilled action. *Child Dev.* 44:1–11.

Bruner, J. S. 1977. Early social interaction and language acquisition. In: H. R. Schaffer (ed.), *Studies in Mother-Infant Interaction*. Academic Press, New York.

Bûhler, K. 1934. *Sprachtheorie*. Fischer, Jena.

Bullowa, M. 1975. When infant and adult communicate, how do they synchronize their behavior? In: A. Kendon, R. M. Harris, and M. R. Key (eds.), *Organization of Behavior in Face-to-Face Interaction*. Mouton (World Anthropology), the Hague.

Bullowa, M. 1979. Introduction. Prelinguistic communication: A field for scientific research. In: M. Bullowa (ed.), *Before Speech*. Cambridge University Press, Cambridge.

Bullowa, M., Fidelholtz, J. L., and Kessler, A. R. 1975. Infant vocalization: Communication before speech. In: T. R. Williams (ed.), *Socialization and Communication in Primary Groups*. Mouton (World Anthropology), the Hague.

Burke, K. 1966. *Language and Symbolic Action*. University of California Press, Berkeley.

Carlson, P., and Anisfeld, M. 1969. Some observations on the linguistic competence of a two-year-old child. *Child Dev.* 40:569–575.

Carson, R. C. 1969. *Interaction Concepts of Personality*. Aldine Publishers, Chicago.

Carter, A. L. 1978. The development of systematic vocalizations prior to words: A case study. In: N. Waterson and C. Snow (eds.), *The Development of Communication*. John Wiley and Sons, Inc., New York.

Chafe, W. L. 1976. Givenness, contrastiveness, definiteness, subjects, topics, and point of view. In: C. N. Li (ed.), *Subject and Topic*. Academic Press, New York.

Chambers, J. K. (1973) Remarks on topicalization in child language. *Found. Lang.* 9:442–446.

Chapple, E. D., and Arnesberg, C. M. 1940. Measuring human relations. *Genet. Psychol. Monog.* 22:3–147.

Chomsky, C. 1969. *The Acquisition of Syntax in Children from 5 to 10*. MIT Press, Cambridge, Mass.

Chomsky, N. 1965. *Aspects of the Theory of Syntax*. MIT Press, Cambridge, Mass.

Chomsky, N., and Halle, M. 1968. *The Sound Pattern of English*. Harper and Row, Inc., New York.

Clark, E. 1973a. How children describe time and order. In: C. Ferguson and D. Slobin (eds.), *Studies of Child Language Development*. Holt, Rinehart & Winston, New York.

Clark, E. 1973b. What's in a word? On the child's acquisition of semantics in his first language. In: T. Moore (ed.), *Cognitive Development and the Acquisition of Language*. Academic Press, New York.

Clark, E. 1974. Some aspects of the conceptual basis for first language acquisition. In: R. Schiefelbusch and L. Lloyd (eds.), *Language Perspectives—Acquisition, Retardation and Intervention*. University Park Press, Baltimore.

Clark, E. 1975. Knowledge, context and strategy in the acquisition of meaning. In: D. Dato (ed.), Proceedings of the 26th Annual Georgetown University Roundtable. *Developmental Psycholinguistics: Theory and Applications*. Georgetown University Press, Washington, D.C.

Clark, H. H., and Clark, E. V. 1968. Semantic distinctions and memory for complex sentences. *Q. J. Exp. Psychol. 20*:129–138.

Cogen, C. 1977. On three aspects of time expression in American Sign Language. In: L. A. Friedman (ed.), *On the Other Hand*. Academic Press, New York.

Cohen, E., Namir, L., and Schlesinger, I. M. 1977. *A New Dictionary of Sign Language*. Mouton, the Hague.

Condon, W. S. 1980. Cultural microrhythms. In: M. Davis (ed.), *Interaction Rhythm*. Proceedings of the First Annual Research Conference of the Institute for Nonverbal Communication Research, Teachers College, Columbia University, 1979. Human Science Press, New York.

Condon, W. S., and Ogston, W. 1966. Sound film analysis of normal and pathological behavior patterns. *J. Nerv. Ment. Dis. 143*:338–347.

Condon, W. S., and Sander, L. W. 1974a. Neonate movement is synchronized with adult speech: Interactional participation and language acquisition. *Science 183*:99–101.

Condon, W. S., and Sander, L. W. 1974b. Synchrony demonstrated between movement of the neonate and adult speech. *Child Dev. 45*:456–462.

Cornford, F. M. 1952. *Principium Sapientiae: The Origins of Greek Philosophical Thought*. Cambridge University Press, Cambridge.

Cox, D. R., and Lewis, P. A. W. 1966. *The Statistical Analysis of Series of Events*. Methuen & Co. Ltd., London.

Cross, T. G. 1975. Some relationship between motherese and linguistic level in accelerated children. Papers on Reports on Child Language Development, No. 10, Stanford University, Stanford, Calif.

Cross, T. G. 1978. Motherese: Its association with rate of syntactic acquisition in young children. In: N. Waterson and C. Snow (eds.), *The Development of Communication: Social and Pragmatic Factors in Language Acquisition*. John Wiley and Sons, Inc., New York.

Dale, P. S. 1980. Is early pragmatic development measurable? *J. Child Lang.* 7:1–12.

Darwin, C. 1929. *The Expression of the Emotions in Man and Animals.* D. Appleton, New York. (Original edition, 1872).

Darwin, C. 1859. *The Origin of the Species by Means of Natural Selection or the Preservation of Favoured Races in the Struggle for Life.* Reprinted in 1968. Penguin Books, Inc., Baltimore.

Deleau, M. 1978. *Imitations des Gestes et Representation Graphique de Corps chez les Enfants Sourds.* Monographies Francaises de Psychologie, No. 42. Centre National de la Recherche Scientifique, Paris.

DeStefano, J. S. 1972. Some parameters of register in adult and child speech. *ITL* 18:31–45. Institute for Applied Linguistics, Louvain, Belgium.

Deutsch, F. 1952. Analytic posturology. *Psychoanal. Q.* 21:196–214.

Deutsch, J. A., and Deutsch, D. 1963. Attention: Some theoretical considerations. *Psychol. Rev.* 20:80–90.

Dittman, A. T. 1966. Speech and body movement: Independent sources of information. Paper presented at the Annual Meeting of the American Psychological Association, New York.

Dittman, A. T. 1972. The body movement–speech rhythm relationship as a cue to speech encoding. In: A. W. Siegman and B. Pope (eds.), *Studies in Dyadic Communication.* Pergamon Press, New York.

Dore, J. 1979. What is so conceptual about the acquisition of linguistic structures? *J. Child Lang.* 6:129–137.

Dore, J., Franklin M. B., Miller, R. T., and Ramer, A. L. H. 1976. Transitional phenomena in early language acquisition. *J. Child Lang.* 3:13–28.

Druker, J. F., and Hagen, J. W. 1969. Developmental trends in processing of task-relevant and task-irrelevant information. *Child Dev.* 40:371–382.

Dukoff, S. 1979. *Notes on children's gestures.* Unpublished manuscript, Department of Psychology, Queens University, Kingston, Ontario, Canada.

Dyer, F. N. 1973. Interference and facilitation for color naming with separate bilateral presentation of word and color. *J. Exp. Psychol.* 99:314–317.

Edge, V., and Herrmann, L. 1977. Verbs and the determination of subject in American Sign Language. In: L. A. Friedman (ed.), *On the Other Hand.* Academic Press, New York.

Efron, D. 1941. *Gesture and Environment.* King's Crown Press, New York.

Ekman, P. 1965. Differential communication of affect by head and body cues. *J. Pers. Soc. Psychol.* 2:726–735.

Ekman, P. 1980. Three classes of nonverbal behavior. In: W. von Raffler-Engel (ed.), *Aspects of Nonverbal Communication.* Swets and Zeitlinger, Amsterdam.

Engquist, G. 1977. Skill and the development of selective behavior perception. Unpublished doctoral dissertation, University of Virginia.

Engquist, G., Newtson, D., and LaCrosse, K. Undated. Prior expectancy and the perceptual segmentation of ongoing behavior. Unpublished manuscript.

Ervin, S. 1964. Imitation and structural change in children's language. In: E. H. Lenneberg (ed.), *New Directions in the Study of Language.* MIT Press, Cambridge.

Eshkol, N. 1973. *Moving Writing Reading.* Movement Notation Society, Tel Aviv.

Fagen, R. M., and Young, D. Y. 1978. Temporal patterns of behaviors. In: P. W. Colgan (ed.), *Quantitative Ethology.* John Wiley and Sons, Inc. New York.

Feldman, H., Goldin-Meadow, S., and Gleitman, L. 1978. Beyond Herodotus: The creation of language by linguistically deprived deaf children. In: A. Lock (ed.), *Action, Gesture and Symbol.* Academic Press, London.

Feuerstein, R. 1979. Ontogeny of learning in man. In: M. Brazier (ed.), *Brain Mechanisms in Memory and Learning: From the Single Neuron to Man.* Raven Press, New York.

Feuerstein, R., and Rand, Y. 1975. Mediated learning experiences: An outline of the proximal etiology for differential development of cognitive functions. *Int. Understanding 9/10:*7–37.

Feuerstein, R., Rand, Y., and Hoffman, M. B. 1979. *The Dynamic Assessment of Retarded Performers: The Learning Potential Assessment Device, Theory, Instruments, and Techniques.* University Park Press, Baltimore.

Feuerstein, R., Rand, Y., Hoffman, M. B., and Miller, R. 1980. *Instrumental Enrichment: An Intervention Program for Cognitive Modifiability.* University Park Press, Baltimore.

Fischer, S. 1973. Two processes of reduplication in the American Sign Language. *Found. Lang. 9:*469–480.

Fischer, S. 1975. Influences on word order changes in American Sign Language. In: C. N. Li (ed.), *Word Order and Word Order Change.* University of Texas Press, Austin.

Fischer, S. 1978. Sign language and creoles. In: F. Siple (ed.), *Understanding Language Through Sign Language Research.* Academic Press, New York.

Fodor, J. A., Bever, T. G., and Garret, M. F. 1974. *The Psychology of Language: An Introduction to Psycholinguistics and Generative Grammar.* McGraw-Hill Book Company, Inc., New York.

Fogel, A. 1977. Temporal organization in mother-infant face-to-face interaction. In: H. R. Schaffer (ed.), *Studies in Mother-Infant Interaction.* Academic Press, New York.

Foster, S. 1979. Topic initiation, one step or two: Some factors involved in mother-child interaction at the prelinguistic stage. *Nottingham Linguist. Circle.*

Foster, S. H. 1979. *Research Summary.* Unpublished manuscript. Department of Linguistics and Psychology, Lancaster University, Lancaster, England.

Fracastoro, G. 1546 *De contagione.* Reprinted in A. Lilienfeld 1976; *Foundations of Epidemiology.* Oxford University Press, New York.

Freedle, R. 1979. Interaction of language use with ethnography and cognition. Paper presented at the *Vanderbilt University Conference on Cognition, Social Behavior, and Environment.*

Freedman, N. 1972. The analysis of movement behavior during the clinical interview. In: A. Siegman and B. Pope (eds.), *Studies in Dyadic Communication.* Pergamon Press, New York.

French, P. 1976. Disintegrating theoretical distinctions and some future directions in psycholinguistics. In: E. C. Carterette and M. P. Friedman (eds.), *Handbook of Perception, Vol. VII. Language and Speech.* Academic press, New York.

French, P. L., and von Raffler-Engel, W. The kinesics of bilingualism. In: W. Mackay (ed.), *Social Aspects of Language Contact.* Laval University Press, Quebec. In press.

Freud, S. 1906. Fragment of an analysis of a case of hysteria. In: *The standard Edition of the Complete Psychological Works of Sigmund Freud,* Vol. 3, pp. 3–122. Reprinted by Hogarth Press Ltd., London, 1953.

Frey, J., and Newtson, D. 1973. Differential attribution in an unequal power situation: Biased inference or biased input? *Proceedings* of the 81st Annual Convention of the American Psychological Association.

Frey, W. H. 1980. Not so idle tears. *Psychol. Today,* January, pp. 91–92.

Friedman, L. A. 1976. The manifestation of subject, object and topic in the American Sign Language. In: L. N. Li (ed.), *Subject and Topic.* Academic Press, New York.

Frost, W. H. 1936. *Snow on Cholera: Being a Reprint of Two Papers by John Snow, M.D.* Commonwealth Fund, New York.

Gewirtz, J. L. 1969. Mechanisms of social learning: Some roles of stimulation and behavior in early human development. *In* D. A. Goslin (ed.), Handbook of Socialization Theory and Research. Rand McNally, Chicago.

Gesell, A., Ilg, F., Ames, L., and Bullis, G. (eds.). 1946. *The Child from Five to Ten.* Harper and Row, Inc., New York.

Geylman, I. 1964. The hand alphabet and speech gestures of deaf-mutes. In: E. Smith (ed.), *Workshop on Interpreting for the Deaf.* Indiana. Transl. from the Russian.

Givon, T. 1979. On Understanding Grammar. Academic Press, New York.

Goffman, E. 1959. *The Presentation of Self in Everyday Life.* Anchor Books, New York.

Golani, I. 1973. *The Golden Jackal.* Movement Notation Society, Tel Aviv.

Goldin-Meadow, S. J. 1975. The representation of semantic relations in manual language created by children of hearing parents: A language you can't dismiss out of hand. Technical report 26. University of Pennsylvania, Philadelphia.

Goldin-Meadow, S. J. 1980. Structure in manual communication system developed without a conventional language model: Language without a helping hand. In: H. Whitaker and H. A. Whitaker (eds.), *Studies in Neurolinguistics. Vol. 4.* Academic Press, New York.

Goldin-Meadow, S. J., Seligman, M., and Gelman, R. 1976. Language and the two year old. *Cognition 4*:189–202.

Grand, S., Freedman, N., and Steingart, I. 1973. A study of the representation of objects in schizophrenia. *J. Am. Psycholanal. Assoc. 21*:399–434.

Grand, S., Freedman, N., Steingart, I., and Buchwald, C. 1975. Communicative behavior in schizophrenia. The relation of adaptive styles to kinetic and linguistic aspects of interview behavior. *J. Nerv. Ment. Dis. 161*:293–306.

Grand, S., Marcos, L. R. Freedman, N., and Barroso, F. 1977. Relation of psychopathology and bilingualism to kinesic aspects of interview behavior in schizoprenia. J. Abnorm. Psychol. 86:492–500.

Greene, J. 1972. *Psycholinguistics and Chomsky.* Penguin Books, Inc., Baltimore.

Greenbaum, S., and Meyer, C. F. 1979. Coordination constructions in English: Judgments of their frequency and acceptability. Department of English, University of Wisconsin, Milwaukee.

Greenberg, J. H. 1963. Some universals of grammar with particular reference to the order of meaningful elements. In: J. H. Greenberg (ed.), *Universals of Language.* 2nd Ed. MIT Press, Cambridge, Mass.

Greenfield, P. 1978. How much is one word? *J. Child Lang. 5*:347–352.

Greenfield, P., and Smith, J. H. 1976. *The Structure of Communication in Early Language Development.* Academic Press, New York.

Gruber, J. S. 1967. Topicalization in Child Language. *Found. Lang. 3*:37–65.

Hagen, J. W. 1967. The effect of distraction on selective attention. *Child Dev. 38*:685–694.

Hall, E. T. 1966. *The Hidden Dimension.* Doubleday & Company, Inc., Garden City, N. Y.

Halliday, M. A. K. 1975. *Learning How to Mean: Explorations in the Development of Language.* Edward Arnold & Co., London.

Hansen, B. 1975. Varieties in Danish Sign Language and grammatical features of the original sign language. *Sign Lang. Stud. 8*:249–256.

Harding, C. G., and Golinkoff, R. M. 1979. The origins of intentional vocalizations in prelinguistic infants. *Child Dev. 50*:33–40.

Hays, W. L. 1963. *Statistics for Psychologists.* Holt, Rinehart & Winston, New York.

Heider, F. 1958. *The Psychology of Interpersonal Relations.* John Wiley and Sons, Inc., New York.

Herzka, S. 1978. *Gesicht und Sprache.* Schwabe & Co., Basel.

Hewes, G. W. 1955. World distribution of certain postural habits. *Am. Anthropol. 57*:231–244.

Hinde, R. A. 1972. *Non-verbal Communication.* Cambridge University Press, Cambridge.

Hippocrates. *On airs, waters, and places.* Reprinted in A. Lilienfeld (ed.), *Foundations of epidemiology.* Oxford University Press, New York. 1976.

Hirsch, A. 1883–1886. *Handbook of Geographical and Historical Pathology. Vols. I–III.* Transl. from the German by C. Creighton. New Sydenham Society, London.

Hoffer, B. 1976. Nonreferential verbal communication. In: W. von Raffler-Engel (ed.), *Child Language—1975.* Special triple issue of *Word 27* (1–3).

Hoffer, B. 1978. The acquisition of English syntax by Mexican Americans: Grades 1–6. In: G. Gilbert (ed.), *Problems in Educational Sociolinguistics.* Walter de Gruyter & Co., Berlin.

Hoffer, B., and Santos, R. 1977. Cultural clashes in kinesics. In: W. von Raffler-Engel and B. Hoffer (eds.), *Aspects of Nonverbal Communication.* Trinity University, San Antonio.

Hoffman, S. P. 1968. An empirical study of representational hand movements. Unpublished doctoral dissertation, New York University.

Holmes, V. M. 1973. Order of main and subordinate clauses in sentence perception. *J. Verb. Learn. Verb. Behav. 12*:285–293.

Hopson-Hasham, B. 1977. The adjustment of the speaker to the hearer. In: W. von Raffler-Engel and B. Hoffer (eds.), *Aspects of Nonverbal Communication.* Trinity University, San Antonio.

Hull, C. L., and Hull, B. I. 1919. Parallel learning curves of an infant in vocabulary and in voluntary control of the bladder. *Pedagog. Semin. 26*:272–283.

Hutcheson, R. H. 1978. Language acquisition in the infant and pre-school child: A pediatrician's viewpoint. In: F. C. C. Peng and W. von Raffler-Engel (eds.), *Language Acquisition and Language Development.* Bunka Hyoron, Hiroshima.

Hutt, C. 1968. Etude d'un Corpus: Dictionnaire de Langage Gestuel chez les Trappistes. *Langages 10*:107–118.

Hymes, D. 1971. Competence and performance in linguistic theory. In: R. Huxley and E. Ingram (eds.), *Language Acquisition: Models and Methods*. Academic Press, London.

Hymes, D. 1972. *Towards Communicative Competence*. University of Pennsylvania Press, Philadelphia.

Ihara, N. 1978. The development of personal space in Japanese children. *Child Dev. 14*:42–51.

Ingram, D. 1971. Transitivity in child language. *Language 47*:888–910.

Ingram, R. M. 1978. Theme, rheme, topic, and comment in the syntax of American Sign Language. *Sign Lang. Stud. 20*:193–218.

Izard, C. 1971. *The Face of Emotion*. Appleton-Century-Crofts, New York.

Jakobson, R. 1963. Implications of language universals for linguistics. In: J. H. Greenberg (ed.), *Universals of Language*. 2 ed. MIT Press, Cambridge, Mass.

Jakobson, R. 1965. The quest for the essence of language. *Diogenes 51*:21–37.

Jakobson, R. 1968. *Child language, aphasia, and phonological universals*. Mouton, the Hague. (German original: 1941).

Jakobson, R., Fant, C., and Halle, M. 1965. *Preliminaries to Speech Analysis*. MIT Press, Cambridge, Mass.

Jarvella, R. 1972. Starting with psychological verbs. Paper presented at the Midwestern Psychological Association, Cleveland.

Jespersen, O. 1922. *Language: Its Nature, Development and Origin*. Holt, Rinehart & Winston, New York.

Jespersen, O. 1924. *The Philosophy of Grammar*. George Allen & Unwin, Ltd., London.

Jones, E., and Davis, K. E. 1965. From acts to dispositions. In: L. Berkowitz (ed.), *Advances in Experimental Social Psychology*. Vol. 2. Academic Press, New York.

Jones, S. E., and Aiello, J. R. 1973. Proxemic behavior of black and white first-, third-, and fifth-grade children. *J. Pers. Soc. Psychol. 25(1)*.

Kagan, J., Moss, H. A., and Siegel, I. E. 1963. Psychological significance of styles of conceptualization. *Monographs of the Society for Research in Child Development*, Vol. 28, No. 2.

Kainz, F. 1960. *Psychologie der Sprache. Vol. 2*. Ferd. Enke Verlag, Stuttgart.

Kakamasu, J. 1968. Urubú sign language. *Int. J. Am. Linguist. 34*:275–281.

Kattiyakulvanich, N. 1975. State minimizing process of chain sequential machine. Unpublished masters thesis, Kansas University.

Katz, E. W., and Brent, S. B. 1968. Understanding connectives. *J. Verb. Learn. Verb. Behav. 7*:501–509.

Kaye, K. 1977. Toward the origin of dialogue. In: H. R. Schaffer (ed.), *Studies in Mother-Infant Interaction*. Academic Press, New York.

Kelley, H. 1967. Attribution theory in social psychology. In: D. Levine (ed.), *Nebraska Symposium on Motivation*. University of Nebraska Press, Lincoln.

Kendon, A. 1970. Movement coordination in social interaction: Some examples described. *Acta Psychol. 32*:1–25.

Key, M. R. 1980. *The Relationship of Verbal and Nonverbal Communication*. Mouton, the Hague.

Kimura, D. 1973. The asymmetry of the human brain. *Sci. Am. 228*:70–78.

Kimura, D. 1976. The neural basis of language qua gesture. In: H. Whitaker and H. D. Whitaker (eds.), *Studies in Neurolinguistics*. Vol. 2. Academic Press, New York.

Kiparsky, P. 1976. Historical linguistics and the origin of language. In: S. R. Harned, H. D. Steklis, and J. Lancaster (eds.), *Origins and Evolution of Language and Speech*. Annals of the New York Academy of Sciences. Vol. 280.

Klein, R. 1974. *Word Order: Dutch Children and Their Mothers*. Institute for General Linguistics, Publication 9, University of Amsterdam.

Kroeber, A. L. 1958. Sign language inquiry. *Int. J. Am. Linguist. 24*:1–19.

Krout, M. H. 1954. An experimental attempt to produce unconscious manual symbolic movements. *J. Genet. Psychol. 51*:93–120.

Kuhn, T. S. 1970. *The Structure of Scientific Revolutions*. University of Chicago Press, Chicago.

Kuschel, R. 1973. The silent inventor: The creation of sign language by the only deaf-mute on a Polynesian island. *Sign Lang. Stud. 3*:1–27.

Lambert, W. E., and Paivio, A. 1956. The influence of noun-adjective order on learning. *Can. J. Psychol. 10*.9–12.

Lehman, E. B. 1972. Selective strategies in children's attention to task-relevant information. *Child Dev. 43*:197–209.

Lehmann, W. P. 1974. *Proto-Indo-European Syntax*. University of Texas Press, Austin.

Lehmann, W. P. 1975. A discussion of compound and word order. In: C. N. Li (ed.), *Word Order and Word Order Change*. University of Texas Press, Austin.

Lehmann, W. P. 1976. From topic to subject in Indo-European. In: C. N. Li (ed.), *Subject and Topic*. Academic Press, New York.

Lempers, J. 1979. Young children's production and comprehension of nonverbal deicitic behaviors. *J. Genet. Psychol. 135*:93–102.

Lenneberg, E. 1967. *Biological Foundations of Language*. John Wiley and Sons, Inc., New York.

Leont'yev, A. A. 1969. Inner speech and the process of grammatical generation of utterance. *Sov. Psychol. 7*:11–16.

Leopold, W. F. 1974. *Speech Development of a Bilingual Child*: A Linguistic Record. 2 vols. Northwestern University Press, Evanston, Ill.

Lewis, J. L. 1970. Semantic processing of unattended messages using dichotic listening. *J. Exp. Psychol. 85*:225–228.

Li, C. N., and Thompson, S. A. 1976. Subject and topic: A new typology of language. In: C. N. Li (ed.), *Subject and Topic.* Academic Press, New York.

Liddell, S. K. 1978. Nonmanual signals and relative clauses in American Sign Language. In: P. Siple (ed.), *Understanding Language Through Sign Language Research.* Academic Press, New York.

Lieberman, P. 1967. *Intonation, Perception, and Language.* MIT Press, Cambridge, Mass.

Livesley, W. J., and Bromley, D. B. 1973. *Person Perception in Childhood and Adolescence.* John Wiley and Sons, Inc., London.

Lock, A. (ed.). 1978. *Action, Gesture, and Symbol.* Academic Press, London.

Lomax, A. 1977. A stylistic analysis of speaking. *Lang. Soc. 6*:1–48.

Lomax, A., et al. 1968. *Folk song style and culture.* American Association for the Advancement of Science, Washington, D.C., Publication 88.

Lounsbury, F. G. 1954. Transitional probability, linguistic structure, and systems of habit-family hierarchies. In: C. E. Osgood and T. Sebeok (eds.), *Psycholinguistics: A Survey of Theory and Research Problems.* Waverly Press, Baltimore.

Maccoby, E. E. 1967. Selective auditory attention in children. In: L. P. Lipsitt and C. C. Spiker (eds.), *Advances in Child Development and Behavior.* Vol. 3. Academic Press, New York.

Maccoby, E. E. (1976). Sex differentiation during childhood. Manuscript 1339. Abstracted in *JSAS Catalog of Selected Documents in Psychology*, Vol. 6, no. 4.

Macleod, C. 1973. A deaf man's sign language: Its nature and position relative to spoken languages. *Linguistics 101*:72–88.

MacWhinney, B. 1976. Hungarian research on the acquisition of morphology and syntax. *J. Child Lang. 3*:397–410.

Maddox, C., and Rea, C. 1980. Nonverbal interaction of Down's syndrome and normal children with their mothers during play. In: R. St. Clair and W. von Raffler-Engel (eds.), *Language and Cognitive Style.* Swets and Zeitlinger, Amsterdam.

Mahl, G. 1968. Gestures and body movements in interviews. In: J. Shlien (ed.), *Research in Psychotherapy. Vol. 3.* American Psychological Association, Washington, D.C.

Mallery, G. 1879–1880. Sign language among the North American Indians, compared with that among other peoples and deafmutes. *First Annual Report of the Bureau of Ethnology to the . . . Smithsonian Institution.*

Manly, L. Nonverbal communication of the blind. In W. von Raffler-Engel (ed.), *Aspects of Nonverbal Communication.* (Japanese Ed.), Taishu-kan, Tokyo. In press.

Marcos, L. R. 1974. The emotional correlates of smiling and laughter. *Am. J. Psychoanal. 34*:33–41.

Marcos, L. R. 1976a. Bilinguals in Psychotherapy: Language as an emotional barrier. *Am. J. Psychother. 30*:552–560.

Marcos, L. R. 1976b. The linguistic dimensions in the bilingual patient. *Am. J. Psychoanal. 36*:347–354.

Marcos, L. R. 1978. Hand movements in relation to the encoding process in bilinguals. *Diss. Abstr. Int. 38*:11.

Marcos, L. R. 1979a. Hand movements and nondominant fluency in bilinguals. *Percept. Mot. Skills, 48*:207–214.

Marcos, L. R. 1979b. Nonverbal behavior and thought processing. *Arch. Gen. Psychiatr. 36*:940–943.

Marcos, L. R., and Alpert, M. 1976. Strategies and risks in the psychotherapy of bilinguals: The phenomenon of language independence. *Am. J. Psychiatr. 133*:1275–1278.

Marcos, L. R., Alpert, M., Urcuyo, L., and Kesselman, M. 1973. The effect of interview language on the evaluation of psychopathology in Spanish-American schizophrenic patients. *Am. J. Psychiatr. 130*:549–553.

Marcos, L. R., Urcuyo, L. Kesselman, M., and Alpert, M. 1973. The language barrier in evaluating Spanish-American patients. *Arch. Gen. Psychiatr. 29*:655–659.

Marx, K. 1973. *Karl Marx: A Bibliography.* Progress Publishers, Moscow.

Marx, L. 1976. *The Machine in the Garden: Technology and the Pastoral Ideal in America.* Oxford University Press, New York.

Mayberry, R. I. 1978. French Canadian Sign Language. In: P. Siple (ed.), *Understanding Language Through Sign Language Research.* Academic Press, New York.

McCall, E. A. 1965. A generative grammar of sign. Unpublished masters thesis, University of Iowa.

McCawley, J. D. 1968. Lexical insertion in a transformational grammar without deep structure. Mimeograph.

McGrew, W. C. 1972. *An Ethological Study of Children's Behavior.* Academic Press, New York.

McNeill, D. 1970. *The Acquisition of Language.* Harper and Row, Inc., New York.

McQuown, N. A. 1964. Discussion section on language teaching. In: T. Sebeok, A. Hayes, and M. Bateson (eds.), *Approaches to Semiotics.* Mouton, the Hague.

Mehrabian, A. 1968. Communication without words. *Psychol. Today 24*:52–55.

Meltzoff, A., and Moore, M. 1977. Imitation of facial and manual gestures by human neonates. *Science 198*:75–78.

Menyuk, P. 1969. *Sentences Children Use*. MIT Press, Cambridge, Mass.

Menyuk, P. 1971. *The Acquisition and Development of Language*. Prentice-Hall, Inc., Englewood Cliffs, N. J.

De la Mettrie, J. 1961. *Man a Machine*. Open Court Publishing, La Salle, Ill.

Miller, G., and Johnson-Laird, P. 1976. *Language and Perception*. Harvard University Press, Cambridge, Mass.

Miller, M. H. 1975. *Zur Logik der frühen Sprachentwicklung*. Deutsche Seminar der Universität Frankfurt.

Moray, N. 1967. Where is capacity limited? A survey and a model. *Acta Psychol. 27*:84–92.

Morris, J. N. 1964. *Uses of Epidemiology*. Livingstone, Ltd., Edinburgh.

Müller, M. 1864. *Lectures on the Science of Language*. Armstrong, London.

Murphy, C. 1978. Pointing in the context of a shared activity. *Child Dev. 49*:371–380.

Namir, L., and Schlesinger, I. M. 1978. The grammar of sign language. In: I. M. Schlesinger and L. Namir (eds.), *Sign Language of the Deaf*. Academic Press, New York.

Neisser, U. 1976. *Cognition and Reality*. W. H. Freeman & Co., Publishers, San Francisco.

Neisser, U., and Becklin, R. 1975. Selective looking: Attending to visually specified events. *Cogn. Psychol. 7*:480–494.

Nelson, K. 1973. Structure and strategy in learning to talk. *Monographs of the Society for Research in Child Development*, Vol. 38.

Nelson, K. 1974. Concept, word and sentence: Interactions in acquisitions and development. *Psychol. Rev. 81*:267–285.

Nelson, K., Rescorla, L., Gruendel, J., and Benedict, H. 1978. Early lexicons: What do they mean? *Child Dev. 49*:960–968.

Neville, H. J., and Bellugi, U. 1978. Patterns of cerebral specialization in congenitally deaf adults. In: P. Siple (ed.), *Understanding Language Through Sign Language Research*. Academic Press, New York.

Newell, K. M. 1978. Some issues on action plans. In: G. E. Stelmach (ed.), *Information Processing in Motor Control and Learning*. Academic Press, New York.

Newtson, D. 1973. Attribution and the unit of perception of ongoing behavior. *J. Pers. Soc. Psychol. 28*:28–38.

Newtson, D. 1976. Foundations of attribution: The unit of perception of ongoing behavior. In: J. Harvey, W. Ickes, and R. Kidd (eds.), *New Direction in Attribution Research*. Lawrence Erlbaum Associates, Hillsdale, N.J.

Newtson, D., and Engquist, G. 1976. The perceptual organization of ongoing behavior. *J. Exp. Soc. Psychol. 12*:436–450.

Newtson, D., Engquist, G., and Bois, J. 1974. The effects of arousal and cognitive interference on unitization and behavioral recall. Unpublished paper.

Newtson, D., Engquist, G., and Bois, J. 1976. The reliability of a measure of behavior perception. *JSAS Catalogue of Selected Documents in Psychology*, Manuscript 1173, Vol. 6:5.

Newtson, D., Engquist, G., and Bois, J. 1977. The objective basis of behavior units. J. Pers. Soc. Psychol. 35:847–862.

Newtson, D., Rindner, R., and Campbell, R. 1976. Observer skill and perceptual organization. Unpublished paper, University of Virginia.

Newtson, D., Gowan, D., and Patterson, C. Undated. The development of action discrimination. Unpublished manuscript.

Nida, E. A. 1949. *Morphology*. 2nd Ed. University of Michigan Press, Ann Arbor.

Nierenberg, G., and Calero, H. 1971. *How to Read a Person Like a Book*. Hawthorn Books, Inc., New York.

Nisbet, R. A. 1969. *Social Change and History: Aspects of the Western Theory of Development*. Oxford University Press, New York.

Odom, R. D. 1972. Effects of perceptual salience on recall of relevant and incidental dimensional values: A developmental study. *J. Exp. Psychol.* 92:285–291.

Orne, M. 1962. On the psychology óf the social psychology. *Am. Psychol.* 17:776–783.

Osgood, C. E., and Bock, J. K. 1977. Salience and sentencing: Some production principles. In: S. Rosenberg (ed.), *Sentence Production*. Lawrence Erlbaum Associates, Hillsdale, N.J.

Osgood, C. E., and Jenkins, J. J. 1954. A psycholinguistic analysis of decoding and encoding. In: C. E. Osgood and T. A. Sebeok (eds.), *Psycholinguistics: A Survey of Theory and Research Problems*. Waverly Press, Baltimore.

Osgood, C. E., and Tanz, C. 1977. Will the real direct object in bitransitives please stand up? In: A. Juilland (ed.), *Linguistic studies in honor of Joseph Greenberg*. Anna Libri, Saratoga, N.Y.

Oster, H., and Ekman, P. 1978. Facial behavior in child development. In: W. Collins (ed.), *Minnesota Symposium on Child Psychology. Vol. 11*. Lawrence Erlbaum Associates, Hillsdale, N.J.

Overall, J. E., and Gorham, D. R. 1962. The brief psychiatric rating scale. *Psychol. Rep. 10*:799–812.

Paivio, A. 1971. *Imagery and Verbal Processes*. Holt, Rinehart & Winston, New York.

Palmer, L. R. 1978. *Descriptive and Comparative Linguistics: A Critical Introduction*. Faber & Faber, Ltd., London.

Park, T. 1970a. The acquisition of German syntax. Unpublished manuscript, University of Münster.

Park, T. 1970b. Language acquisition in a Korean child. Unpublished manuscript, University of Münster.

Parton, D. A. 1976. Learning to imitate in infancy. *Child Dev.* 47:14–31.

Patterson, G., and Cobb, J. 1971. A dyadic analysis of "aggressive" behaviors. In: J. P. Hill (ed.), *Minnesota Symposia on Child Psychology.* Vol. 5. University of Minnesota Press, Minneapolis.

Paz, A. 171. *Introduction to Probabilistic Automata.* Academic Press, New York.

Pederson, H. 1959. *Linguistic Science in the Nineteenth Century.* Indiana University Press, Bloomington.

Peel, J. D. (ed.). 1972. *Herbert Spencer on Social Evolution.* University of Chicago Press, Chicago.

Peng, F. C. C. 1975. *Body motions of a Japanese child in a Tokyo nursery school.* Videotape in Vanderbilt University archives, Nashville.

Peng, F. C. C. 1978. On the problem of language-specific innatism. In: F. C. C. Peng and W. von Raffler-Engel (eds.), *Language Acquisition and Developmental Kinesics.* Bunka Hyoron, Hiroshima.

Peng, F. C. C., and W. von Raffler-Engel (eds.). 1978. *Language Acquisition and Developmental Kinesics.* Bunka Hyoron, Hiroshima.

Piaget, J. 1926. *The Language and Thought of the Child.* Harcourt, Brace, Jovanovich, New York.

Piaget, J. 1928. *Judgement and Reasoning in the Child.* Routledge & Kegan Paul, London.

Piaget, J. 1952. *The Origins of Intelligence in Children.* International Universities Press, New York.

Piaget, J. 1954. *The Construction of Reality in the Child.* Basic Books, Inc., New York.

Pick, A., Frankel, D., and Hess, V. 1975. Children's attention: The development of selectivity. In: E. Hetherington (ed.), *Review of Child Development Research. Vol. 5.* Academic Press, New York.

Pike, K. 1945. *The Intonation of American English.* University of Michigan Press, Ann Arbor.

Pike, K. 1947. *Phonemics.* University of Michigan Press, Ann Arbor.

Pike, K. 1966. On the grammar of intonation. *Proceedings of the Fifth International Congress of Phonetic Sciences.* Karger, Basel.

Poizner, H., Battison, R., and Lane, H. 1979. Cerebral asymmetry for American Sign Language: The effects of moving stimuli. *Brain Lang.* 7:351–362.

Poizner, H., and Bellugi, U. Psycholinguistic studies of American Sign Language. In: B. Frokjaer-Jensen (ed.), *Selected Papers from the NATO ASI: Sign Language Research.* A special issue of *Logos.* In press.

Poizner, H., and Lane, H. 1979. Cerebral asymmetry in the perception of American Sign Language. *Brain Lang.* 7:210–226.

Posada, C. D. 1980. Unpublished doctoral thesis.

Poulton, E. C. 1957. On prediction in skilled movements. *Psycholog. Bull.* 54:467–479.

Prescott, J. W. 1979. Alienation and affection. *Psychol. Today* December, p. 124.

Preyer, W. 1900. *Die Seele des Kindes, Beobachtungen über die geistige Entwicklung des Menschen in den ersten Lebenjahren.* Lipsia (1st Ed., 1882.)

Reber, A. S. 1973. On psycho-linguistic paradigms. *J. Psycholinguist. Res.* 2:289–319.

Reich, W. 1958. *Character analysis.* Vision Press, London. (1st Ed., 1928.)

Restak, R. 1979. *The brain: The Last Frontier.* Doubleday & Company, Inc., New York.

Rosenberg, S., and Sedlak, A. 1965. Structural representation of implicit personality theory. In: L. Berkowitz (ed.), *Advances in Experimental Social Psychology. Vol. 5.* Academic Press, New York.

Rosenfeld, H. M. 1971. Development of social competence. Kansas Center for Research in Early Childhood Education, Project report 1HOKO1. Subreports as follows: 1) Apparatus for videotaping and time-coding social interaction; 2) A comprehensive code for temporal analysis of mother-infant interaction; 3) Computer analysis of time-coded mother-infant interactions.

Rosenfeld, H. M. 1972. The experimental analysis of interpersonal influence processes. *J. Commun.* 22:424–442.

Rosenfeld, H. M. 1973. Time series analysis of mother-infant interaction. Paper presented at the Symposium on the Analysis of Mother-Infant Interaction Sequences, Annual Meeting of the Society for Research in Child Development, Philadelphia.

Rosenfeld, H. M. 1980. Whither interactional synchrony? In: K. Bloom (ed.), *Prospective Issues in Infancy Research.* Lawrence Erlbaum Associates, Hillsdale, N.J.

Rosenfeld, H. M., Shea, M., and Greenbaum, P. 1979. Facial emblems of "right" and "wrong": Topographical analysis and derivation of a recognition test. *Semiotica* 26:15–34.

Ruesch, J., and Bateson, G. 1968. *Communication: The Social Matrix of Psychiatry.* W. W. Norton & Company, Inc., New York.

Sackett, G. P. 1978. The lag sequential analysis of contingency and cyclicity in behavioral interaction research. In: J. D. Osofsky (ed.), *Handbook of Infant Development.* John Wiley and Sons, Inc., New York.

Sallagoïty, P. 1975. The sign language of Southern France. *Sign Lang. Stud.* 7:181–202.

Sayre, K. M. 1969. *Consciousness: A Philosophic Study of Minds and Machines.* Random House, Inc., New York.

Sayre, K. M., and Crosson, F. J. (eds.). 1968. *The Modeling of Mind:*

Computers and Intelligence. Clarion Books, Simon & Schuster, Inc., New York.

Schaffer, H. R. (ed.). 1977. *Studies in Mother-Infant Interaction.* Academic Press, New York.

Schaffer, H. R., and Emerson, P. 1964. *The development of social attachments in infancy.* Monographs of the Society for Research in *Child Development,* Vol. 29, no. 3.

Schank, R. C. 1972. Conceptual dependency: A theory of natural language understanding. *Cog. Psychol. 3*:522–631.

Scheflen, A. E. 1963. Communication and regulation in psychotherapy. *Psychiatry 26*:126–136.

Schleicher, A. 1863. *Die darwinische Theorie und die Sprachwissenschaft.* Hermann Bohlan, Weimar.

Schlesinger, I. M. 1971a. The grammar of sign language and the problem of language universals. In: J. Morton (eds.), *Biological and Social Factors in Psycholinguistics.* Logos Press, London.

Schlesinger, I. M. 1971b. Production of utterances and language acquisition. In: D. Slobin (ed.), The Ontogenesis of Grammar. Academic Press, New York.

Schlesinger, I. M. 1976. Is there a natural word order? In: W. von Raffler-Engel and Y. Lebrun (eds.), *Babytalk and Infant Speech.* Swets and Zeitlinger, Amsterdam.

Schlesinger, I. M. 1977a. On universals of language change. In: J. Macnamara (ed.), *Language Learning and Thought.* Academic Press, New York.

Schlesinger, I. M. 1977b. Production and comprehension of utterances. Lawrence Erlbaum Associates, Hillsdale, N.J.

Schlesinger, I. M. *Steps to Language: Toward a Theory of Language Acquisition.* Lawrence Erlbaum Associates, Hillsdale, N.J. In press.

Scholer, H., and Zufle, K. 1978. *Macht der Ton die Musik? Zur Verarbeitung inkonsistenter Informationen bei Kindern.* Universität Mannheim.

Schwartz, R., and Leonard, L. B. 1980. Words, objects and actions in early lexical acquisition. Paper presented at the twelfth Annual Child Language Research Forum, March.

Sears, R. R., and Feldman, S. S. (eds.), 1964. *The Seven Stages of Man: A Survey of Human Development—Body, · Personality, Activity— Through Life.* William Kaufmann, Los Altos, Calif.

Shannon, C., and Weaver, W. 1949. *The Mathematical Theory of Communication.* University of Illinois Press, Urbana.

Shopen, T. 1972. *A Generative Theory of Ellipsis.* Indiana University Linguistic Club, Bloomington.

Shwayder, D. S. 1965. *The Stratification of Behavior.* Routledge & Kegan Paul Ltd., London.

Sinclair, J. McH., and Coulthard, R. M. 1975. *Towards an Analysis of Discourse*. Oxford University Press, Oxford.

Slobin, D. I. 1966. The acquisition of Russian as a native language. In: F. S. Smith and G. A. Miller (eds.), *The Genesis of Language: A Psycholinguistic Approach*. MIT Press, Cambridge, Mass.

Slobin, D. I. 1973. Cognitive prerequisites for the development of grammar. In: C. A. Ferguson and D. I. Slovin (eds.), *Studies of Child Language Development*. Holt, Rinehart and Winston, New York.

Slobin, D. I. 1976. Universal and particular in the acquisition of language. Paper prepared for Workshop Conference, "Language Acquisition: State of Art," University of Pennsylvania, May 19–22.

Slobin, D. I. 1977a. Language change in childhood and in history. In: J. Macnamara (ed.), *Language Learning and Thought*. Academic Press, New York.

Smith, A. 1776. *An Inquiry into the Nature and Causes of the Wealth of Nations*. Reprinted by Random House, Inc., New York, 1937.

Smith, F., and Miller, G. A. (eds.). 1966. *The Genesis of Language: A Psycholinguistic Approach*. MIT Press, Cambridge, Mass.

Smoczyńska, M. 1979. Uniformities and individual variations in early syntactic development. Unpublished paper, Jagellonian University, Krakow.

Snow, E. C., and Ferguson, C. A. (eds.). 1977. *Talking to Children: Language Input and Organization*. Cambridge University Press, Cambridge.

Snow, J. 1855. *On the Mode of Communication of Cholera*. John Churchill, London. Reprinted in W. H. Frost (1936). *Snow on Cholera: Being a Reprint of Two Papers by John Snow, M.D.* Commonwealth Fund, New York.

Spencer, H. 1876. *Principles of Sociology*. Reprinted by CTL Archon Books, Hamden, 1969.

Spitz, R. 1965. *The First Year of Life; A Psychoanalytic Study of Normal and Deviant Development of Object Relations*. International University Press, New York.

St. Clair, R., and von Raffler-Engel, W. (eds.). 1980. *Language and Cognitive Style*. Swets and Zeitlinger, Amsterdam.

Steckol, K. F., and Leonard L. B. 1979. Sensorimotor development and prelinguistic communication. Paper presented at the American Speech-Language and Hearing Association Convention, November.

Steingart, I., and Freedman, M. 1976. The organization of body-focused kinesic behavior and language construction in schizophrenic and depressed states. In: D. P. Spence (ed.), *Psychoanalysis and Contemporary Science*. Vol. 4. International Universities Press, New York.

Stern, C. and Stern, W. 1928. *Die Kindersprache: Eine psychologische und sprachtheoretiche Untersuchung.* Wissenschaftliche Buchgesellschaft, Darmstadt.

Stokoe, W. C., Jr. 1972. *Semiotics and Human Sign Language.* Approaches to Semiotics. Vol. 21, Mouton, the Hague.

Stokoe, W. C., Jr., Casterline, D. C., and Croneberg, C. G. 1965. *A Dictionary of American Sign Language on Linguistic Principles.* Gallaudet College Press, Washington, D.C.

Stone, L. 1961. *The Psychoanalytic Situation.* International Universities Press, New York.

Stroop, J. R. 1935. Studies of interference in serial verbal reaction. *J. Exp. Psychol. 18*:643–662.

Sugarman, S. The development of preverbal communication: Its contribution and limits in promoting the development of language. In: R. L. Schiefelbusch and J. Pickar (eds.), *Communicative Competence: Acquisition and Intervention.* University Park Press, Baltimore. In press.

Sugarman-Bell, S. 1978. Some organizational aspects of pre-verbal communication. In: I. Markova (ed.), *The Social Context of Language.* John Wiley and Sons, Inc. London.

Sully J. 1924. *Studies in Childhood.* Longmans Green & Co., Ltd., London.

Supalla, T., and Newport, E. L. 1978. How many seats in a chair? The derivation of nouns and verbs in American Sign Language. In: P. Siple (ed.), *Understanding Language Through Sign Language Research.* Academic Press, New York.

Tagiuri, R. 1954. Person perception. In: G. Lindsey and E. Aronson (eds.), *Handbook of Social Psychology.* Vol. 3. Addison-Wesley, London.

Tamir, L. Interrogative in dialogue: Case study of mother and child 16–19 months. *J. Psycholinguist. Res.* To appear.

TenHouten, W. D. 1980. Social correlates of cerebral lateralization: A neurosociological approach. In: R. St. Clair and W. von Raffler-Engel (eds.), *Language and Cognitive Styles.* Swets and Zeitlinger, Amsterdam.

Tervoort, B. T. 1961. Esoteric symbolism in the communication behavior of young deaf children. *Am. Ann. Deaf 106*:436–480.

Tervoort, B. T. 1974. *Could There Be a Human Sign Language?* Institute of General Linguistics, University of Amsterdam, Amsterdam.

Thompson, H. 1977. The lack of subordination in American Sign Language. In: L. A. Friedman (ed.), *On the Other Hand.* Academic Press, New York.

Togeby, K. 1951. *Structure Immanente de la Langage Francaise.* 6:7–282. Traveaux de la Cercle Linguistique de Copenhague, Copenhagen.

Trager, G. 1958. Paralanguage: A first approximation. *Stud. Linguist. 13*:1–12.

Trager, G., and Smith, H. 1957. *An outline of English Structure*. Studies in Linguistics: Occasional Papers 3. (1st Ed., 1951.)

Travarthen, C. 1977. Descriptive analyses of infant communicative behavior. In: H. R. Schaffer (ed.), *Studies in Mother-Infant Interaction*. Academic Press, New York.

Triesman, A. 1964. Selective attention in man. *Br. Med. Bull. 20*:12–16.

Trubetskoy, N. S. 1939. *Principles of Phonology*. Reprinted by University of California Press, Berkeley, 1969.

Tylor, E. B. 1881. The gesture language. *Am. Ann. Deaf 23*:162–178; 251–260.

Uzgiris, I., and Hunt, J. 1975. *Assessment in Infancy: Ordinal Scales of Psychological Development*. University of Illinois Press, Urbana.

Van Coetsen, F., and Kufner, H. L. 1972. *Towards a Grammar of Proto-Germanic*. Niemeyer. Tübingen.

Van der Geest, T. 1970. *Some non-verbal aspects in language acquisition*. In: Proceedings if the Fourth International Congress on Education of the Deaf, Stockholm, August.

Van der Geest, T. 1974. *Evaluation of Theories on Child Grammar*. Mouton, the Hague.

Van der Geest, T. 1975. *Some Aspects of Communicative Competence and Their Implications for Language Acquisition*. Van Gorcum, Amsterdam.

Van der Geest, T. 1977. Some interactional aspects of language acquisition. In: C. Snow and C. Ferguson, *Talking to Children*. Cambridge University Press, Cambridge.

Van der Geest, T. 1978a. *Entwicklung der Kommunikation; Verbale Interaktion im ersten Schuljahr*. Kamp Verlag, Bochum.

Van der Geest, T. 1978b. *Mother-child interactions and their researchers*. Unpublished manuscript.

Von Raffler-Engel, W. 1964. *Il Prelinguaggio Infantile*. Studi grammaticali e linguistici 7. Paideia, Brescia.

Von Raffler-Engel, W. 1968. Suprasegmental and substitution tests in first language acquisition. *Folio Linguistic. 2*:166–175.

Von Raffler-Engel, W. 1970a. Competence, a term in search of a concept. In: J. Dierickx and Y. Lebrun (eds.), *Linguististique Contemporaine*. Editions de l'Institut de Sociologie, Brussels.

Von Raffler-Engel, W. 1970b. The function of repetition in child language as a part of an integrated theory of developmental linguistics. *Boll. Psicol. Appl. 97–99*:27–32.

Von Raffler-Engel, W. 1972. The relationship of intonation to the first vowel articulation in infants. *Philologica 1*:197–202.

Von Raffler-Engel, W. 1973. A preliminary report on research in progress on the language development of monolingual and bilingual children ages

5–7. In: G. Rondeau (ed.), *Some Aspects of Canadian Applied Linguistics*. Centre Educatif et Culturel, Montreal, Quebec.

Von Raffler-Engel, W. 1974a. *Children's Acquisition of Kinesics. (Film.)* Campus Film Distributors, Scarsdale, N.Y.

Von Raffler-Engel, W. 1974b. The concept of critical age in language acquisition; A position paper. (Paper presented at the Eighth Annual Meeting of the Societa Linguistica Europea, University of Jyvaskyka, Finland, 1974.) In *Folia Linguist. 9 (1–4)*:17–27.

Von Raffler-Engel, W. 1974c. Language in context: Situationally conditioned style change in Black English. In: L. Heilmann (ed.), *Proceedings of the Eleventh International Congress of Linguists*. Il Mulino, Bologna.

Von Raffler-Engel, W. 1975. Introductory remarks to the section on kinesics. In: *Third International Child Language Symposium*. Unpublished manuscript, University of London.

Von Raffler-Engel, W. 1976a. Developmental kinesics: Cultural differences. (Paper presented at the 25th Anniversary Meeting, International Communication Association, Chicago, 1975.) In: W. von Raffler-Engel (ed.), *Child Language—1975*. International Linguistic Association, New York. Special triple issue of *Word 27 (1–3)*.

Von Raffler-Engel, W. 1976b. Some rules of socio-kinesics. In: G. Nickel (ed.), *Proceedings of the Fourth International Congress of Applied Linguistics*. Vol. 2 Hochschul Verlag, Stuttgart.

Von Raffler-Engel, W. 1976c. We talk in several ways. In: S. Neel (ed.), *Decisions 1976: The Changing Role of the Handicapped*. Bill Wilkerson Hearing and Speech Center, Language Development Program, Nashville.

Von Raffler-Engel, W. 1976d. A pluri-modal communicative approach to language acquisition. In: W. von Raffler-Engel and Y. Lebrun (eds.), *Baby Talk and Infant Speech*. Neurologuistics Series. Vol. 5. Swets and Zeitlinger. (Proceedings of the International Symposium on First Language Acquisition, Florence, 1972.)

Von Raffler-Engel, W. 1976e. Introduction. In: W. von Raffler-Engel (ed.), *Child Language—1975*. International Linguistic Association, New York. Special triple issue of *Word 27 (1–3)*.

Von Raffler-Engel, W. 1977. We do not talk only with our mouths. *Verbatim 4 (3)*.

Von Raffler-Engel, W. 1978a. The acquisition of kinesics by the child. In: F. C. Peng and W. von Raffler-Engel (eds.), *Language Acquisition and Developmental Kinesics*. Bunka Hyoron, Hiroshima.

Von Raffler-Engel, W. 1978b. The nonverbal adjustment of adults to children's communicative styles. In: D. Lance (ed.), *Proceedings of the Mid-America Conference on Linguistics*. University of Missouri, Columbia.

Von Raffler-Engel, W. 1979. The unconscious element in intercultural communication. In: R. St. Clair and H. Giles (eds.), *The Social and Psychological Context of Language*. Lawrence Erlbaum Associates, Hillsdale, N.J. (Short version of this article: Kinesic awareness in intercultural interaction. In: A. G. Lozano (ed.), *Bilingual and Biliterate Perspectives*. University of Colorado, Boulder, 1978.)

Von Raffler-Engel, W. (ed.) 1980. *Aspects of Nonverbal Communication*. Swets and Zeitlinger, Amsterdam.

Von Raffler-Engel, W., and Hoffer, B. (eds.) 1977. *Aspects of Nonverbal Communication*. Trinity University, San Antonio.

Von Raffler-Engel, W., and Hutcheson, R. 1975. *Language Intervention Programs in the United States*. Van Gorcum, Amsterdam.

Von Raffler-Engel, W., and Y. Lebrun. (eds.). 1976. *Baby Talk and Infant Speech*. Swets and Zeitlinger, Amsterdam.

Von Raffler-Engel, W., Mewman, K., Foster, R., and Gantz, F. 1980. The relationship of nonverbal behavior to verbal behavior in the evaluation of job applicants. In: W. von Raffler-Engel (ed.), *Aspects of Nonverbal Communication*. Swets and Zeitlinger, Amsterdam.

Von Raffler-Engel, W., and Rea, C. 1978. *The influence of the child's communicative style on the conversational behavior of the adult*. Paper presented at the First International Congress on Child Language, Tokyo, 1978. ERIC ED 163 755, Center for Applied Linguistics, Arlington, Va.

Von Raffler-Engel, W., and Weinstein, S. 1977. *Metakinesic behavior in the description of non-verbal behavior*. University of Trier, Linguistic Agency, Trier. Series B, Paper 2. (Short version appeared in: W. U. Dressler and W. Meid (eds.), *Proceedings of the Twelfth International Congress of Linguists*. University of Vienna, 1977. Institut für Sprachwissenschaft der Universität Innsbruck, Innsbruck, 1978.

Walters, B. R. 1978. Gender language: Codes in cross-sex competition and their effects on sex-typed behavior. In: F. C. C. Peng and W. von Raffler-Engel (eds.), *Language Acquisition and Developmental Kinesics*. Bunka Hyoron, Hiroshima.

Wapner, S., and Werner, H. 1957. *Perceptual Development*. Clark University Press, Worcester, Mass.

Warren, N. K. 1978. Aspect marking in American Sign Language. In: P. Siple (ed.), *Understanding Language Through Sign Language Research*. Academic Press, New York.

Washabaugh, W. 1979. Hearing and deaf signers on Providence Island. *Sign Lang. Stud. 24*:191–214.

Washabaugh, W. The manufacturing of a language. *Semiotica*. In press.

Wasow, T. 1973. The innateness hypothesis and grammatical relations. *Synthese 26*:38–56.

Waterhouse, L., and Fein, D. 1978. Patterns of kinesic synchrony in autistic and schizophrenic children. In: F. C. C. Peng and W. von Raffler-Engel (eds.), *Language Acquisition and Developmental Kinesics*. Bunka Hyoron, Hiroshima.

Watzlawick, P., Beavin, J. H., and Jackson, D. D. 1967. *Pragmatics of Human Communication*. W. W. Norton & Company, Inc., New York.

Weir, R. 1966. Some questions on the child's learning of phonology. In: F. Smith and G. A. Miller (eds.), *The Genesis of Language*. MIT Press, Cambridge, Mass.

Weisenburger, J. L. 1976. A choice of words: Two-year-old speech from a situational point of view. *J. Child Lang. 3*:275–281.

Weitz, S. 1974. *Nonverbal Communication*. Oxford University Press, New York.

Werner, H., and Kaplan, B. 1963. *Symbol Formation: An Organismic-Developmental Approach to Language and the Expression of Thought*. John Wiley and Sons, Inc., New York.

West, L., Jr. 1960. *The Sign Language: An Analysis*. Vols. I and II. University Microfilms, Ann Arbor, Mich.

Wexler, K., Culicover, P., and Hamburger, H. 1975. Learning theoretic foundations of linguistic universals. *Theor. Linguist. 2*:215–253.

Willows, D. M. 1974. Reading between the lines: Selective attention in good and poor readers. *Child Dev. 45*:408–415.

Wolff, C. 1952. *The Hand in Psychological Diagnosis*. Philosophical Library, New York.

Wood, B. S. 1976. *Children and Communication; Verbal and Nonverbal Language Development*. Prentice-Hall, Inc., Englewood Cliffs, N.J.

Yando, R., Seitz, V., and Zigler, E. 1978. *Imitation: A Developmental Perspective*. John Wiley and Sons, Inc., New York.

Yau, S. C. 1978. Natural Word Order in Child Language. Centre National de la Recherche Scientifique, Paris.

Yoder, C. K. 1980. Two systems in synchrony: A study of early language development. In: R. St. Clair and W. von Raffler-Engel (eds.), *Language and Cognitive Styles*. Swets and Zeitlinger, Amsterdam.

Young Browne, G. 1972. Infant crying: An exploratory analysis of maternal elicitors in naturally occurring mother-infant interactions. Doctoral dissertation, University of Kansas.

Zajonc, R. B. 1975. Birth order and intelligence: Dumber by the dozen. *Psychol. Today 3*:37–41.

Zazzo, R. 1962. *Conduites et Conscience*. Vol. I. *Psychologie de l'Enfant et Methode Génétique*. Delachaux & Niestle, Neuchatel.

Index